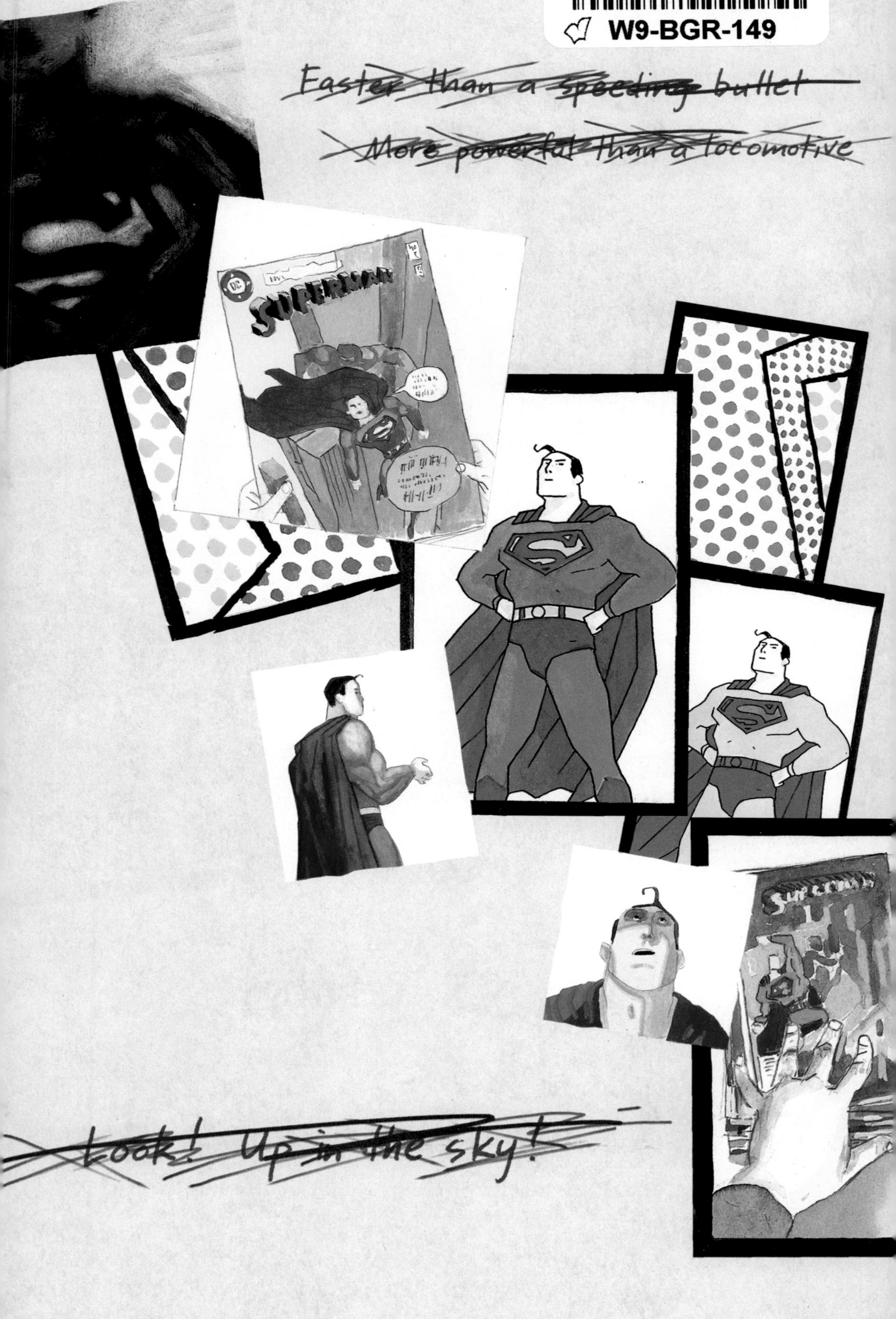
Faster than a speeding bullet
More powerful than a locomotive
SUPERMAN
SUPERMAN
Look! Up in the sky!

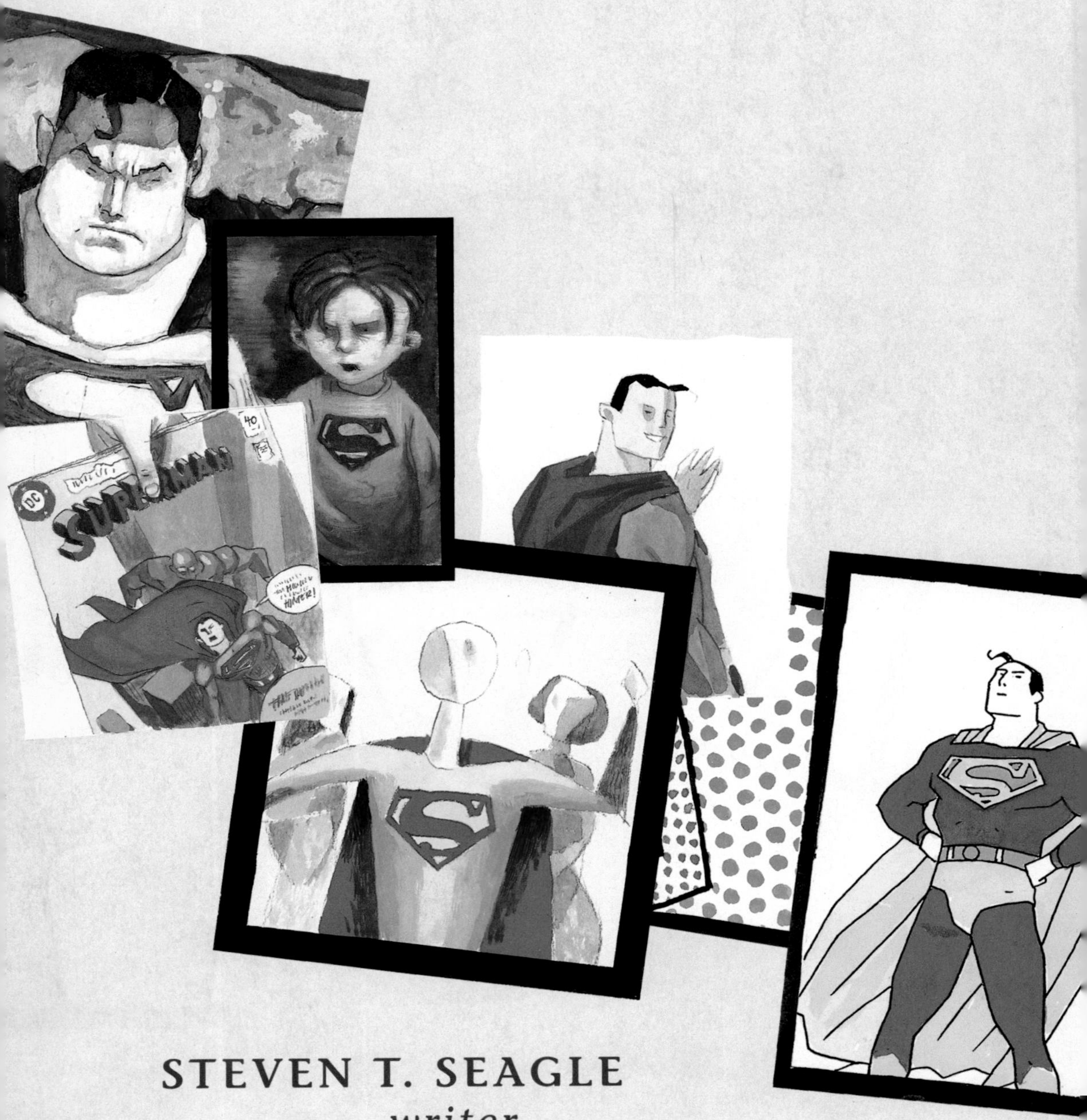

STEVEN T. SEAGLE
writer

TEDDY KRISTIANSEN
artist

TODD KLEIN
letterer

SUPERMAN *created by* **Jerry Siegel** *and* **Joe Shuster**
By special arrangement with the Jerry Siegel family

It's a Bird...

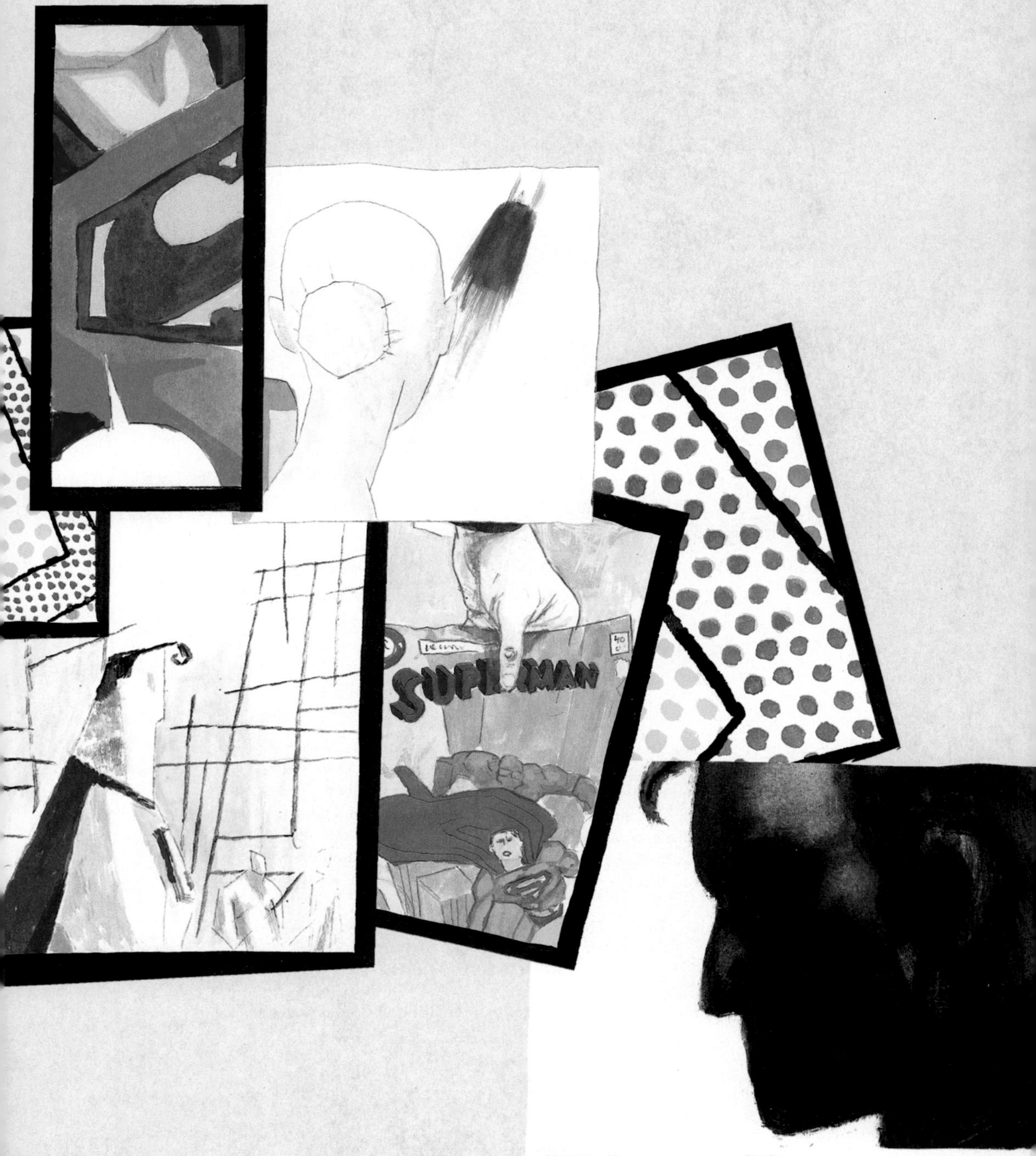

KAREN BERGER *Editor*
PORNSAK PICHETSHOTE *Assistant Editor*
JAMIE S. RICH *Group Editor – Vertigo Comics*
JEB WOODARD *Group Editor – Collected Editions*
ERIKA ROTHBERG *Editor – Collected Edition*
STEVE COOK *Design Director – Books*
AMIE BROCKWAY-METCALF *Publication Design*

DIANE NELSON *President*
DAN DiDIO *Publisher*
JIM LEE *Publisher*
GEOFF JOHNS *President & Chief Creative Officer*
AMIT DESAI *Executive VP – Business & Marketing Strategy,*
Direct to Consumer & Global Franchise Management
SAM ADES *Senior VP – Direct to Consumer*
BOBBIE CHASE *VP – Talent Development*
MARK CHIARELLO *Senior VP – Art, Design & Collected Editions*
JOHN CUNNINGHAM *Senior VP – Sales & Trade Marketing*
ANNE DePIES *Senior VP – Business Strategy, Finance & Administration*
DON FALLETTI *VP – Manufacturing Operations*
LAWRENCE GANEM *VP – Editorial Administration & Talent Relations*
ALISON GILL *Senior VP – Manufacturing & Operations*
HANK KANALZ *Senior VP – Editorial Strategy & Administration*
JAY KOGAN *VP – Legal Affairs*
THOMAS LOFTUS *VP – Business Affairs*
JACK MAHAN *VP – Business Affairs*
NICK J. NAPOLITANO *VP – Manufacturing Administration*
EDDIE SCANNELL *VP – Consumer Marketing*
COURTNEY SIMMONS *Senior VP – Publicity & Communications*
JIM (SKI) SOKOLOWSKI *VP – Comic Book Specialty Sales & Trade Marketing*
NANCY SPEARS *VP – Mass, Book, Digital Sales & Trade Marketing*

IT'S A BIRD...

DC Comics, 2900 West Alameda Ave., Burbank, CA 91505
Printed in the United States. First Printing.
ISBN: 978-1-4012-7288-3

Library of Congress Cataloging-in-Publication Data is available.

PEFC Certified
Printed on paper from
sustainably managed
forests, controlled
sources
PEFC/29-31-337   www.pefc.org

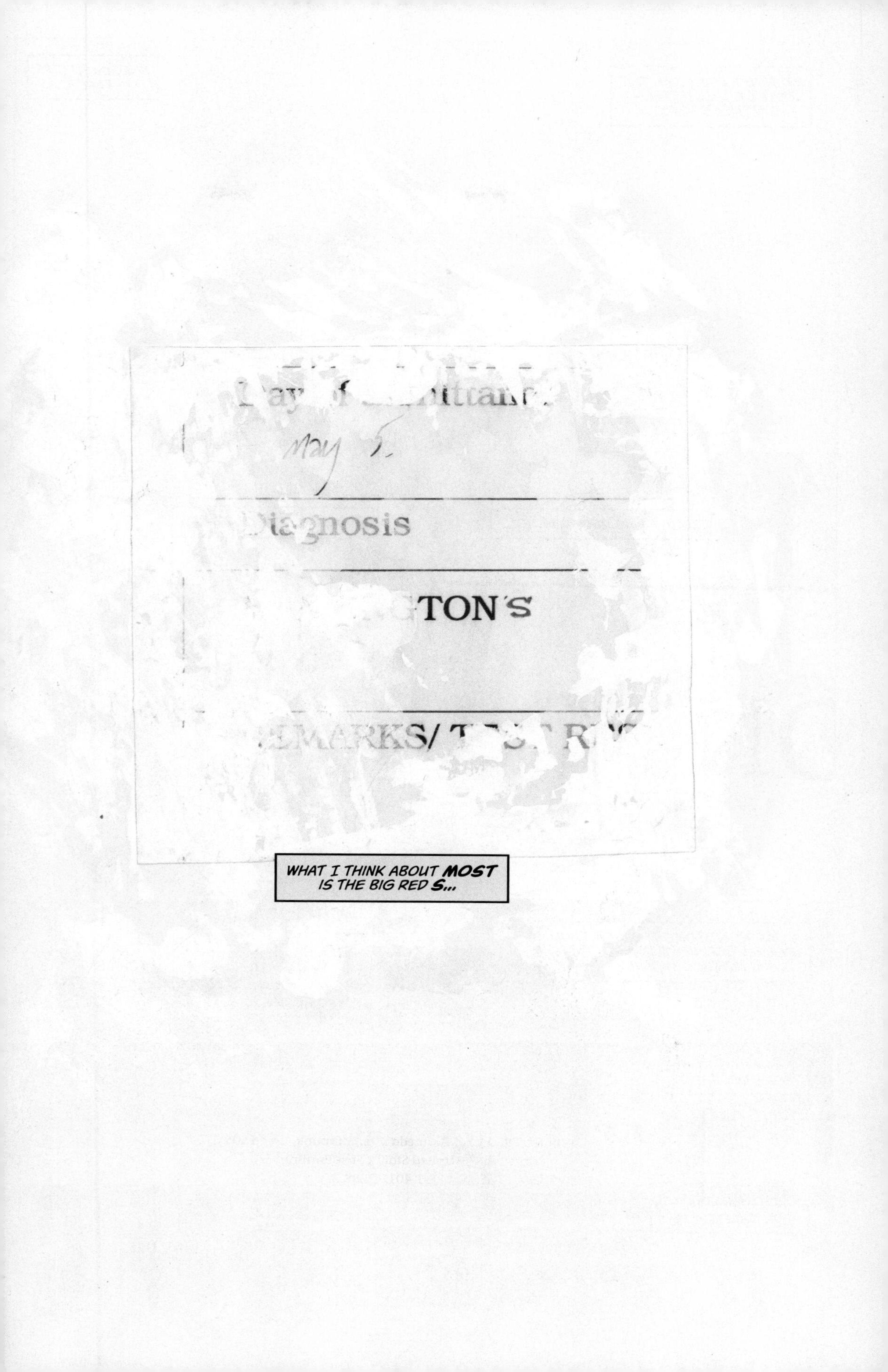

Day of Entrance:

May 5.

Diagnosis

...TON'S

...EMARKS/T...R...

WHAT I THINK ABOUT **MOST**
IS THE BIG RED **S**...

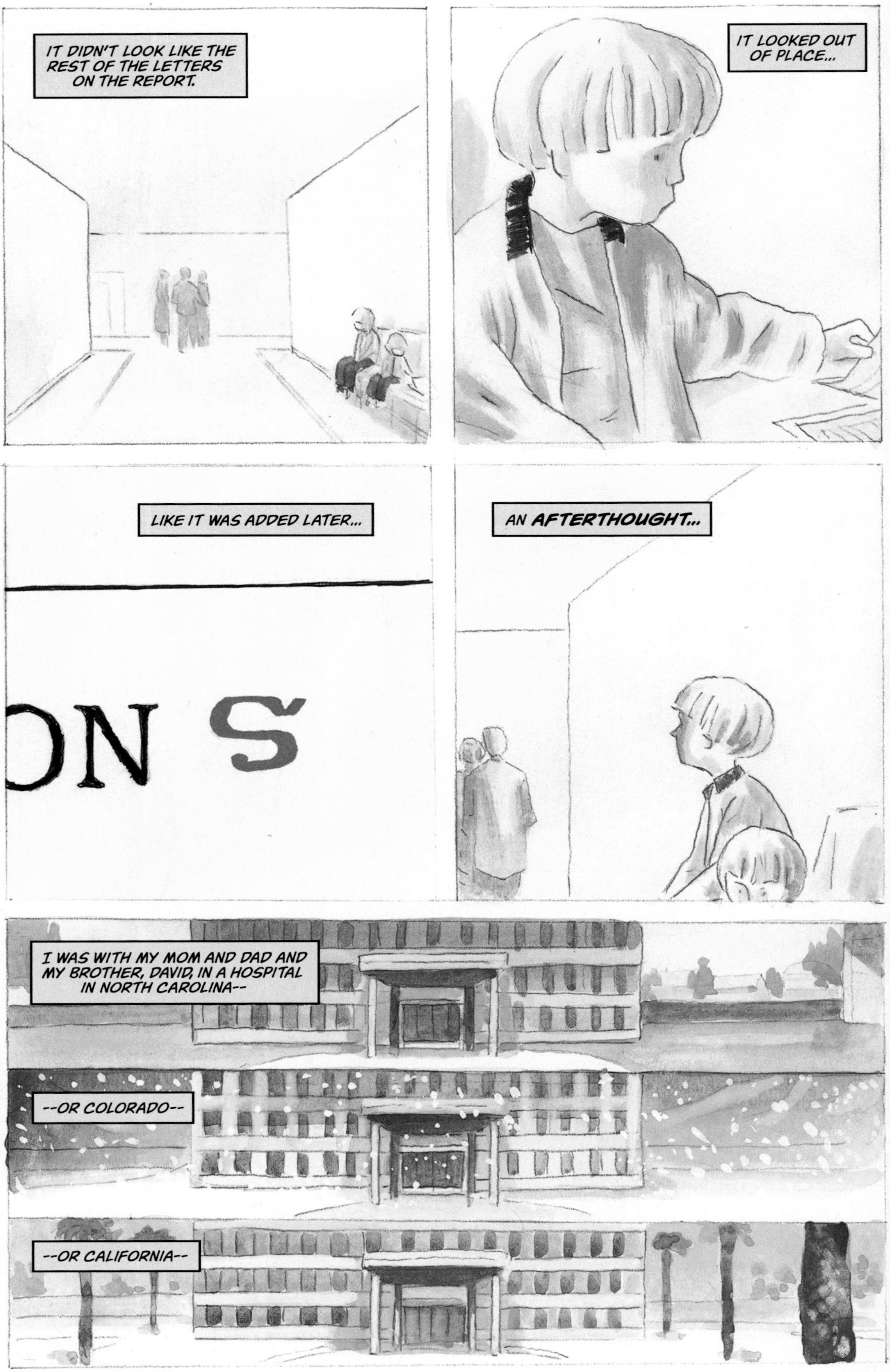
IT DIDN'T LOOK LIKE THE REST OF THE LETTERS ON THE REPORT.
IT LOOKED OUT OF PLACE...
LIKE IT WAS ADDED LATER...
ON S
AN AFTERTHOUGHT...
I WAS WITH MY MOM AND DAD AND MY BROTHER, DAVID, IN A HOSPITAL IN NORTH CAROLINA--
--OR COLORADO--
--OR CALIFORNIA--

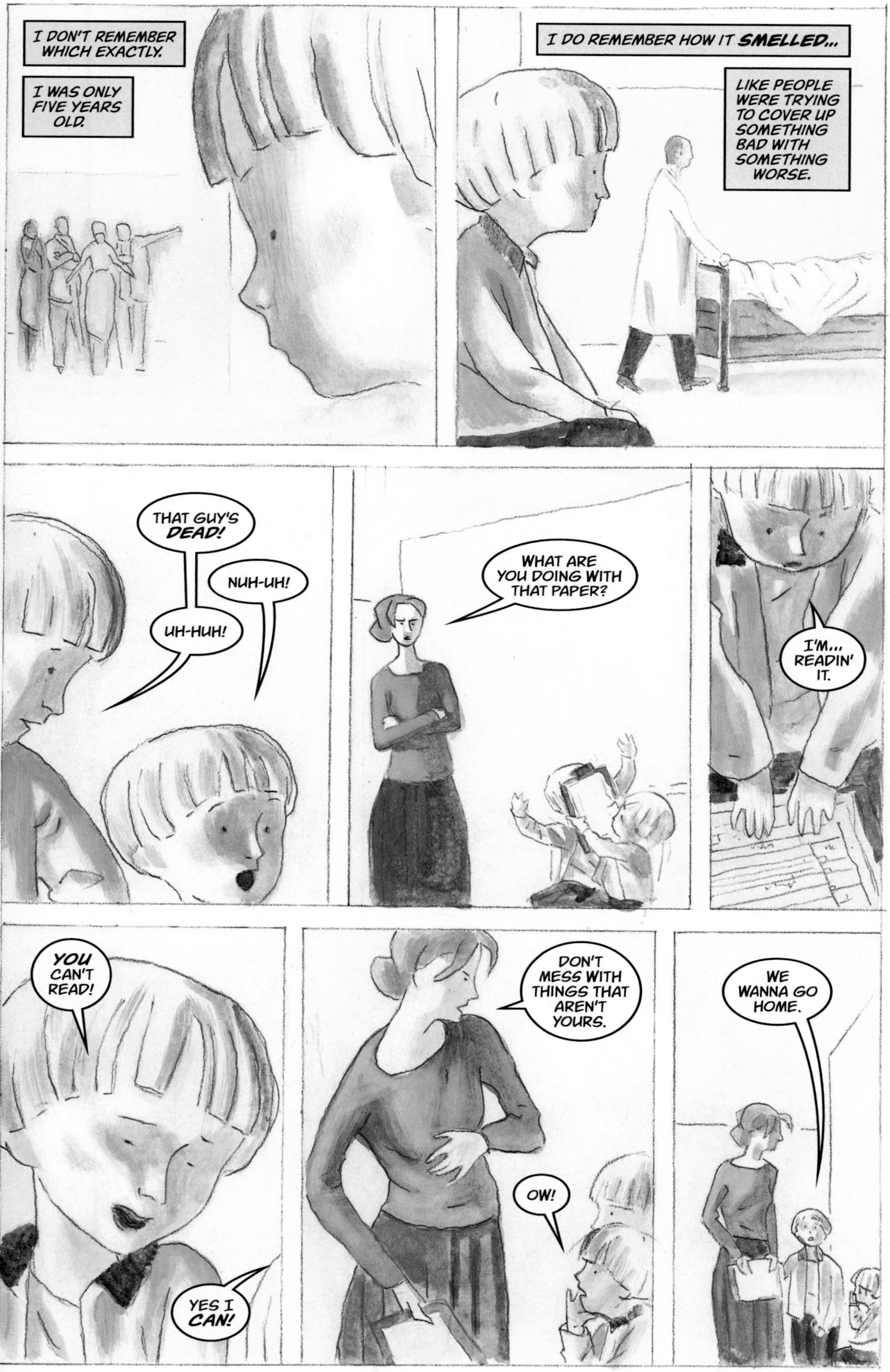

I DON'T REMEMBER WHICH EXACTLY.
I WAS ONLY FIVE YEARS OLD.
I DO REMEMBER HOW IT SMELLED...
LIKE PEOPLE WERE TRYING TO COVER UP SOMETHING BAD WITH SOMETHING WORSE.
THAT GUY'S DEAD!
NUH-UH!
UH-HUH!
WHAT ARE YOU DOING WITH THAT PAPER?
I'M... READIN' IT.
YOU CAN'T READ!
YES I CAN!
DON'T MESS WITH THINGS THAT AREN'T YOURS.
OW!
WE WANNA GO HOME.

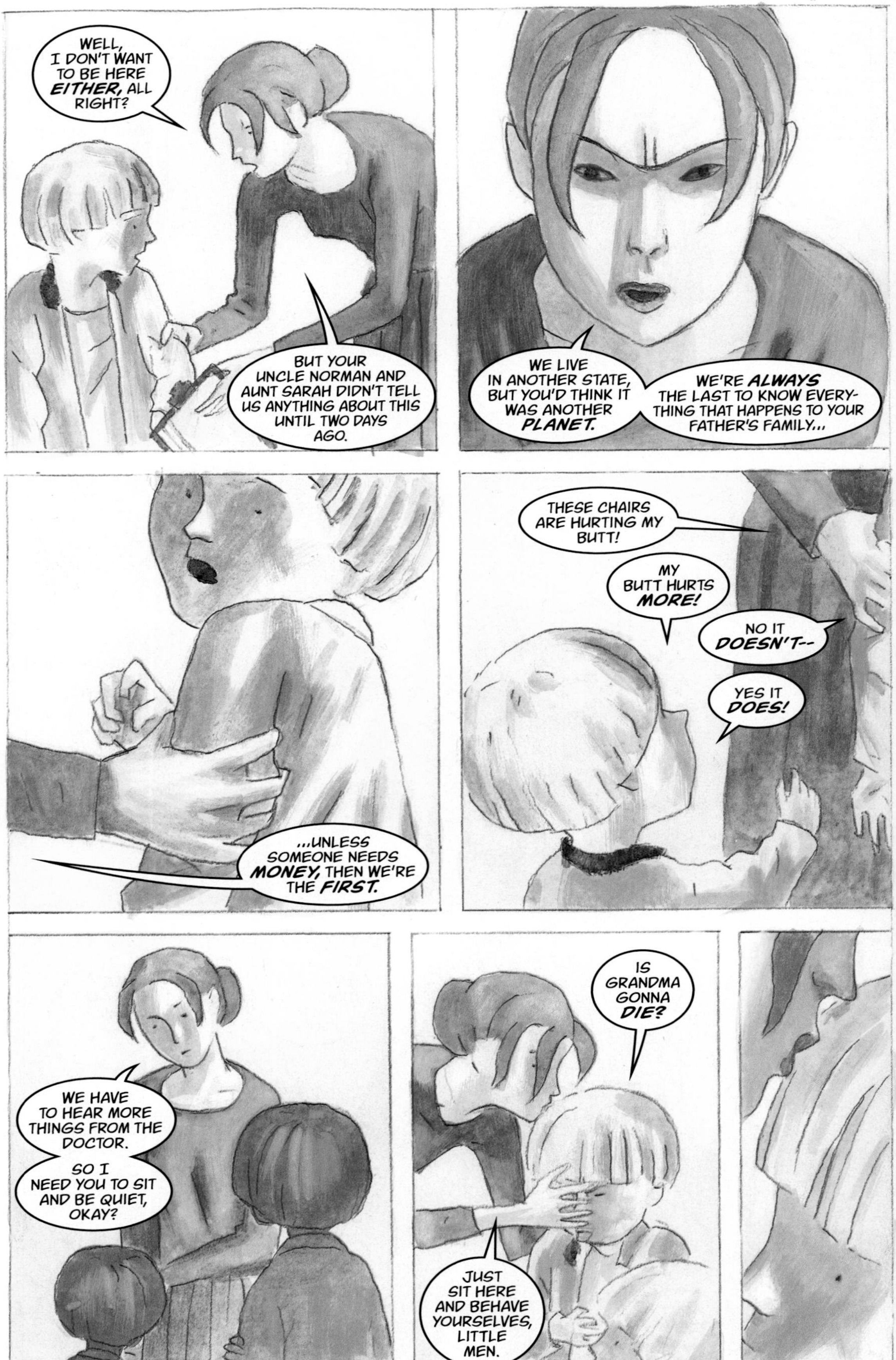
WELL, I DON'T WANT TO BE HERE *EITHER*, ALL RIGHT?
BUT YOUR UNCLE NORMAN AND AUNT SARAH DIDN'T TELL US ANYTHING ABOUT THIS UNTIL TWO DAYS AGO.
WE LIVE IN ANOTHER STATE, BUT YOU'D THINK IT WAS ANOTHER *PLANET.*
WE'RE *ALWAYS* THE LAST TO KNOW EVERY-THING THAT HAPPENS TO YOUR FATHER'S FAMILY...
...UNLESS SOMEONE NEEDS *MONEY,* THEN WE'RE THE *FIRST.*
THESE CHAIRS ARE HURTING MY BUTT!
MY BUTT HURTS *MORE!*
NO IT *DOESN'T--*
YES IT *DOES!*
WE HAVE TO HEAR MORE THINGS FROM THE DOCTOR.
SO I NEED YOU TO SIT AND BE QUIET, OKAY?
IS GRANDMA GONNA *DIE?*
JUST SIT HERE AND BEHAVE YOURSELVES, LITTLE MEN.

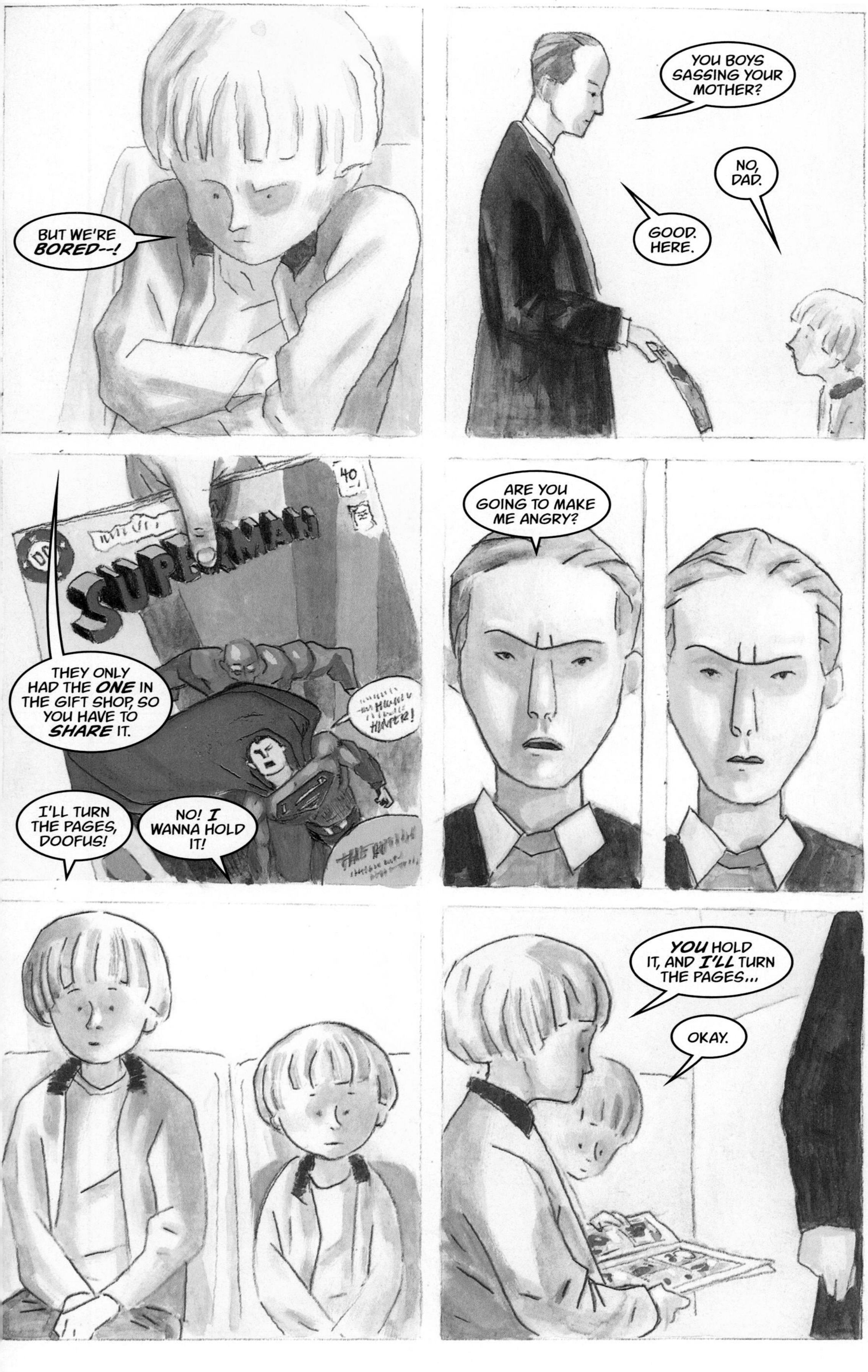
BUT WE'RE *BORED*--!
YOU BOYS SASSING YOUR MOTHER?
NO, DAD.
GOOD. HERE.
THEY ONLY HAD THE *ONE* IN THE GIFT SHOP, SO YOU HAVE TO *SHARE* IT.
I'LL TURN THE PAGES, DOOFUS!
NO! *I* WANNA HOLD IT!
ARE YOU GOING TO MAKE ME ANGRY?
YOU HOLD IT, AND *I'LL* TURN THE PAGES...
OKAY.

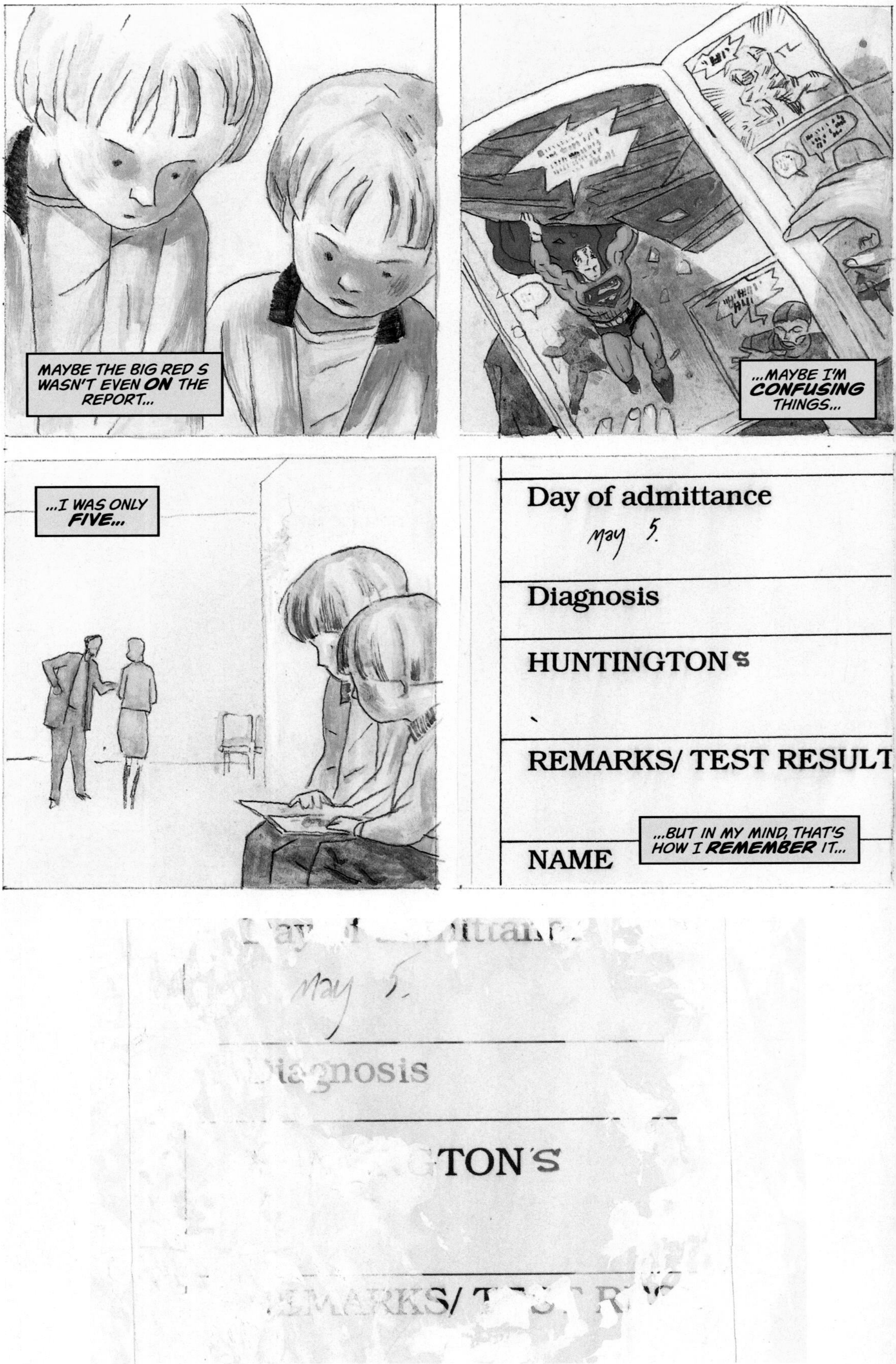
MAYBE THE BIG RED S WASN'T EVEN ON THE REPORT...
...MAYBE I'M CONFUSING THINGS...
...I WAS ONLY FIVE...
Day of admittance
may 5.
Diagnosis
HUNTINGTON's
REMARKS/ TEST RESULT
NAME
...BUT IN MY MIND, THAT'S HOW I REMEMBER IT...
may 5.
Diagnosis

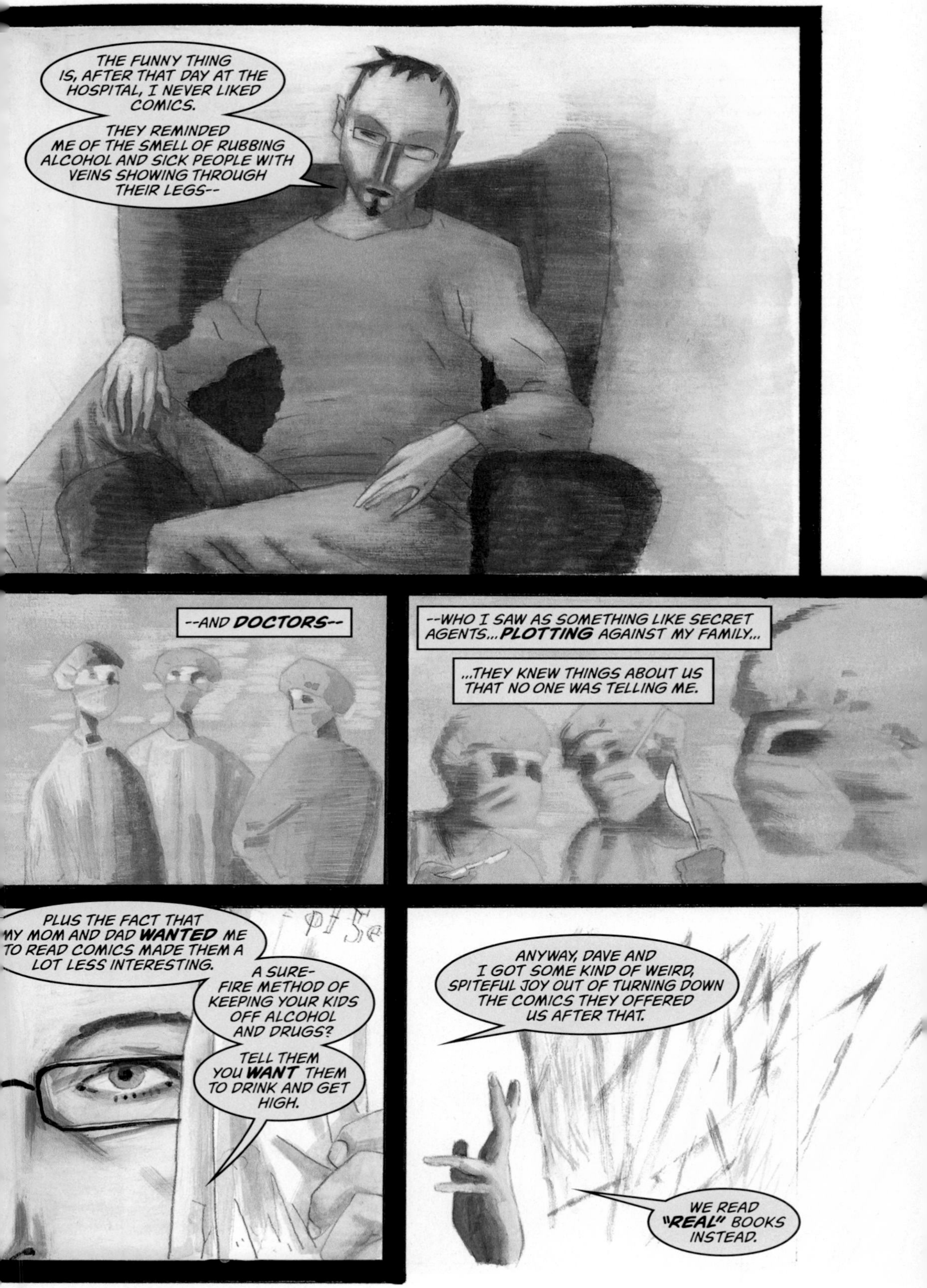
THE FUNNY THING IS, AFTER THAT DAY AT THE HOSPITAL, I NEVER LIKED COMICS.
THEY REMINDED ME OF THE SMELL OF RUBBING ALCOHOL AND SICK PEOPLE WITH VEINS SHOWING THROUGH THEIR LEGS--
--AND DOCTORS--
--WHO I SAW AS SOMETHING LIKE SECRET AGENTS... PLOTTING AGAINST MY FAMILY...
...THEY KNEW THINGS ABOUT US THAT NO ONE WAS TELLING ME.
PLUS THE FACT THAT MY MOM AND DAD WANTED ME TO READ COMICS MADE THEM A LOT LESS INTERESTING.
A SURE-FIRE METHOD OF KEEPING YOUR KIDS OFF ALCOHOL AND DRUGS?
TELL THEM YOU WANT THEM TO DRINK AND GET HIGH.
ANYWAY, DAVE AND I GOT SOME KIND OF WEIRD, SPITEFUL JOY OUT OF TURNING DOWN THE COMICS THEY OFFERED US AFTER THAT.
WE READ "REAL" BOOKS INSTEAD.

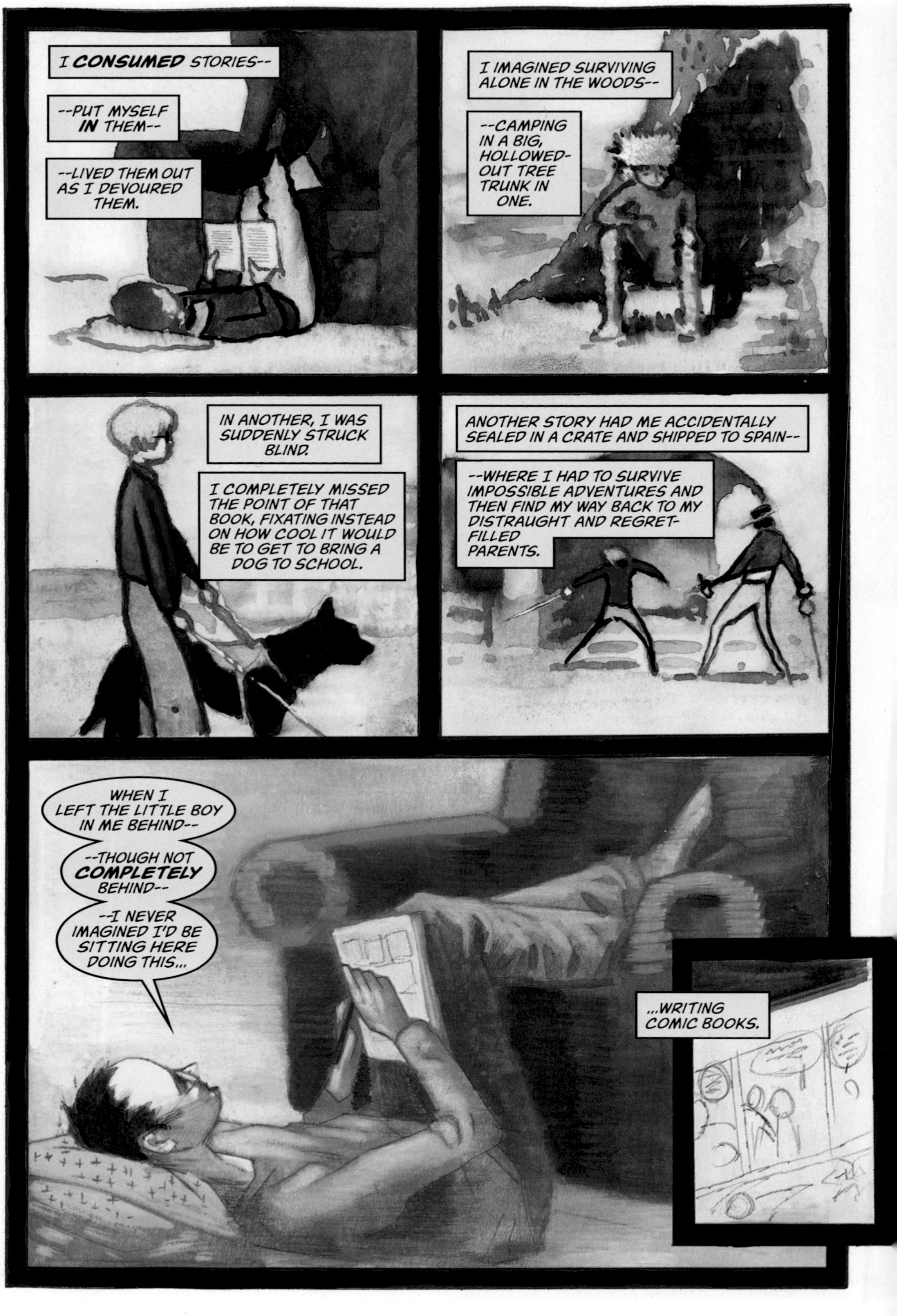
I CONSUMED STORIES--
--PUT MYSELF IN THEM--
--LIVED THEM OUT AS I DEVOURED THEM.
I IMAGINED SURVIVING ALONE IN THE WOODS--
--CAMPING IN A BIG, HOLLOWED-OUT TREE TRUNK IN ONE.
IN ANOTHER, I WAS SUDDENLY STRUCK BLIND.
I COMPLETELY MISSED THE POINT OF THAT BOOK, FIXATING INSTEAD ON HOW COOL IT WOULD BE TO GET TO BRING A DOG TO SCHOOL.
ANOTHER STORY HAD ME ACCIDENTALLY SEALED IN A CRATE AND SHIPPED TO SPAIN--
--WHERE I HAD TO SURVIVE IMPOSSIBLE ADVENTURES AND THEN FIND MY WAY BACK TO MY DISTRAUGHT AND REGRET-FILLED PARENTS.
WHEN I LEFT THE LITTLE BOY IN ME BEHIND--
--THOUGH NOT COMPLETELY BEHIND--
--I NEVER IMAGINED I'D BE SITTING HERE DOING THIS...
...WRITING COMIC BOOKS.

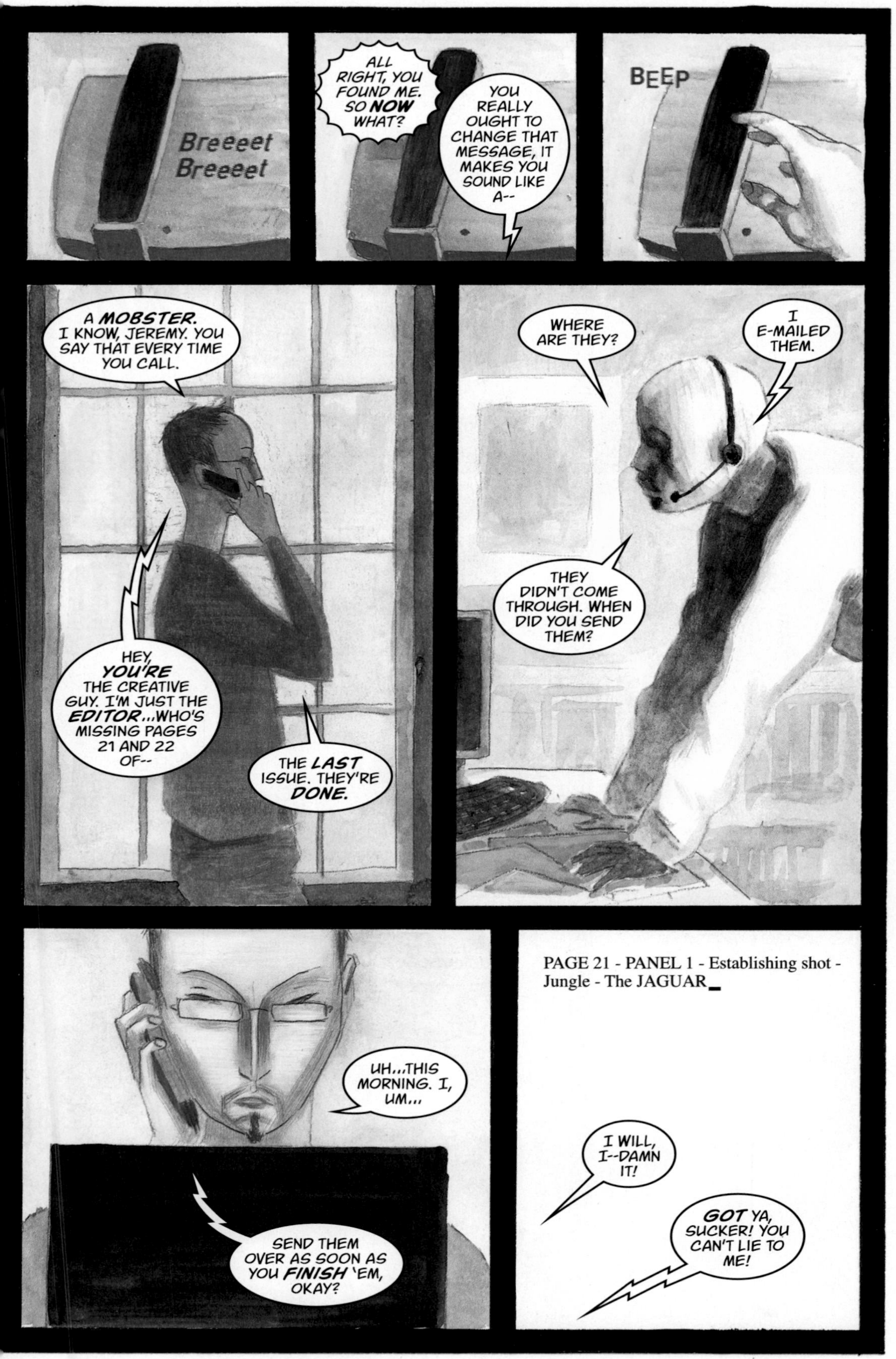
Breeeet
Breeeet
ALL RIGHT, YOU FOUND ME. SO NOW WHAT?
YOU REALLY OUGHT TO CHANGE THAT MESSAGE, IT MAKES YOU SOUND LIKE A--
BEEP
A MOBSTER. I KNOW, JEREMY. YOU SAY THAT EVERY TIME YOU CALL.
HEY, YOU'RE THE CREATIVE GUY. I'M JUST THE EDITOR...WHO'S MISSING PAGES 21 AND 22 OF--
THE LAST ISSUE. THEY'RE DONE.
WHERE ARE THEY?
I E-MAILED THEM.
THEY DIDN'T COME THROUGH. WHEN DID YOU SEND THEM?
UH...THIS MORNING. I, UM...
SEND THEM OVER AS SOON AS YOU FINISH 'EM, OKAY?
PAGE 21 - PANEL 1 - Establishing shot - Jungle - The JAGUAR_
I WILL, I--DAMN IT!
GOT YA, SUCKER! YOU CAN'T LIE TO ME!

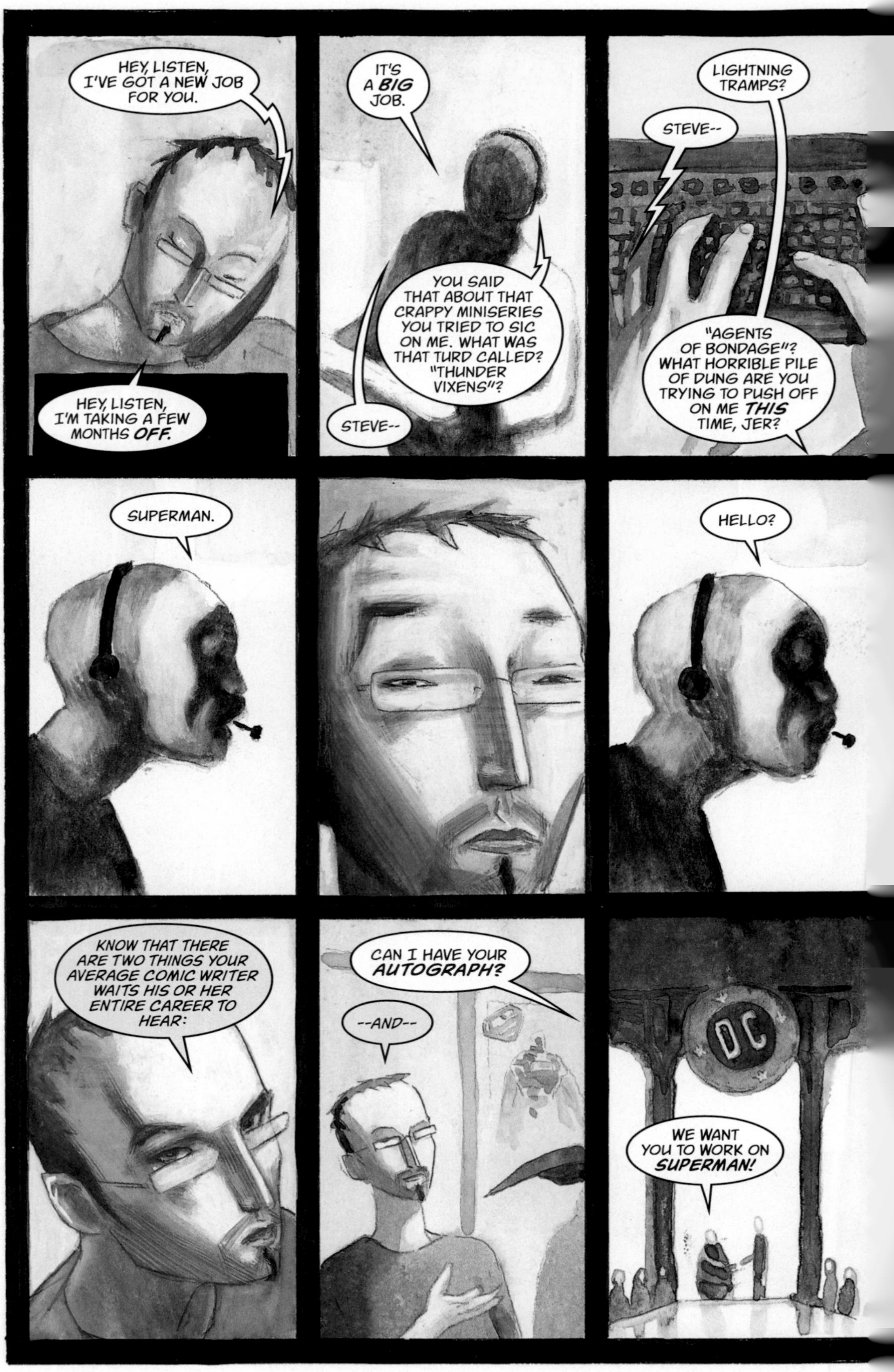
HEY, LISTEN, I'VE GOT A NEW JOB FOR YOU.
HEY, LISTEN, I'M TAKING A FEW MONTHS OFF.
IT'S A BIG JOB.
YOU SAID THAT ABOUT THAT CRAPPY MINISERIES YOU TRIED TO SIC ON ME. WHAT WAS THAT TURD CALLED? "THUNDER VIXENS"?
STEVE--
LIGHTNING TRAMPS?
STEVE--
"AGENTS OF BONDAGE"? WHAT HORRIBLE PILE OF DUNG ARE YOU TRYING TO PUSH OFF ON ME THIS TIME, JER?
SUPERMAN.
HELLO?
KNOW THAT THERE ARE TWO THINGS YOUR AVERAGE COMIC WRITER WAITS HIS OR HER ENTIRE CAREER TO HEAR:
CAN I HAVE YOUR AUTOGRAPH?
--AND--
DC
WE WANT YOU TO WORK ON SUPERMAN!

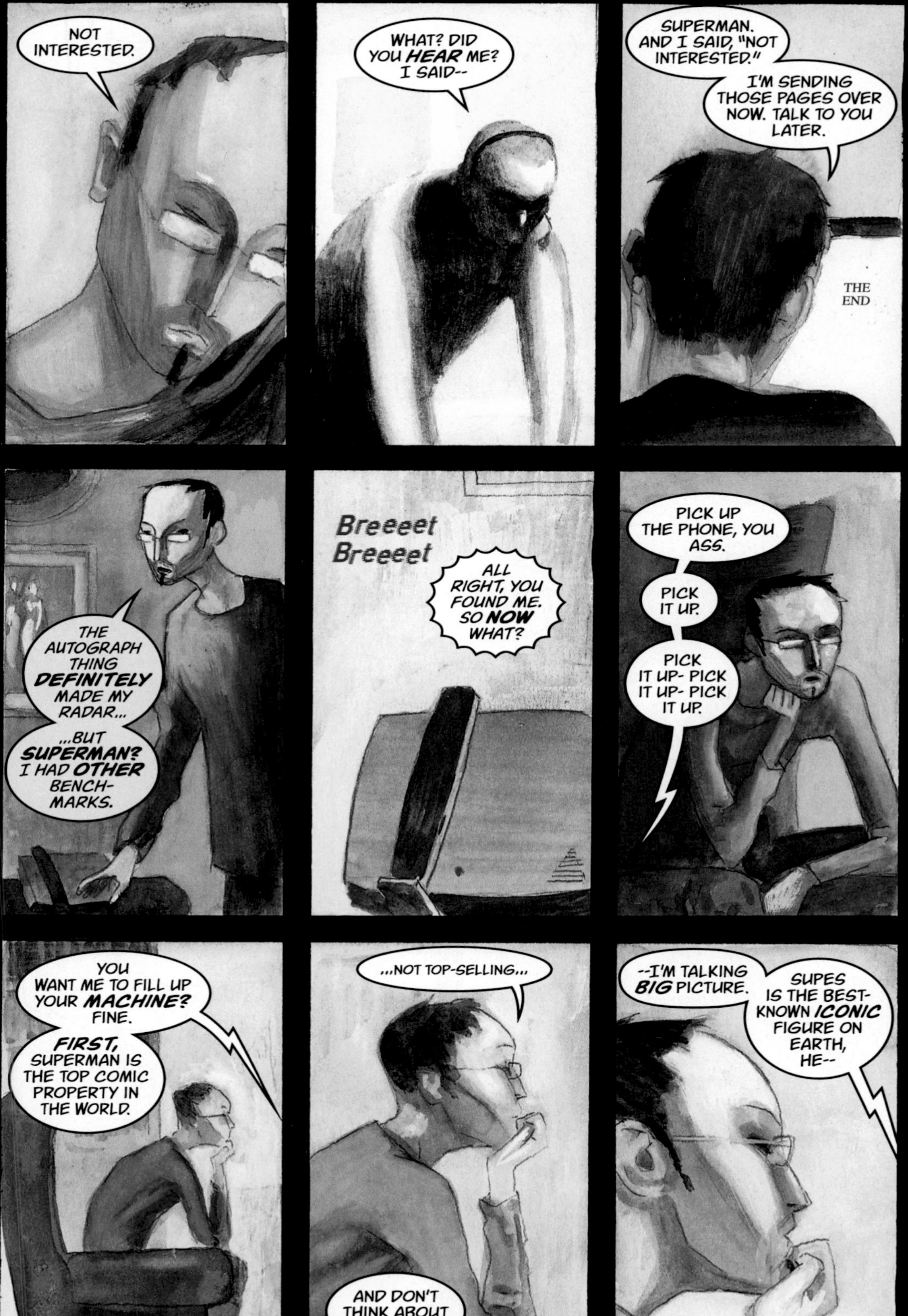
NOT INTERESTED.
WHAT? DID YOU HEAR ME? I SAID--
SUPERMAN. AND I SAID, "NOT INTERESTED."
I'M SENDING THOSE PAGES OVER NOW. TALK TO YOU LATER.
THE END
THE AUTOGRAPH THING DEFINITELY MADE MY RADAR...
...BUT SUPERMAN? I HAD OTHER BENCH-MARKS.
Breeeet Breeeet
ALL RIGHT, YOU FOUND ME. SO NOW WHAT?
PICK UP THE PHONE, YOU ASS.
PICK IT UP.
PICK IT UP- PICK IT UP- PICK IT UP.
YOU WANT ME TO FILL UP YOUR MACHINE? FINE.
FIRST, SUPERMAN IS THE TOP COMIC PROPERTY IN THE WORLD.
...NOT TOP-SELLING...
AND DON'T THINK ABOUT SALES--
--I'M TALKING BIG PICTURE.
SUPES IS THE BEST-KNOWN ICONIC FIGURE ON EARTH, HE--

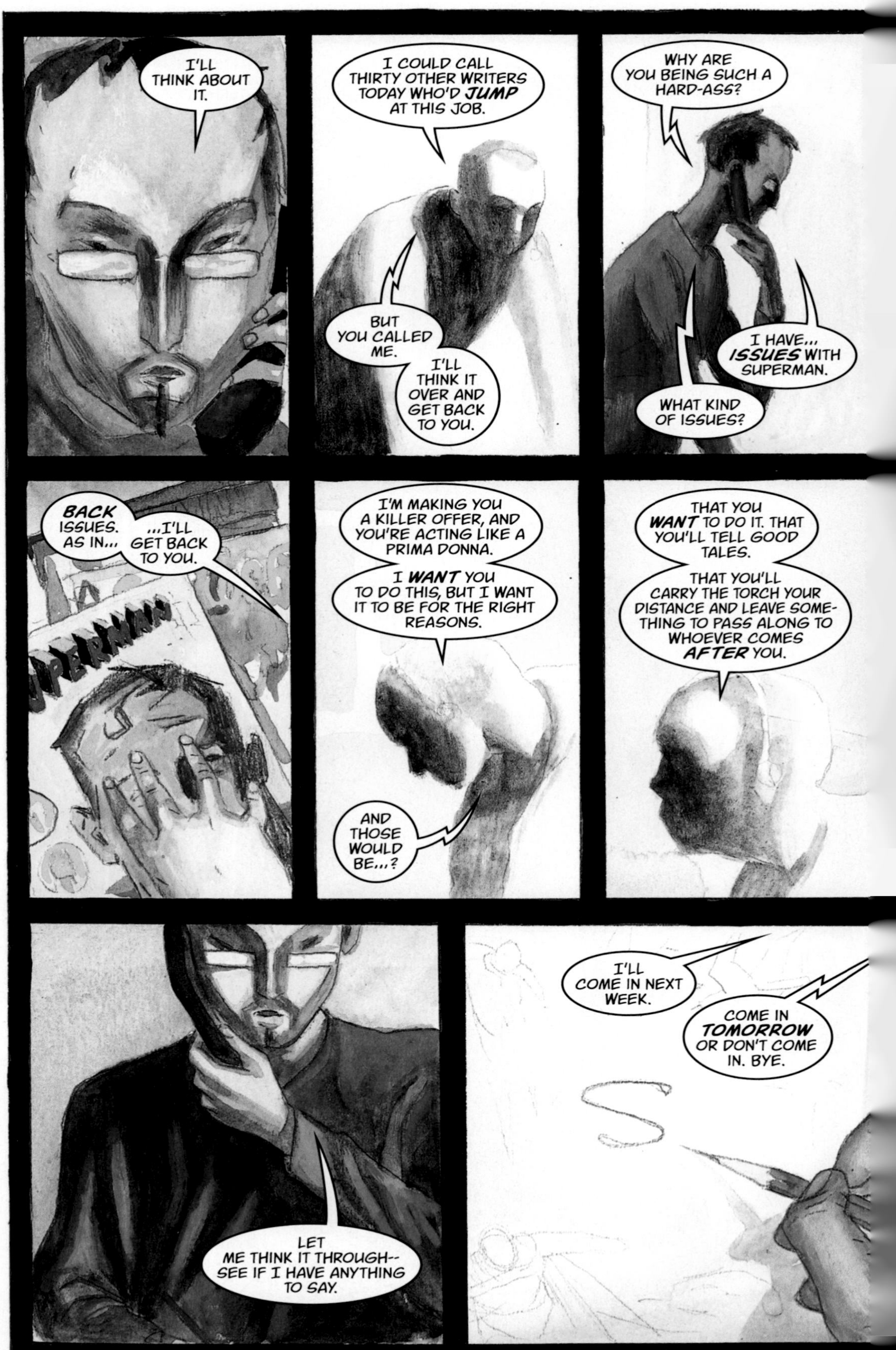
I'LL THINK ABOUT IT.
I COULD CALL THIRTY OTHER WRITERS TODAY WHO'D JUMP AT THIS JOB.
BUT YOU CALLED ME.
I'LL THINK IT OVER AND GET BACK TO YOU.
WHY ARE YOU BEING SUCH A HARD-ASS?
I HAVE... ISSUES WITH SUPERMAN.
WHAT KIND OF ISSUES?
BACK ISSUES. AS IN...
...I'LL GET BACK TO YOU.
SUPERMAN
I'M MAKING YOU A KILLER OFFER, AND YOU'RE ACTING LIKE A PRIMA DONNA.
I WANT YOU TO DO THIS, BUT I WANT IT TO BE FOR THE RIGHT REASONS.
AND THOSE WOULD BE...?
THAT YOU WANT TO DO IT. THAT YOU'LL TELL GOOD TALES.
THAT YOU'LL CARRY THE TORCH YOUR DISTANCE AND LEAVE SOME-THING TO PASS ALONG TO WHOEVER COMES AFTER YOU.
LET ME THINK IT THROUGH-- SEE IF I HAVE ANYTHING TO SAY.
I'LL COME IN NEXT WEEK.
COME IN TOMORROW OR DON'T COME IN. BYE.

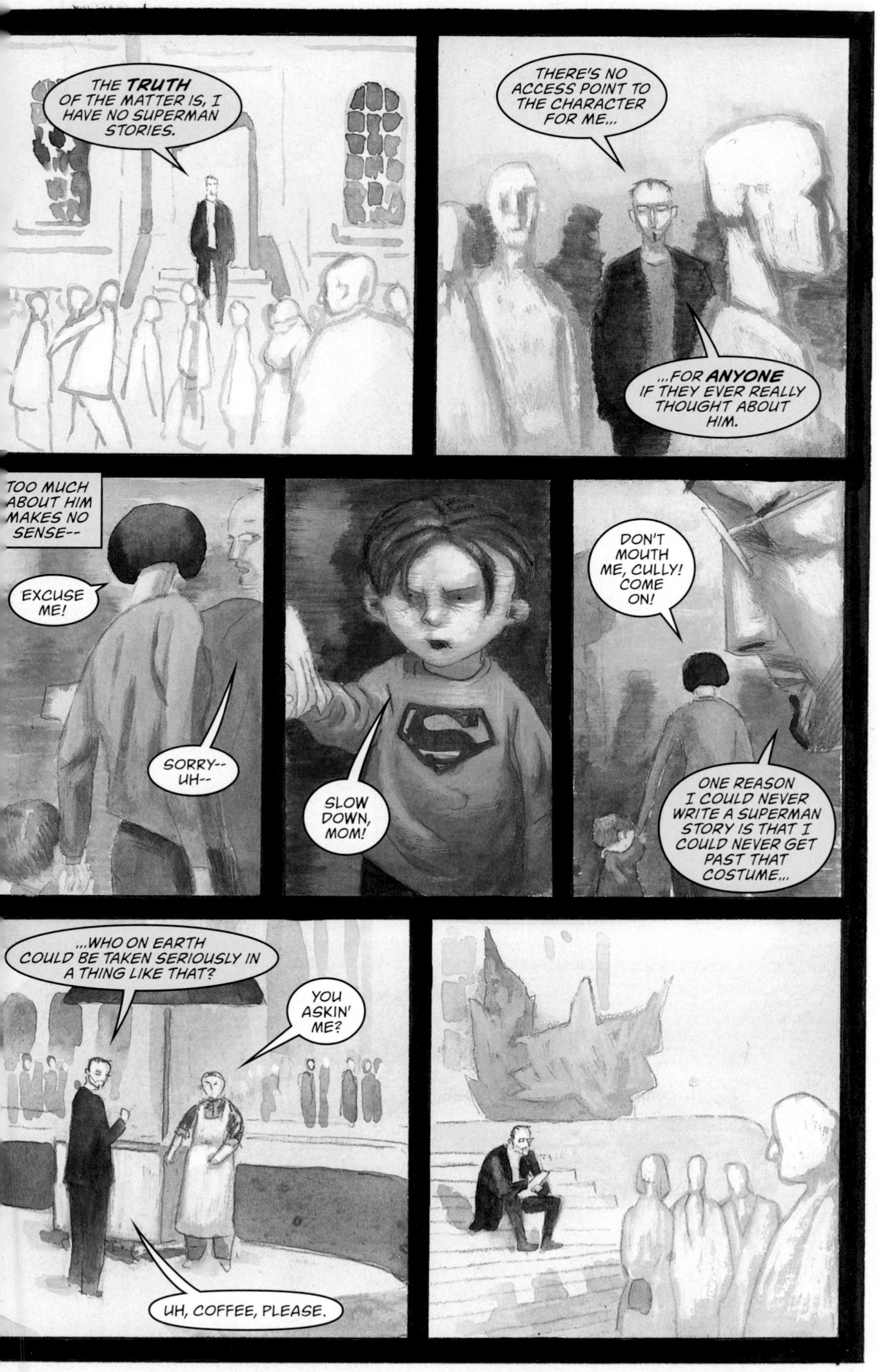
THE TRUTH OF THE MATTER IS, I HAVE NO SUPERMAN STORIES.
THERE'S NO ACCESS POINT TO THE CHARACTER FOR ME...
...FOR ANYONE IF THEY EVER REALLY THOUGHT ABOUT HIM.
TOO MUCH ABOUT HIM MAKES NO SENSE--
EXCUSE ME!
SORRY-- UH--
SLOW DOWN, MOM!
DON'T MOUTH ME, CULLY! COME ON!
ONE REASON I COULD NEVER WRITE A SUPERMAN STORY IS THAT I COULD NEVER GET PAST THAT COSTUME...
...WHO ON EARTH COULD BE TAKEN SERIOUSLY IN A THING LIKE THAT?
YOU ASKIN' ME?
UH, COFFEE, PLEASE.

THE COSTUME

SEVENTH GRADE WAS WHERE IT ALL STARTED TO GET WEIRD. SOME OF THE BOYS LOOKED LIKE KIDS, WHILE THEIR FRIENDS THE SAME AGE LOOKED LIKE MEN.

SOME OF THE GIRLS STILL PLAYED WITH DOLLS, BUT OTHERS BEGAN TO DRESS LIKE THEIR OLDER SISTERS.

AND THINGS THAT DIDN'T USED TO MATTER SUDDENLY DID.

THE KIDS CONGREGATED INTO GROUPS THAT WOULD ENDURE UNTIL GRADUATION DAY: THE JOCKS...THE BRAINS...THE GEEKS.

UNFORTUNATELY, JASON DOBSON WASN'T LUCKY ENOUGH TO FIT IN WITH ANY OF THEM. HE SAT ALONE AT LUNCH, PAINFULLY AWARE THAT EVEN THE GEEKS HAD SOMEONE TO EAT WITH.

JASON DOBSON SAT IN THE BACK OF CLASS ANSWERING HISTORY QUESTIONS WRONG.

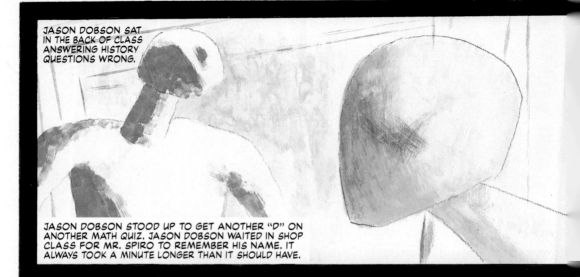

JASON DOBSON STOOD UP TO GET ANOTHER "D" ON ANOTHER MATH QUIZ. JASON DOBSON WAITED IN SHOP CLASS FOR MR. SPIRO TO REMEMBER HIS NAME. IT ALWAYS TOOK A MINUTE LONGER THAN IT SHOULD HAVE.

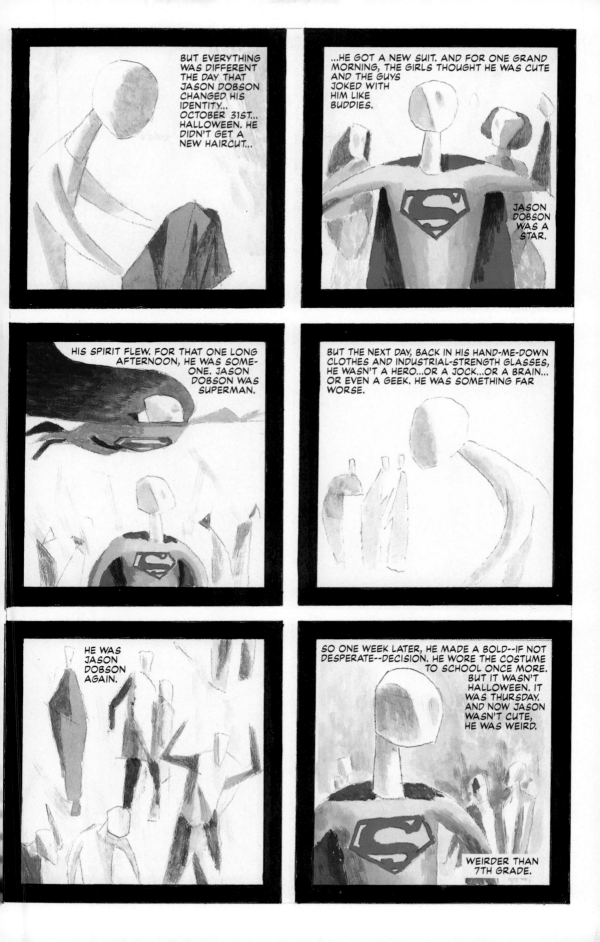

BUT EVERYTHING WAS DIFFERENT THE DAY THAT JASON DOBSON CHANGED HIS IDENTITY... OCTOBER 31ST... HALLOWEEN. HE DIDN'T GET A NEW HAIRCUT...

...HE GOT A NEW SUIT. AND FOR ONE GRAND MORNING, THE GIRLS THOUGHT HE WAS CUTE AND THE GUYS JOKED WITH HIM LIKE BUDDIES.

JASON DOBSON WAS A STAR.

HIS SPIRIT FLEW. FOR THAT ONE LONG AFTERNOON, HE WAS SOMEONE. JASON DOBSON WAS SUPERMAN.

BUT THE NEXT DAY, BACK IN HIS HAND-ME-DOWN CLOTHES AND INDUSTRIAL-STRENGTH GLASSES, HE WASN'T A HERO...OR A JOCK...OR A BRAIN... OR EVEN A GEEK. HE WAS SOMETHING FAR WORSE.

HE WAS JASON DOBSON AGAIN.

SO ONE WEEK LATER, HE MADE A BOLD--IF NOT DESPERATE--DECISION. HE WORE THE COSTUME TO SCHOOL ONCE MORE. BUT IT WASN'T HALLOWEEN. IT WAS THURSDAY. AND NOW JASON WASN'T CUTE, HE WAS WEIRD.

WEIRDER THAN 7TH GRADE.

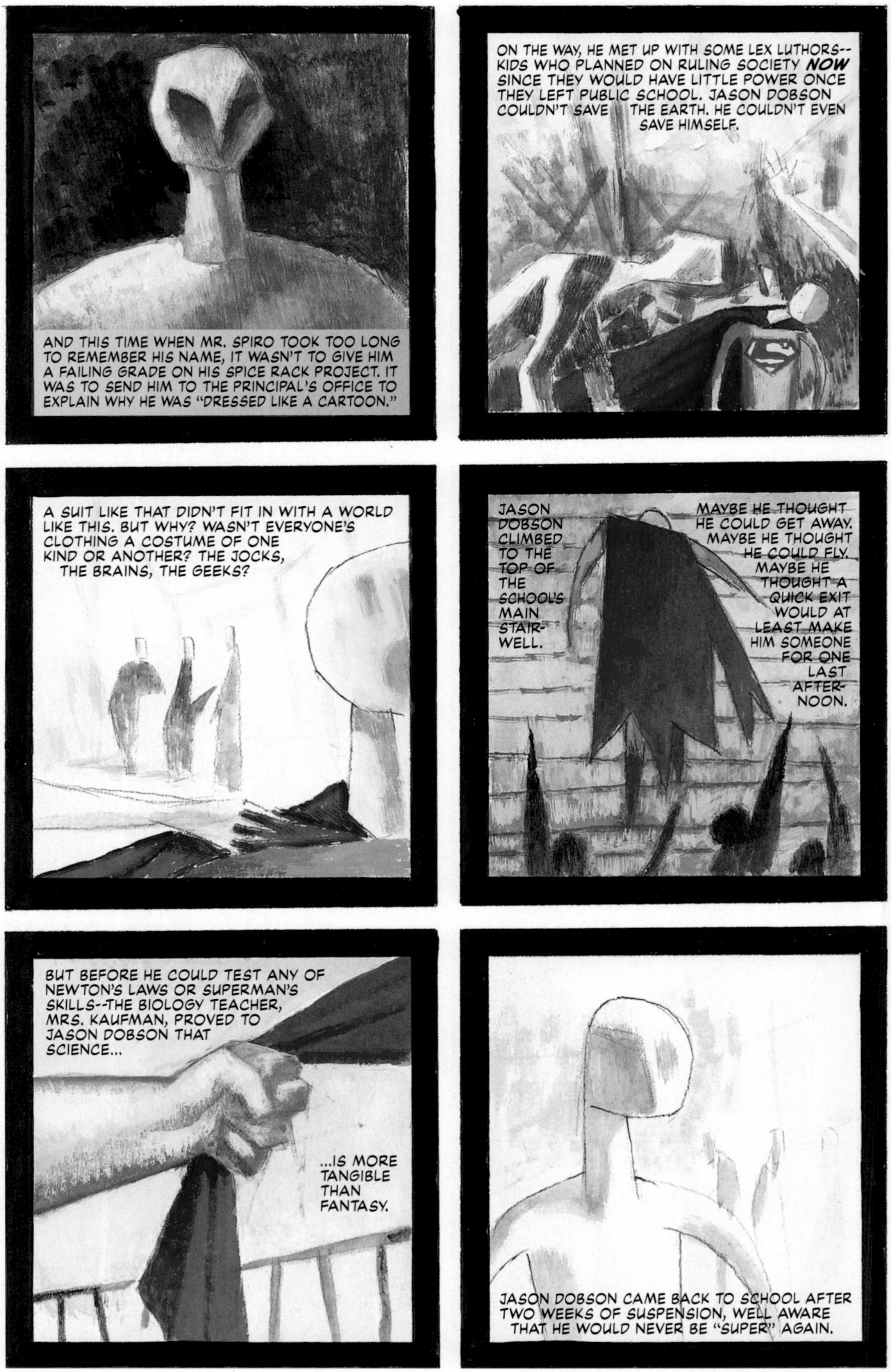
AND THIS TIME WHEN MR. SPIRO TOOK TOO LONG TO REMEMBER HIS NAME, IT WASN'T TO GIVE HIM A FAILING GRADE ON HIS SPICE RACK PROJECT. IT WAS TO SEND HIM TO THE PRINCIPAL'S OFFICE TO EXPLAIN WHY HE WAS "DRESSED LIKE A CARTOON."
ON THE WAY, HE MET UP WITH SOME LEX LUTHORS--KIDS WHO PLANNED ON RULING SOCIETY NOW SINCE THEY WOULD HAVE LITTLE POWER ONCE THEY LEFT PUBLIC SCHOOL. JASON DOBSON COULDN'T SAVE THE EARTH. HE COULDN'T EVEN SAVE HIMSELF.
A SUIT LIKE THAT DIDN'T FIT IN WITH A WORLD LIKE THIS. BUT WHY? WASN'T EVERYONE'S CLOTHING A COSTUME OF ONE KIND OR ANOTHER? THE JOCKS, THE BRAINS, THE GEEKS?
JASON DOBSON CLIMBED TO THE TOP OF THE SCHOOL'S MAIN STAIRWELL.
MAYBE HE THOUGHT HE COULD GET AWAY. MAYBE HE THOUGHT HE COULD FLY. MAYBE HE THOUGHT A QUICK EXIT WOULD AT LEAST MAKE HIM SOMEONE FOR ONE LAST AFTERNOON.
BUT BEFORE HE COULD TEST ANY OF NEWTON'S LAWS OR SUPERMAN'S SKILLS--THE BIOLOGY TEACHER, MRS. KAUFMAN, PROVED TO JASON DOBSON THAT SCIENCE...
...IS MORE TANGIBLE THAN FANTASY.
JASON DOBSON CAME BACK TO SCHOOL AFTER TWO WEEKS OF SUSPENSION, WELL AWARE THAT HE WOULD NEVER BE "SUPER" AGAIN.

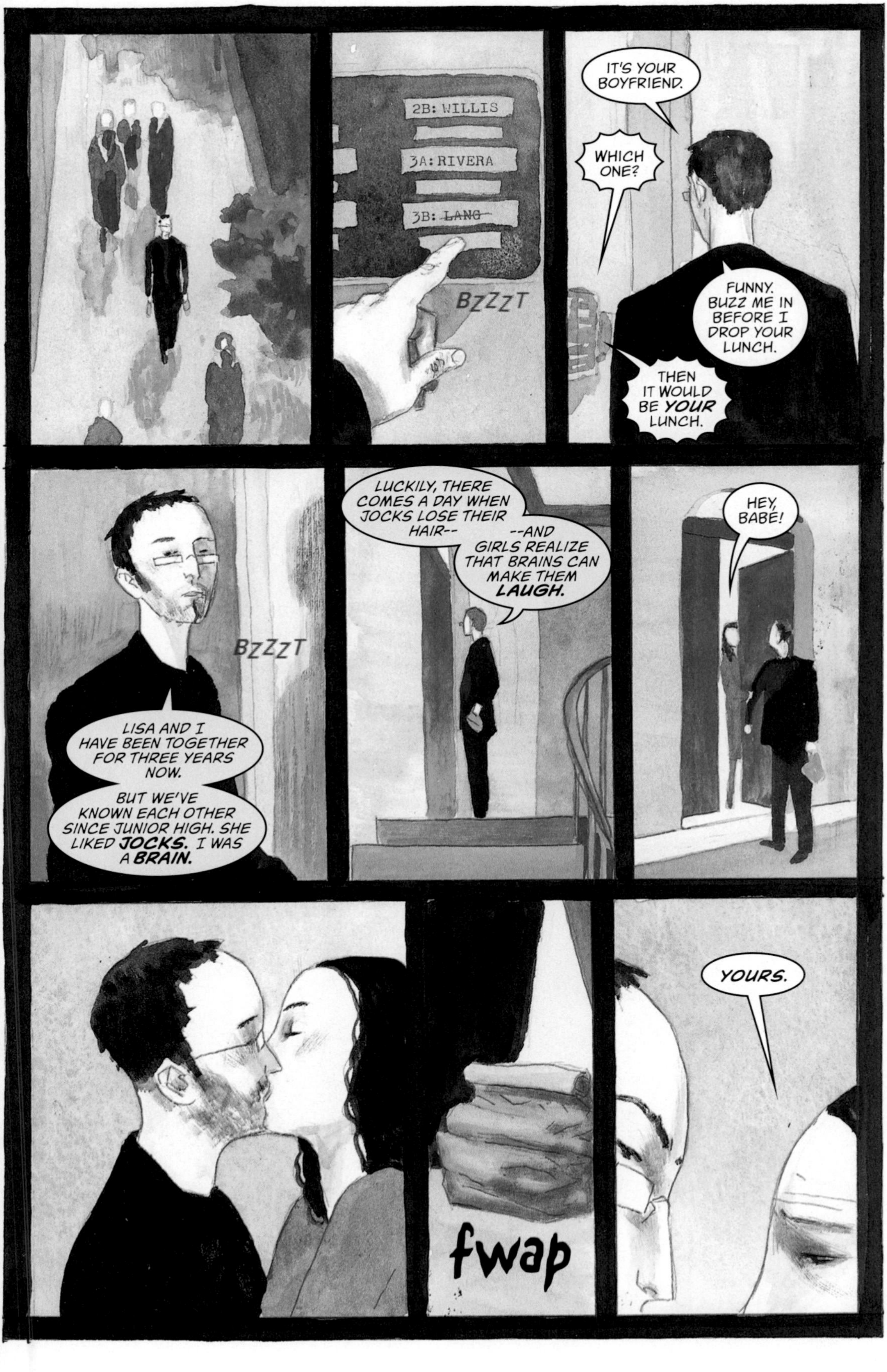
2B: WILLIS
3A: RIVERA
3B: LANG
BZZZT
IT'S YOUR BOYFRIEND.
WHICH ONE?
FUNNY. BUZZ ME IN BEFORE I DROP YOUR LUNCH.
THEN IT WOULD BE *YOUR* LUNCH.
BZZZT
LISA AND I HAVE BEEN TOGETHER FOR THREE YEARS NOW.
BUT WE'VE KNOWN EACH OTHER SINCE JUNIOR HIGH. SHE LIKED **JOCKS.** I WAS A **BRAIN.**
LUCKILY, THERE COMES A DAY WHEN JOCKS LOSE THEIR HAIR--
--AND GIRLS REALIZE THAT BRAINS CAN MAKE THEM **LAUGH.**
HEY, BABE!
fwap
YOURS.

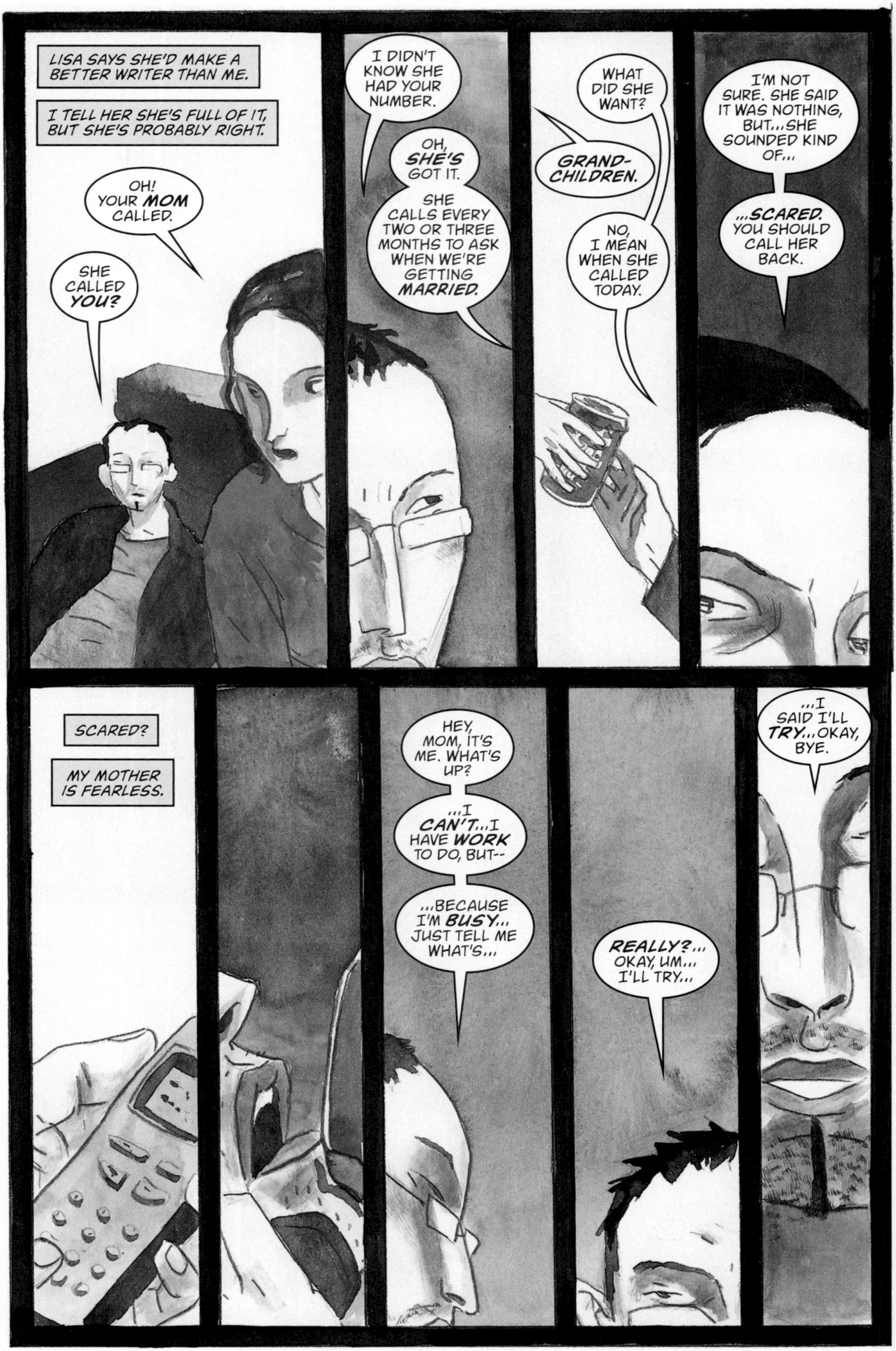
LISA SAYS SHE'D MAKE A BETTER WRITER THAN ME.
I TELL HER SHE'S FULL OF IT, BUT SHE'S PROBABLY RIGHT.
OH! YOUR MOM CALLED.
SHE CALLED YOU?
I DIDN'T KNOW SHE HAD YOUR NUMBER.
OH, SHE'S GOT IT.
SHE CALLS EVERY TWO OR THREE MONTHS TO ASK WHEN WE'RE GETTING MARRIED.
WHAT DID SHE WANT?
GRAND-CHILDREN.
NO, I MEAN WHEN SHE CALLED TODAY.
I'M NOT SURE. SHE SAID IT WAS NOTHING, BUT...SHE SOUNDED KIND OF...
...SCARED. YOU SHOULD CALL HER BACK.
SCARED?
MY MOTHER IS FEARLESS.
HEY, MOM, IT'S ME. WHAT'S UP?
...I CAN'T...I HAVE WORK TO DO, BUT--
...BECAUSE I'M BUSY... JUST TELL ME WHAT'S...
REALLY?... OKAY, UM... I'LL TRY...
...I SAID I'LL TRY...OKAY, BYE.

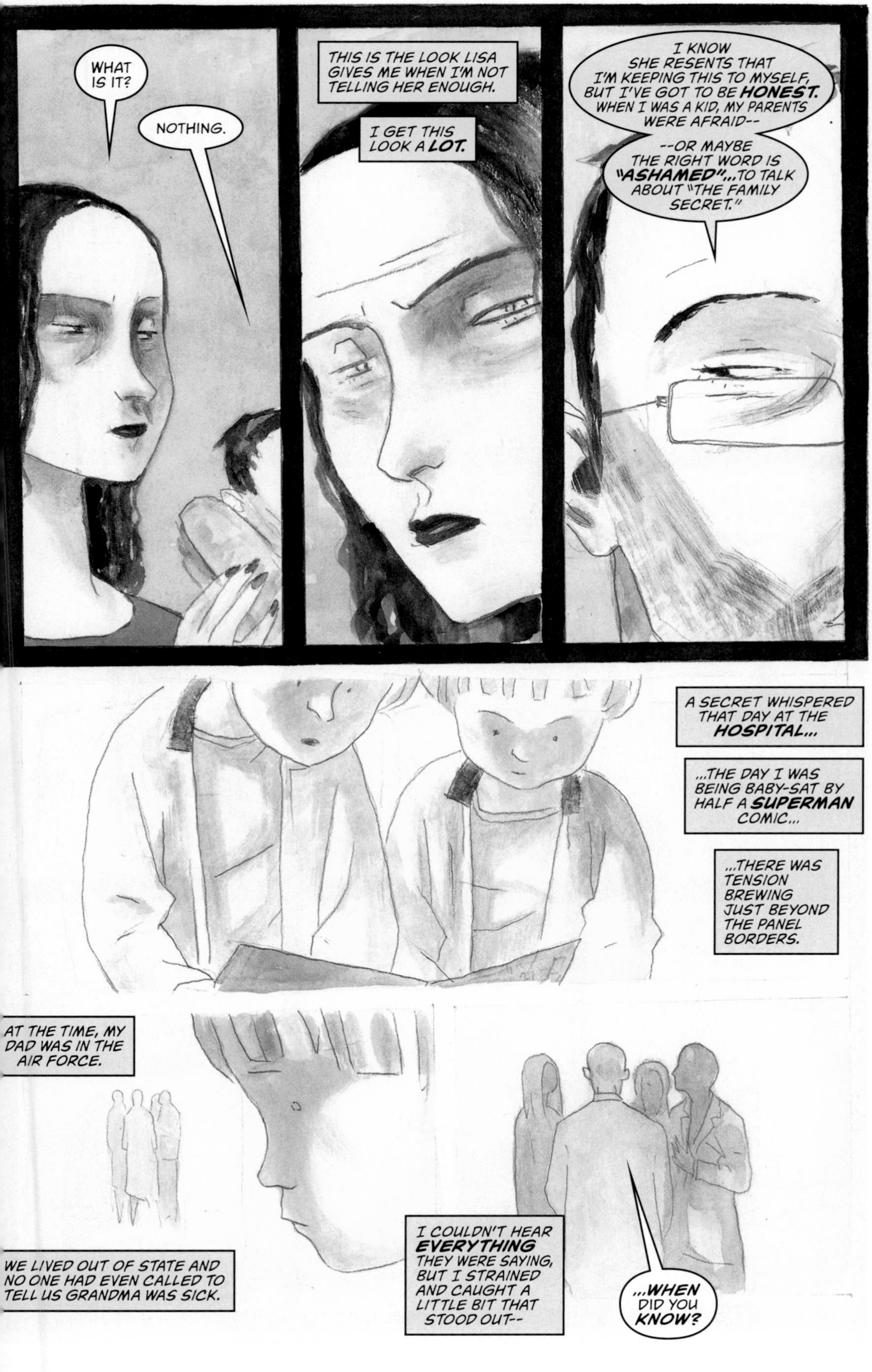
WHAT IS IT?
NOTHING.
THIS IS THE LOOK LISA GIVES ME WHEN I'M NOT TELLING HER ENOUGH.
I GET THIS LOOK A LOT.
I KNOW SHE RESENTS THAT I'M KEEPING THIS TO MYSELF, BUT I'VE GOT TO BE HONEST. WHEN I WAS A KID, MY PARENTS WERE AFRAID--
--OR MAYBE THE RIGHT WORD IS "ASHAMED"...TO TALK ABOUT "THE FAMILY SECRET."
A SECRET WHISPERED THAT DAY AT THE HOSPITAL...
...THE DAY I WAS BEING BABY-SAT BY HALF A SUPERMAN COMIC...
...THERE WAS TENSION BREWING JUST BEYOND THE PANEL BORDERS.
AT THE TIME, MY DAD WAS IN THE AIR FORCE.
WE LIVED OUT OF STATE AND NO ONE HAD EVEN CALLED TO TELL US GRANDMA WAS SICK.
I COULDN'T HEAR EVERYTHING THEY WERE SAYING, BUT I STRAINED AND CAUGHT A LITTLE BIT THAT STOOD OUT--
...WHEN DID YOU KNOW?

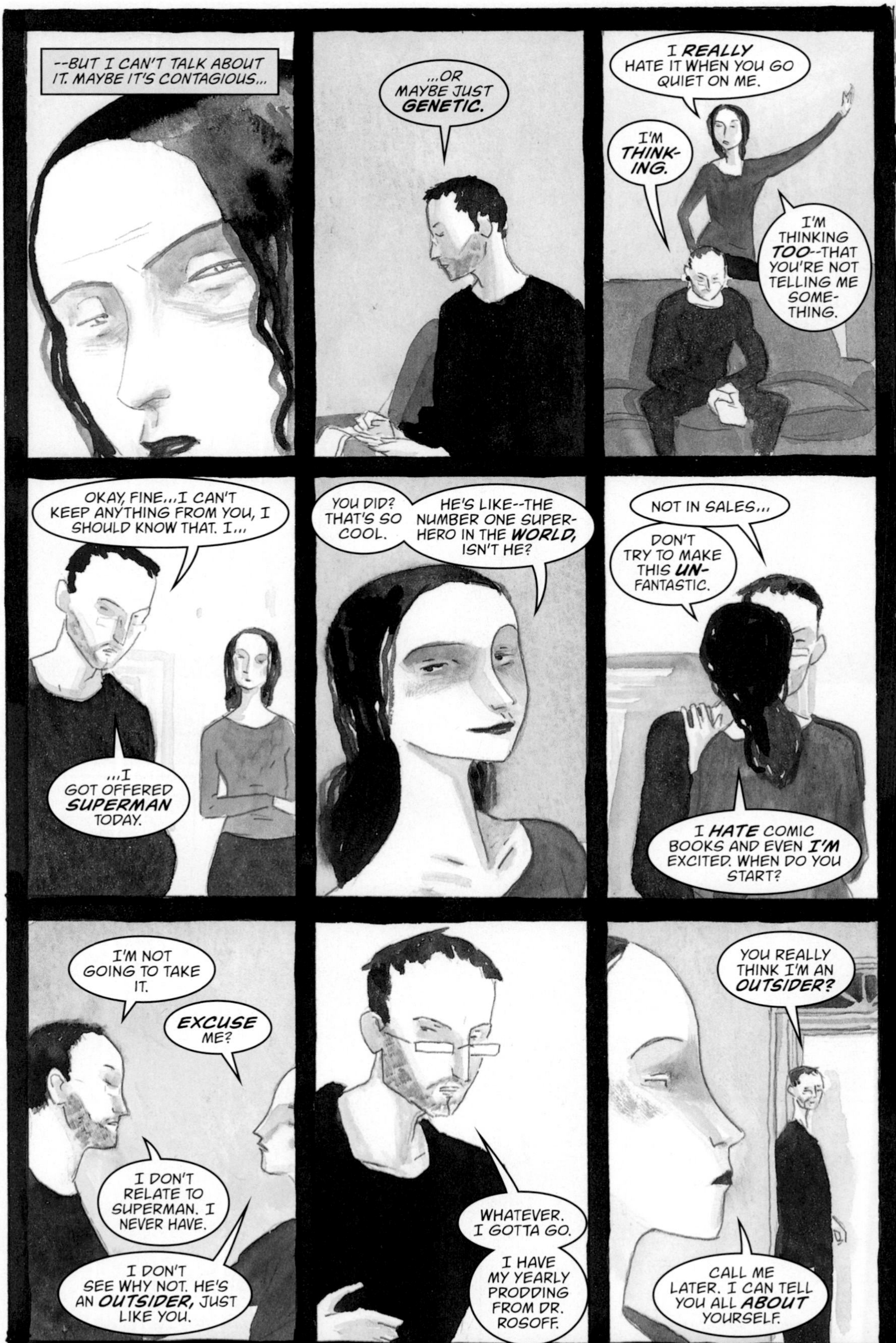
--BUT I CAN'T TALK ABOUT IT. MAYBE IT'S CONTAGIOUS...
...OR MAYBE JUST GENETIC.
I REALLY HATE IT WHEN YOU GO QUIET ON ME.
I'M THINKING.
I'M THINKING TOO--THAT YOU'RE NOT TELLING ME SOMETHING.
OKAY, FINE...I CAN'T KEEP ANYTHING FROM YOU, I SHOULD KNOW THAT. I...
...I GOT OFFERED SUPERMAN TODAY.
YOU DID? THAT'S SO COOL.
HE'S LIKE--THE NUMBER ONE SUPERHERO IN THE WORLD, ISN'T HE?
NOT IN SALES...
DON'T TRY TO MAKE THIS UN-FANTASTIC.
I HATE COMIC BOOKS AND EVEN I'M EXCITED. WHEN DO YOU START?
I'M NOT GOING TO TAKE IT.
EXCUSE ME?
I DON'T RELATE TO SUPERMAN. I NEVER HAVE.
I DON'T SEE WHY NOT. HE'S AN OUTSIDER, JUST LIKE YOU.
WHATEVER. I GOTTA GO.
I HAVE MY YEARLY PRODDING FROM DR. ROSOFF.
YOU REALLY THINK I'M AN OUTSIDER?
CALL ME LATER. I CAN TELL YOU ALL ABOUT YOURSELF.

THE OUTSIDER

Suit and Tie
Hat and Glasses
Clark Kent fits
right in
To the Walk-a-day
Work-a-day
Chit-chat
Clickity-clack
Paycheck and
Collar-stay
Water-cooler
world of
Metropolis.

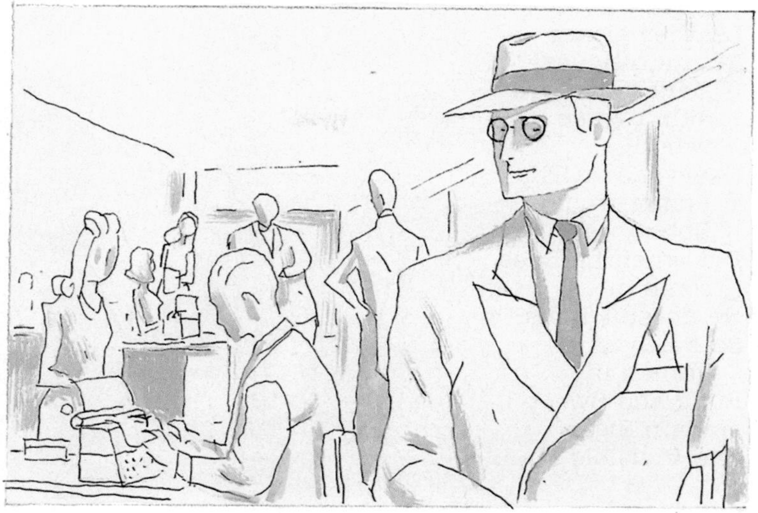

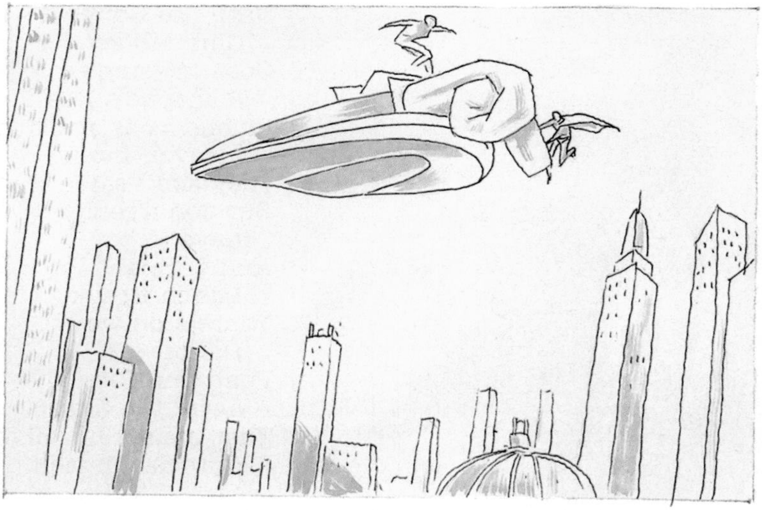

On that Oh-so-
anticipated
Lunch Break
There's always
time for a
Quick Change
A Quick Flight
Quick Work
For Would-be
World-crushers
And then right
back to
Suit and Tie
Hat and Glasses
Oh yes, Clark Kent
fits right in.

But down in
Accounting
Columns and Rows
And Linda Goldberg
knows
The "Ha ha ha's" at
the Water Cooler
Are Jokes about
how "Her People"
Are always "the ones
handling Money."
No Lunch Break
long enough
To allow her a
Quick Change
From her Heritage
or its Critics.

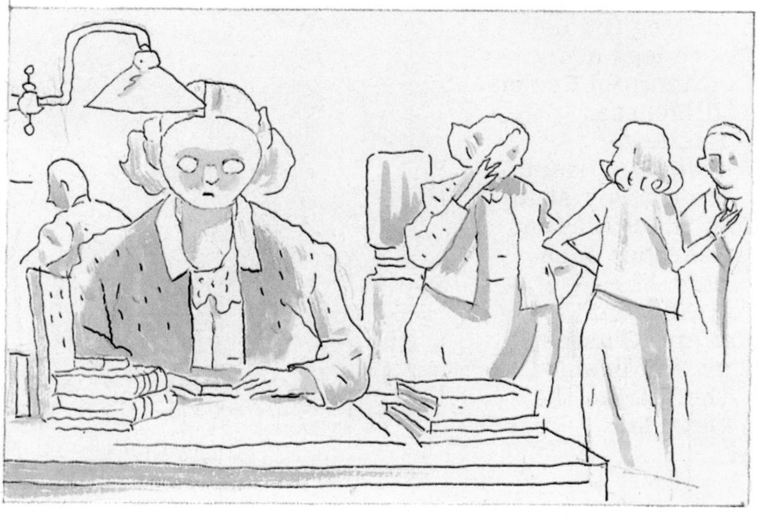

Leather gloves
Denim fatigues
If DeRon Sanford
didn't come to
work
Everyone on The
Planet would
Notice
But when he Does
come in
He doesn't Blend in
So much as
Vanish in
Push and Sweep
Plain Sight
The Invisible Man.

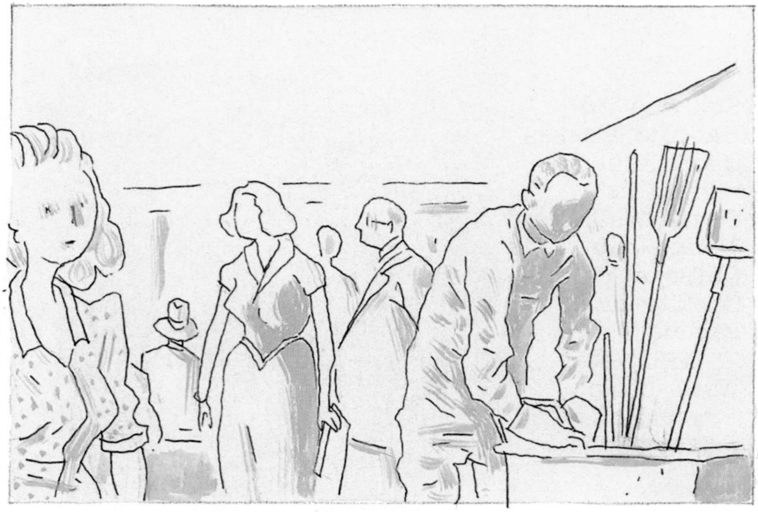

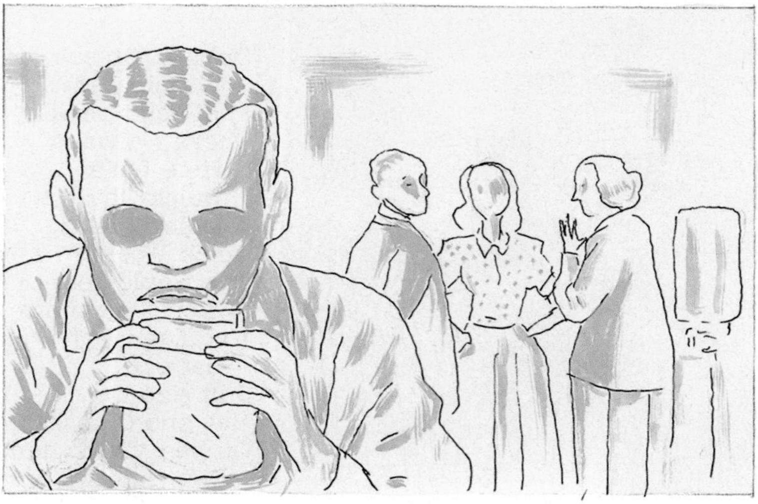

Until the Coffee
Club Money
Goes Missing from
Someone's Desk
No one looks at Clark,
or even Linda
They don't say a Word
But don't really
have to
And on his
Lunch Break
There's no way
DeRon can
Push and Sweep
away the Skin
That makes him live
Outside Himself.

And Greg Giddley
Whose legs are
Aluminum Spokes
And Melissa
Bandeau
Whose "Boyfriend"
isn't a Boy at all
Join the Staff that
Searches each
day
For Suit and Tie
Hat and Glasses
That will bring
them from the
Outside
In.

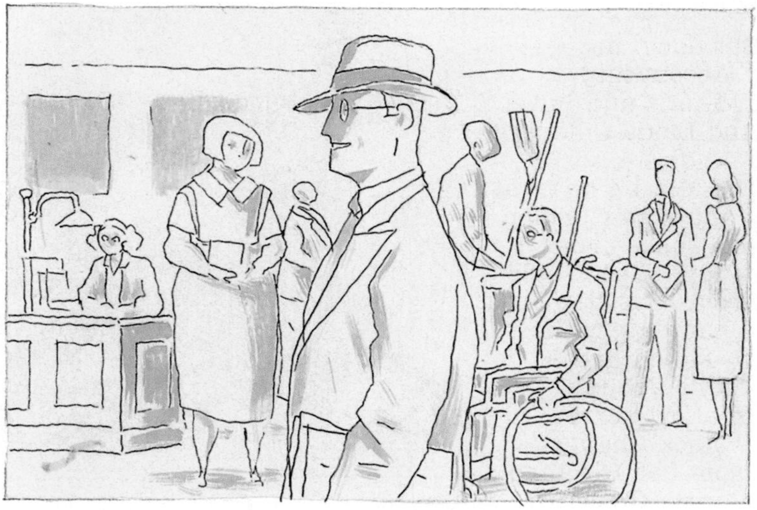

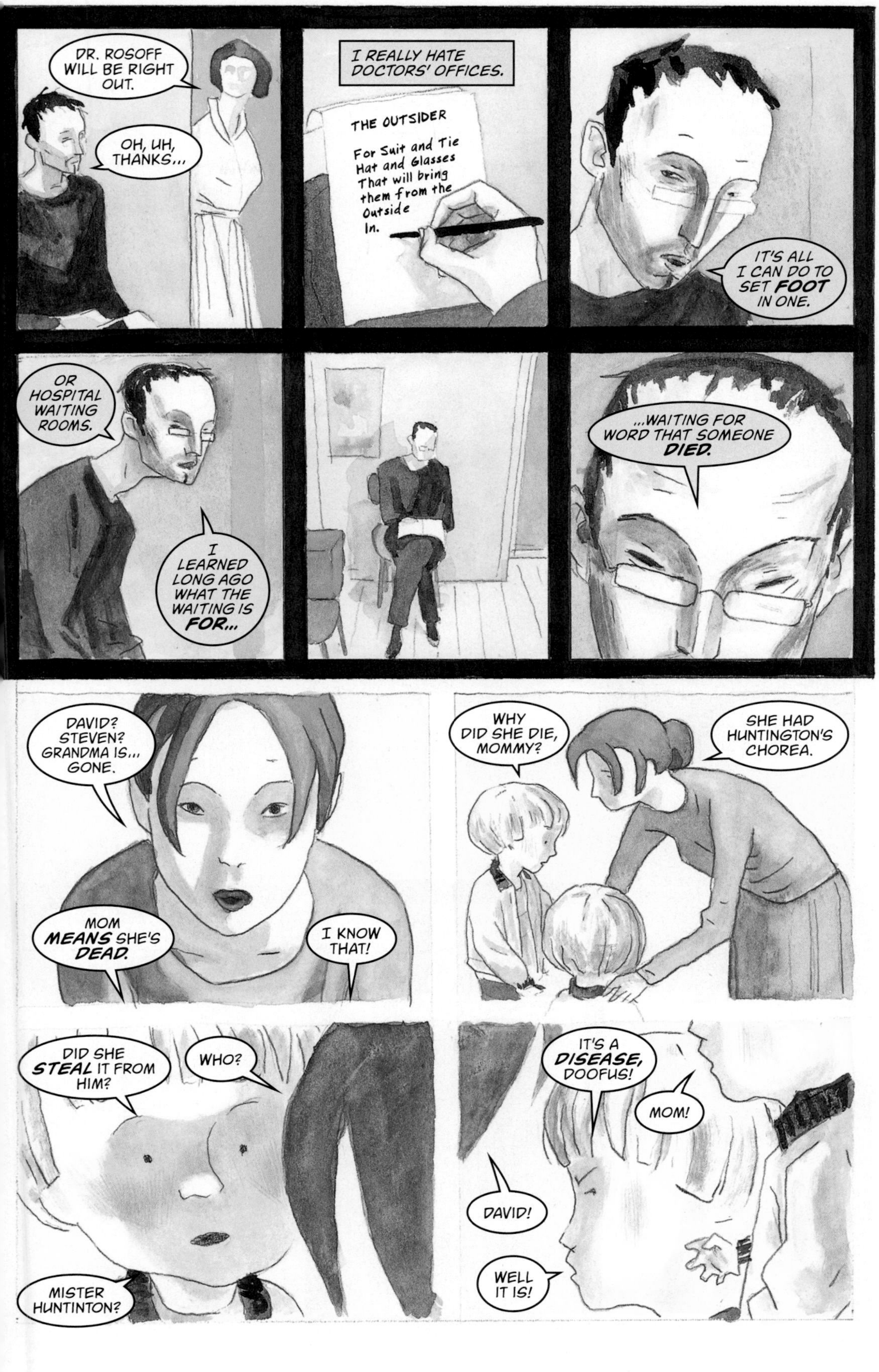
DR. ROSOFF WILL BE RIGHT OUT.
OH, UH, THANKS...
I REALLY HATE DOCTORS' OFFICES.
THE OUTSIDER
For Suit and Tie Hat and Glasses That will bring them from the Outside In.
IT'S ALL I CAN DO TO SET FOOT IN ONE.
OR HOSPITAL WAITING ROOMS.
I LEARNED LONG AGO WHAT THE WAITING IS FOR...
...WAITING FOR WORD THAT SOMEONE DIED.
DAVID? STEVEN? GRANDMA IS... GONE.
MOM MEANS SHE'S DEAD.
I KNOW THAT!
WHY DID SHE DIE, MOMMY?
SHE HAD HUNTINGTON'S CHOREA.
DID SHE STEAL IT FROM HIM?
WHO?
MISTER HUNTINTON?
IT'S A DISEASE, DOOFUS!
MOM!
DAVID!
WELL IT IS!

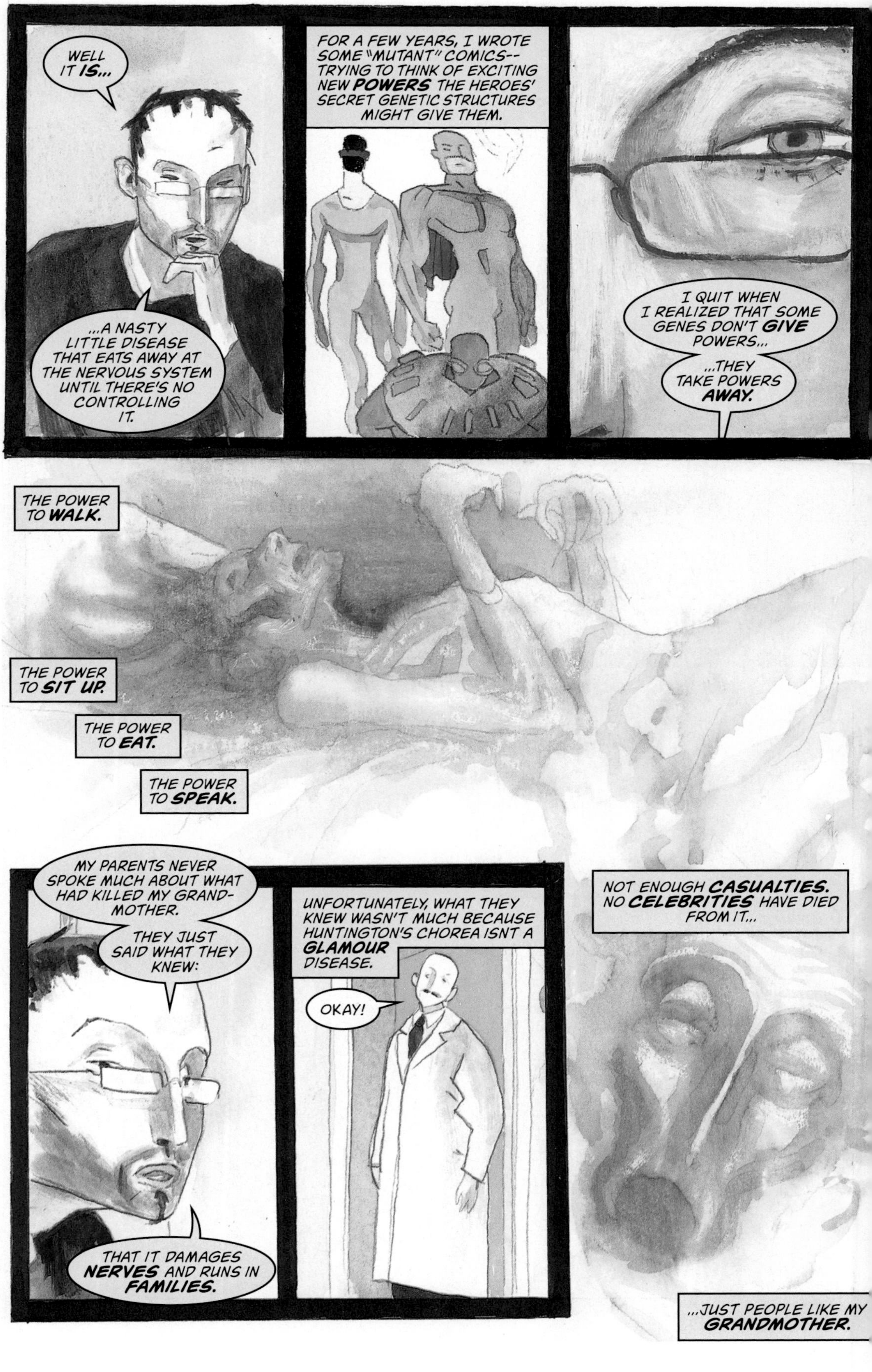
WELL IT IS...
...A NASTY LITTLE DISEASE THAT EATS AWAY AT THE NERVOUS SYSTEM UNTIL THERE'S NO CONTROLLING IT.
FOR A FEW YEARS, I WROTE SOME "MUTANT" COMICS-- TRYING TO THINK OF EXCITING NEW POWERS THE HEROES' SECRET GENETIC STRUCTURES MIGHT GIVE THEM.
I QUIT WHEN I REALIZED THAT SOME GENES DON'T GIVE POWERS...
...THEY TAKE POWERS AWAY.
THE POWER TO WALK.
THE POWER TO SIT UP.
THE POWER TO EAT.
THE POWER TO SPEAK.
MY PARENTS NEVER SPOKE MUCH ABOUT WHAT HAD KILLED MY GRAND-MOTHER.
THEY JUST SAID WHAT THEY KNEW:
THAT IT DAMAGES NERVES AND RUNS IN FAMILIES.
UNFORTUNATELY, WHAT THEY KNEW WASN'T MUCH BECAUSE HUNTINGTON'S CHOREA ISNT A GLAMOUR DISEASE.
OKAY!
NOT ENOUGH CASUALTIES. NO CELEBRITIES HAVE DIED FROM IT...
...JUST PEOPLE LIKE MY GRANDMOTHER.

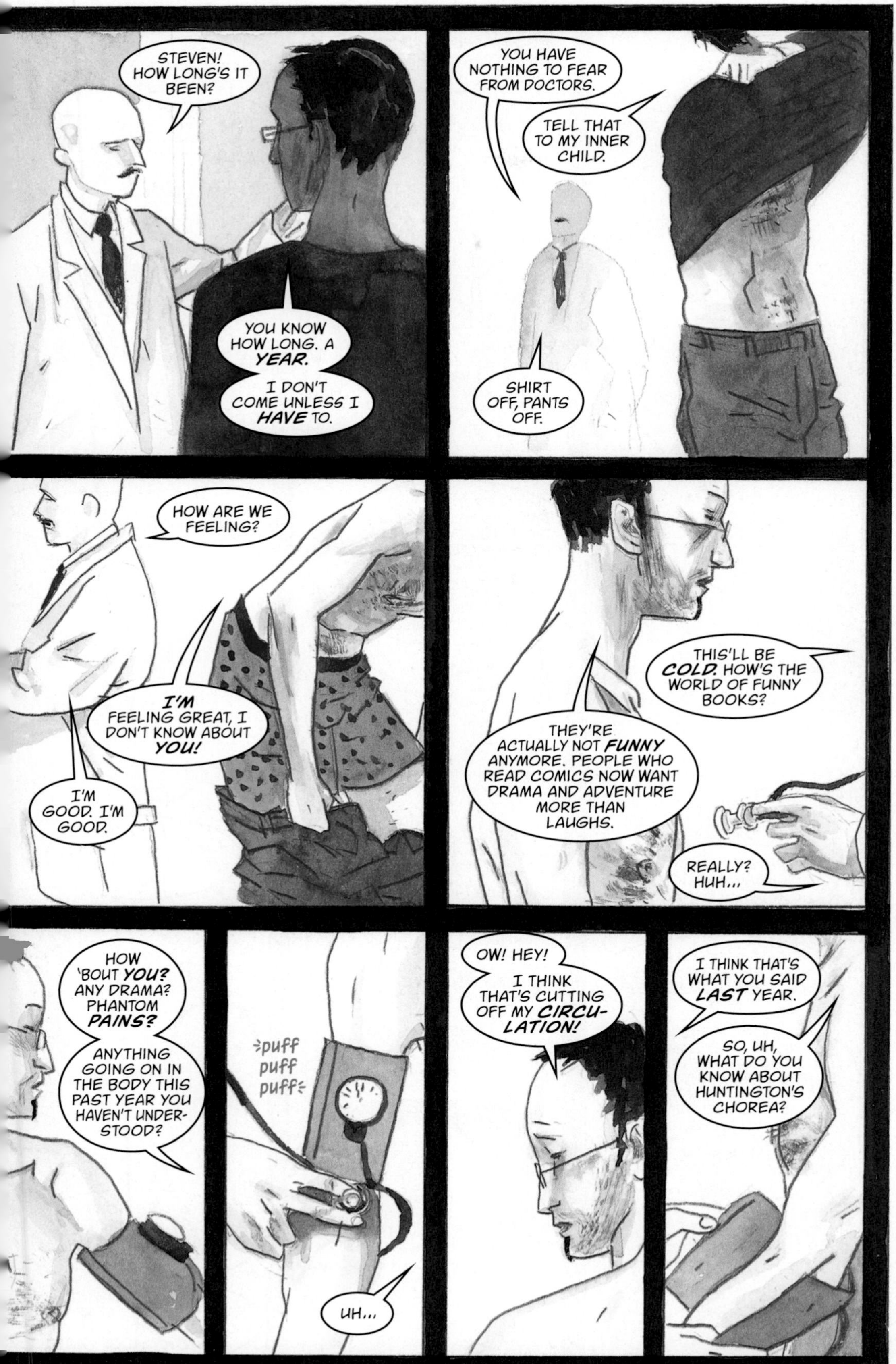
STEVEN! HOW LONG'S IT BEEN?
YOU KNOW HOW LONG. A YEAR.
I DON'T COME UNLESS I HAVE TO.
YOU HAVE NOTHING TO FEAR FROM DOCTORS.
TELL THAT TO MY INNER CHILD.
SHIRT OFF, PANTS OFF.
HOW ARE WE FEELING?
I'M FEELING GREAT, I DON'T KNOW ABOUT YOU!
I'M GOOD. I'M GOOD.
THIS'LL BE COLD. HOW'S THE WORLD OF FUNNY BOOKS?
THEY'RE ACTUALLY NOT FUNNY ANYMORE. PEOPLE WHO READ COMICS NOW WANT DRAMA AND ADVENTURE MORE THAN LAUGHS.
REALLY? HUH...
HOW 'BOUT YOU? ANY DRAMA? PHANTOM PAINS?
ANYTHING GOING ON IN THE BODY THIS PAST YEAR YOU HAVEN'T UNDERSTOOD?
puff puff puff
UH...
OW! HEY!
I THINK THAT'S CUTTING OFF MY CIRCULATION!
I THINK THAT'S WHAT YOU SAID LAST YEAR.
SO, UH, WHAT DO YOU KNOW ABOUT HUNTINGTON'S CHOREA?

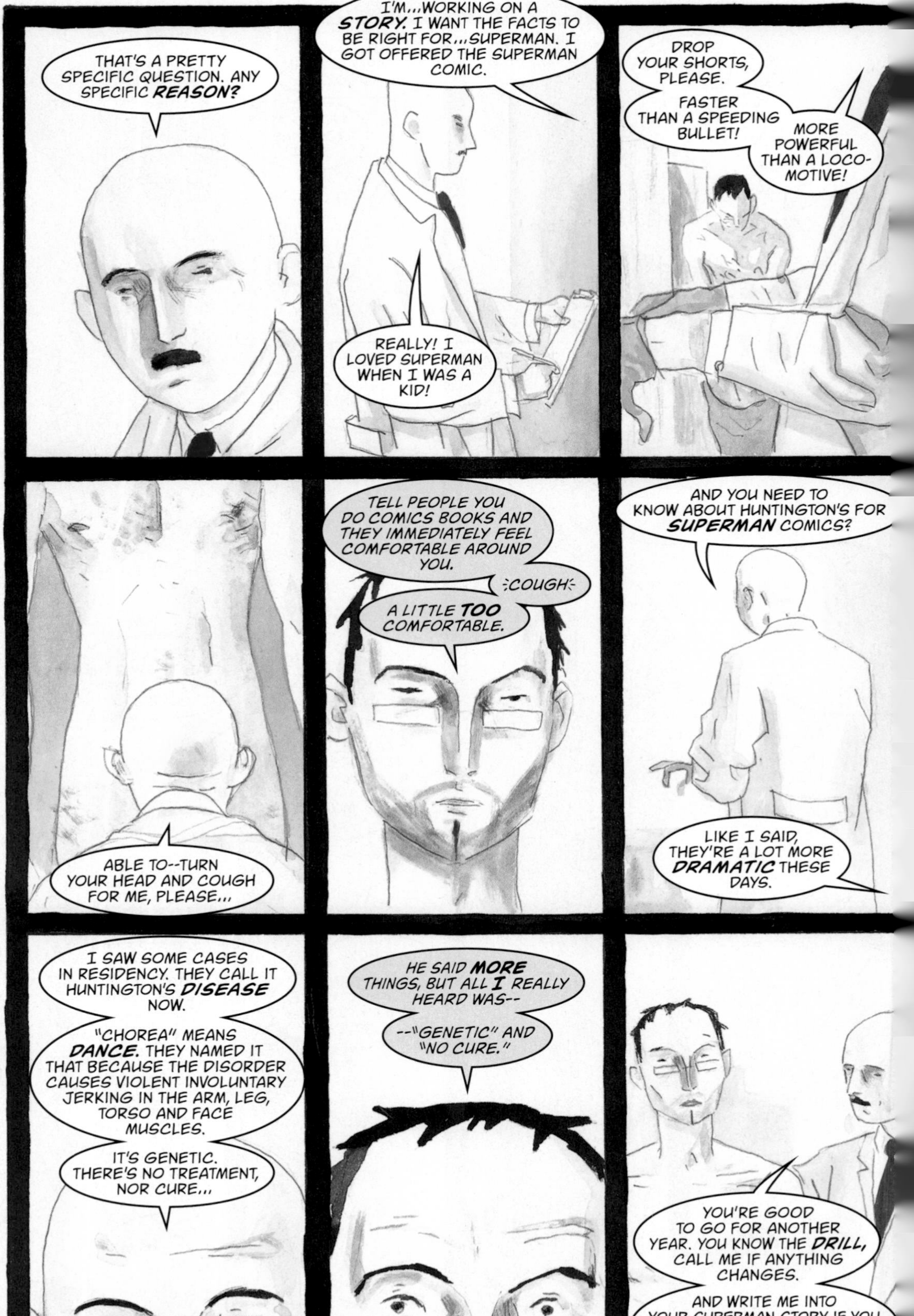
THAT'S A PRETTY SPECIFIC QUESTION. ANY SPECIFIC REASON?
I'M...WORKING ON A STORY. I WANT THE FACTS TO BE RIGHT FOR...SUPERMAN. I GOT OFFERED THE SUPERMAN COMIC.
REALLY! I LOVED SUPERMAN WHEN I WAS A KID!
DROP YOUR SHORTS, PLEASE.
FASTER THAN A SPEEDING BULLET!
MORE POWERFUL THAN A LOCO-MOTIVE!
ABLE TO--TURN YOUR HEAD AND COUGH FOR ME, PLEASE...
TELL PEOPLE YOU DO COMICS BOOKS AND THEY IMMEDIATELY FEEL COMFORTABLE AROUND YOU.
COUGH
A LITTLE TOO COMFORTABLE.
AND YOU NEED TO KNOW ABOUT HUNTINGTON'S FOR SUPERMAN COMICS?
LIKE I SAID, THEY'RE A LOT MORE DRAMATIC THESE DAYS.
I SAW SOME CASES IN RESIDENCY. THEY CALL IT HUNTINGTON'S DISEASE NOW.
"CHOREA" MEANS DANCE. THEY NAMED IT THAT BECAUSE THE DISORDER CAUSES VIOLENT INVOLUNTARY JERKING IN THE ARM, LEG, TORSO AND FACE MUSCLES.
IT'S GENETIC. THERE'S NO TREATMENT, NOR CURE...
HE SAID MORE THINGS, BUT ALL I REALLY HEARD WAS--
--"GENETIC" AND "NO CURE."
YOU'RE GOOD TO GO FOR ANOTHER YEAR. YOU KNOW THE DRILL, CALL ME IF ANYTHING CHANGES.
AND WRITE ME INTO YOUR SUPERMAN STORY IF YOU CAN. MY KIDS WOULD GET A KICK OUT OF THAT!

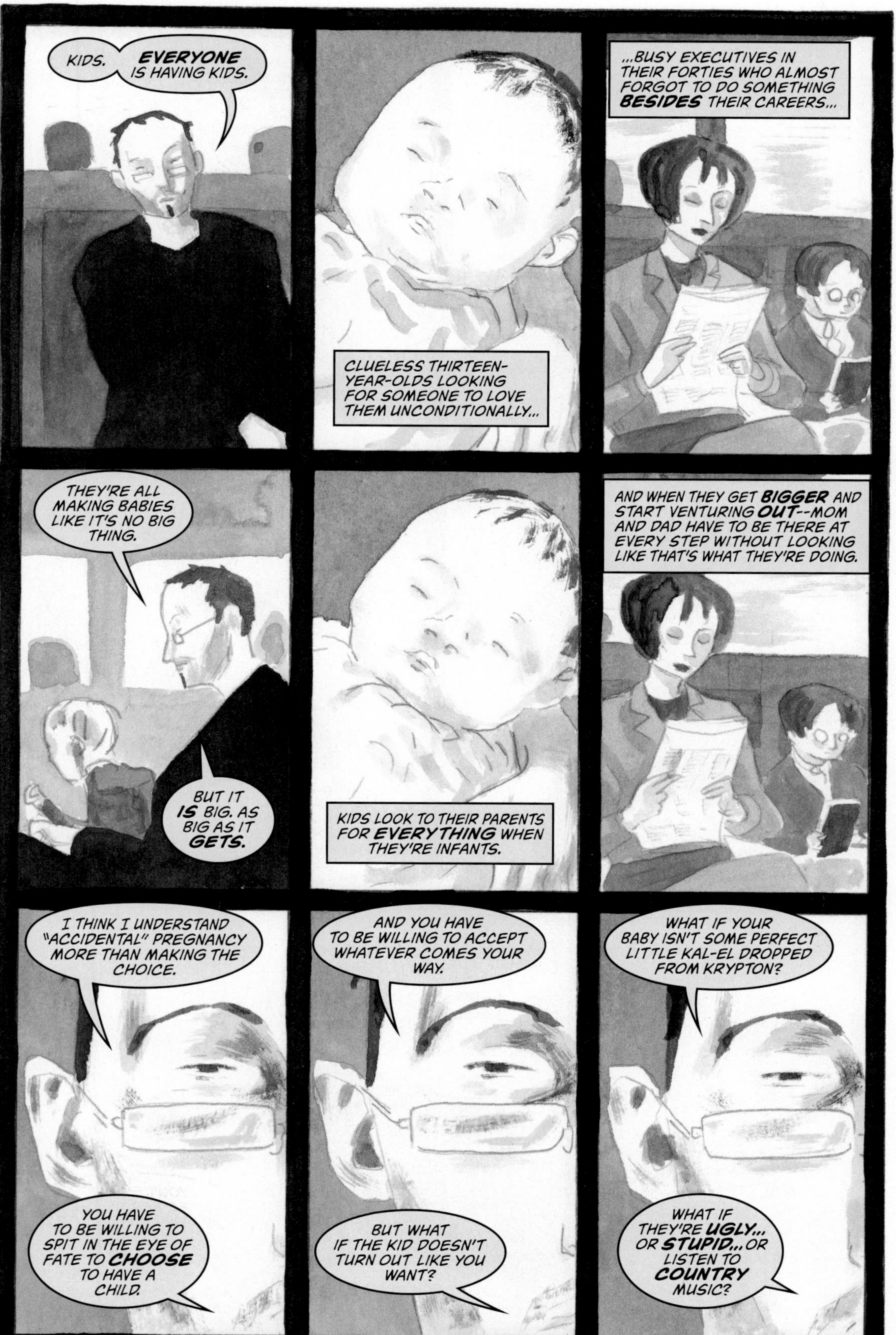
KIDS.
EVERYONE IS HAVING KIDS.
CLUELESS THIRTEEN-YEAR-OLDS LOOKING FOR SOMEONE TO LOVE THEM UNCONDITIONALLY...
...BUSY EXECUTIVES IN THEIR FORTIES WHO ALMOST FORGOT TO DO SOMETHING BESIDES THEIR CAREERS...
THEY'RE ALL MAKING BABIES LIKE IT'S NO BIG THING.
BUT IT IS BIG. AS BIG AS IT GETS.
KIDS LOOK TO THEIR PARENTS FOR EVERYTHING WHEN THEY'RE INFANTS.
AND WHEN THEY GET BIGGER AND START VENTURING OUT--MOM AND DAD HAVE TO BE THERE AT EVERY STEP WITHOUT LOOKING LIKE THAT'S WHAT THEY'RE DOING.
I THINK I UNDERSTAND "ACCIDENTAL" PREGNANCY MORE THAN MAKING THE CHOICE.
YOU HAVE TO BE WILLING TO SPIT IN THE EYE OF FATE TO CHOOSE TO HAVE A CHILD.
AND YOU HAVE TO BE WILLING TO ACCEPT WHATEVER COMES YOUR WAY.
BUT WHAT IF THE KID DOESN'T TURN OUT LIKE YOU WANT?
WHAT IF YOUR BABY ISN'T SOME PERFECT LITTLE KAL-EL DROPPED FROM KRYPTON?
WHAT IF THEY'RE UGLY... OR STUPID... OR LISTEN TO COUNTRY MUSIC?

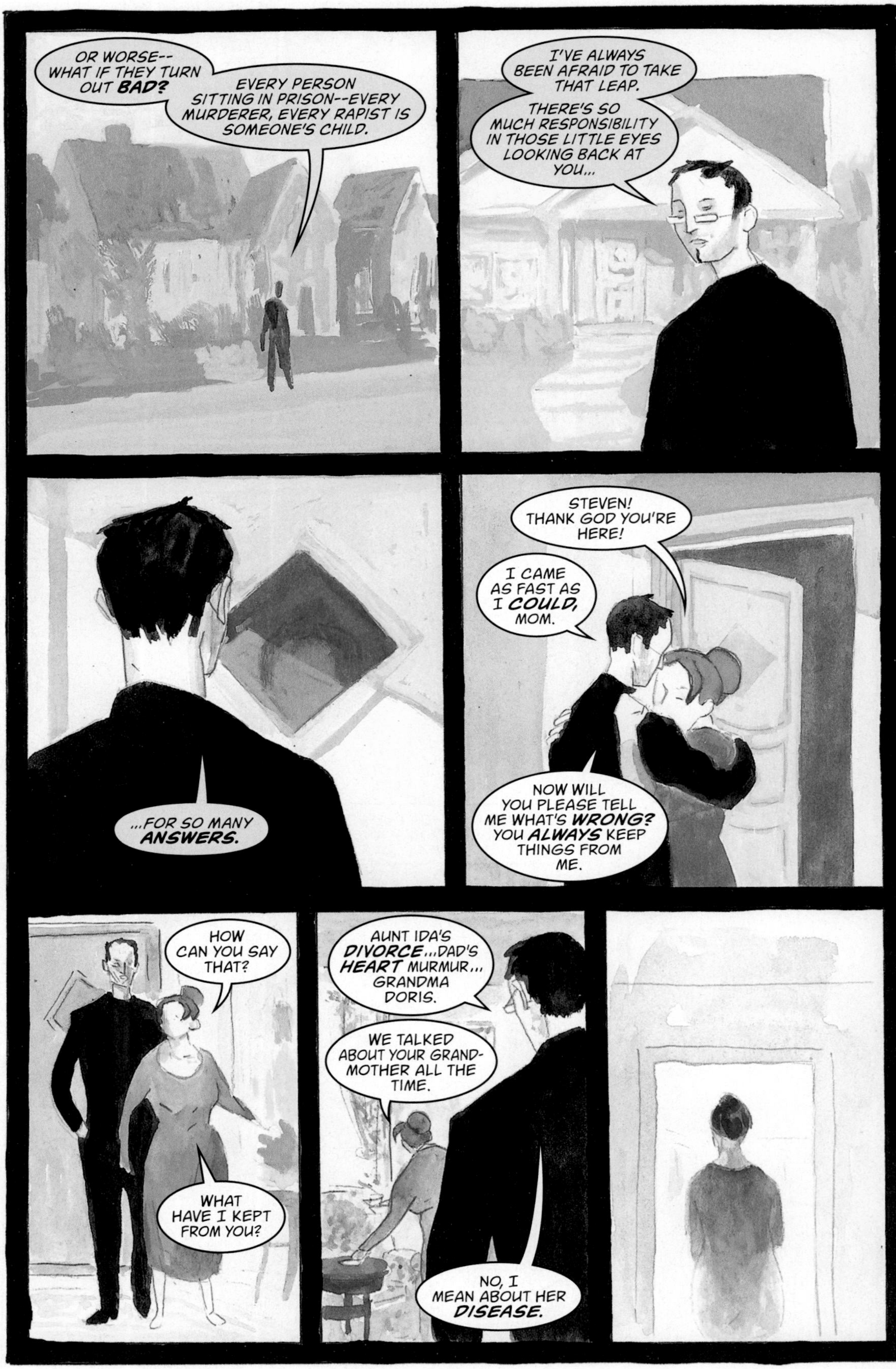
OR WORSE-- WHAT IF THEY TURN OUT **BAD?**
EVERY PERSON SITTING IN PRISON--EVERY MURDERER, EVERY RAPIST IS SOMEONE'S CHILD.
I'VE ALWAYS BEEN AFRAID TO TAKE THAT LEAP.
THERE'S SO MUCH RESPONSIBILITY IN THOSE LITTLE EYES LOOKING BACK AT YOU...
...FOR SO MANY **ANSWERS.**
STEVEN! THANK GOD YOU'RE HERE!
I CAME AS FAST AS I **COULD,** MOM.
NOW WILL YOU PLEASE TELL ME WHAT'S **WRONG?** YOU **ALWAYS** KEEP THINGS FROM ME.
HOW CAN YOU SAY THAT?
WHAT HAVE I KEPT FROM YOU?
AUNT IDA'S **DIVORCE**...DAD'S **HEART** MURMUR... GRANDMA DORIS.
WE TALKED ABOUT YOUR GRAND-MOTHER ALL THE TIME.
NO, I MEAN ABOUT HER **DISEASE.**

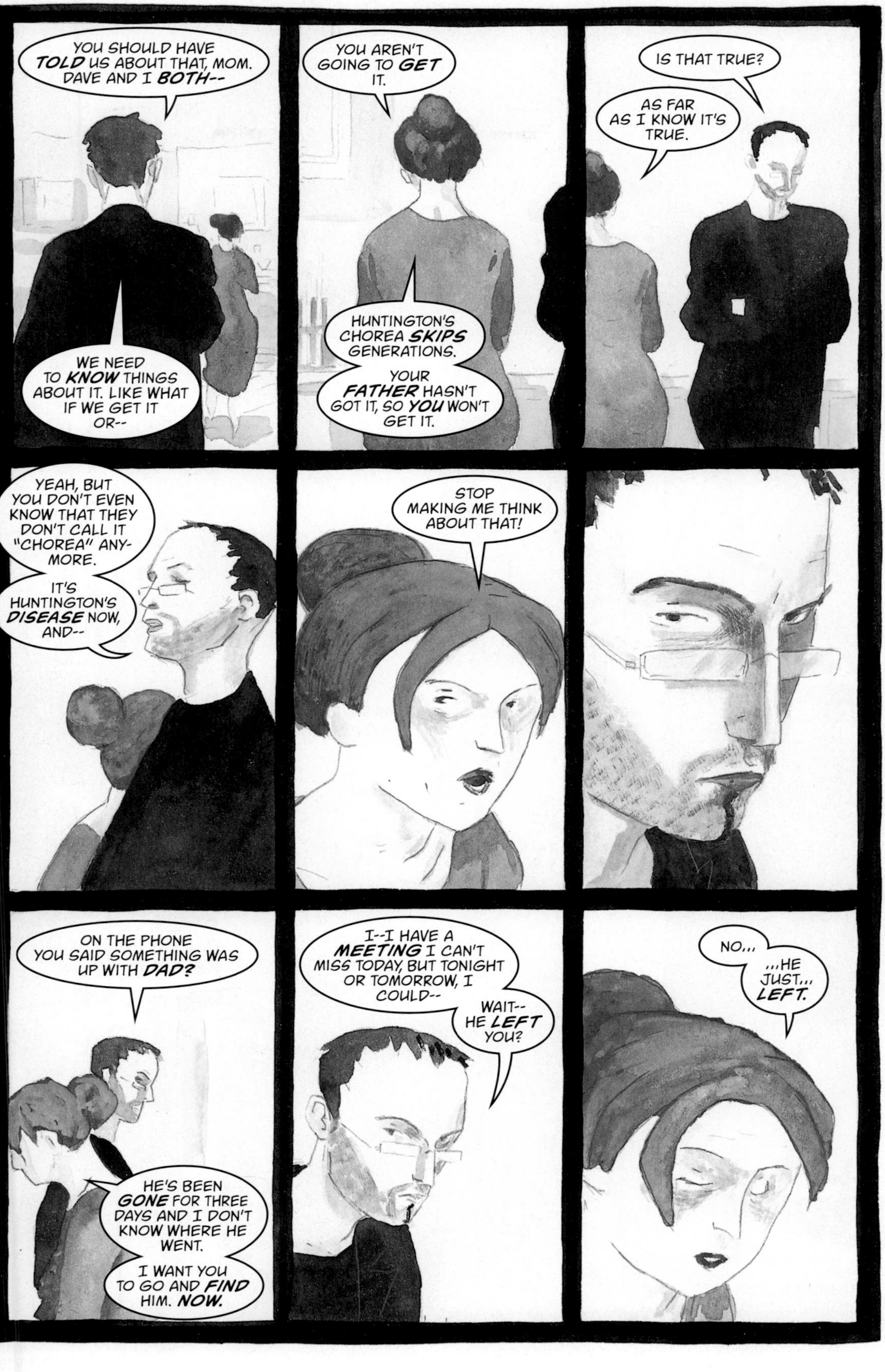
YOU SHOULD HAVE TOLD US ABOUT THAT, MOM. DAVE AND I BOTH--
WE NEED TO KNOW THINGS ABOUT IT. LIKE WHAT IF WE GET IT OR--
YOU AREN'T GOING TO GET IT.
HUNTINGTON'S CHOREA SKIPS GENERATIONS.
YOUR FATHER HASN'T GOT IT, SO YOU WON'T GET IT.
IS THAT TRUE?
AS FAR AS I KNOW IT'S TRUE.
YEAH, BUT YOU DON'T EVEN KNOW THAT THEY DON'T CALL IT "CHOREA" ANYMORE.
IT'S HUNTINGTON'S DISEASE NOW, AND--
STOP MAKING ME THINK ABOUT THAT!
ON THE PHONE YOU SAID SOMETHING WAS UP WITH DAD?
HE'S BEEN GONE FOR THREE DAYS AND I DON'T KNOW WHERE HE WENT.
I WANT YOU TO GO AND FIND HIM. NOW.
I--I HAVE A MEETING I CAN'T MISS TODAY, BUT TONIGHT OR TOMORROW, I COULD--
WAIT-- HE LEFT YOU?
NO...
...HE JUST... LEFT.

LEAVING KRYPTON (Life on another world)

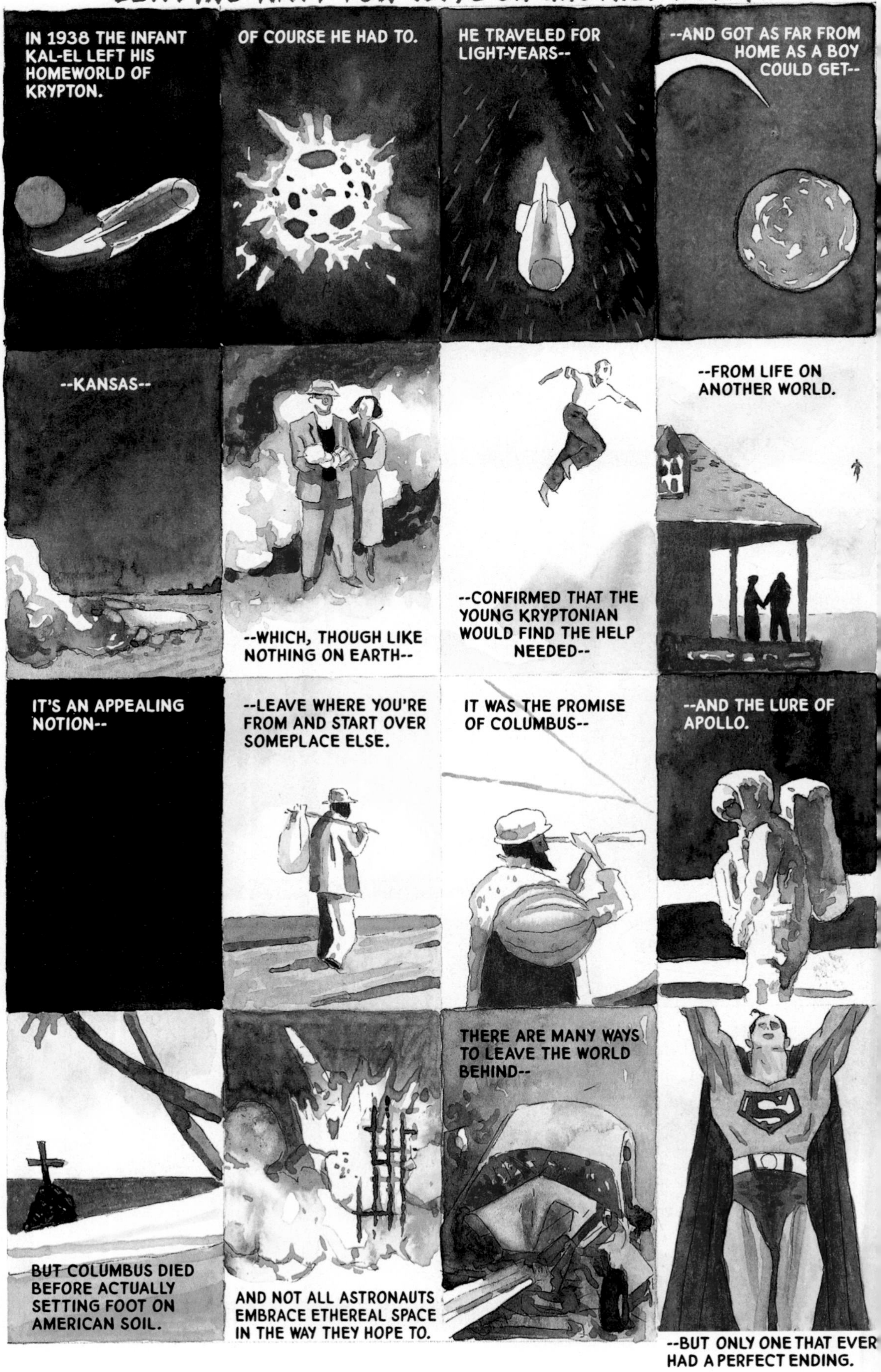
IN 1938 THE INFANT KAL-EL LEFT HIS HOMEWORLD OF KRYPTON.
OF COURSE HE HAD TO.
HE TRAVELED FOR LIGHT-YEARS--
--AND GOT AS FAR FROM HOME AS A BOY COULD GET--
--KANSAS--
--WHICH, THOUGH LIKE NOTHING ON EARTH--
--CONFIRMED THAT THE YOUNG KRYPTONIAN WOULD FIND THE HELP NEEDED--
--FROM LIFE ON ANOTHER WORLD.
IT'S AN APPEALING NOTION--
--LEAVE WHERE YOU'RE FROM AND START OVER SOMEPLACE ELSE.
IT WAS THE PROMISE OF COLUMBUS--
--AND THE LURE OF APOLLO.
BUT COLUMBUS DIED BEFORE ACTUALLY SETTING FOOT ON AMERICAN SOIL.
AND NOT ALL ASTRONAUTS EMBRACE ETHEREAL SPACE IN THE WAY THEY HOPE TO.
THERE ARE MANY WAYS TO LEAVE THE WORLD BEHIND--
--BUT ONLY ONE THAT EVER HAD A PERFECT ENDING.

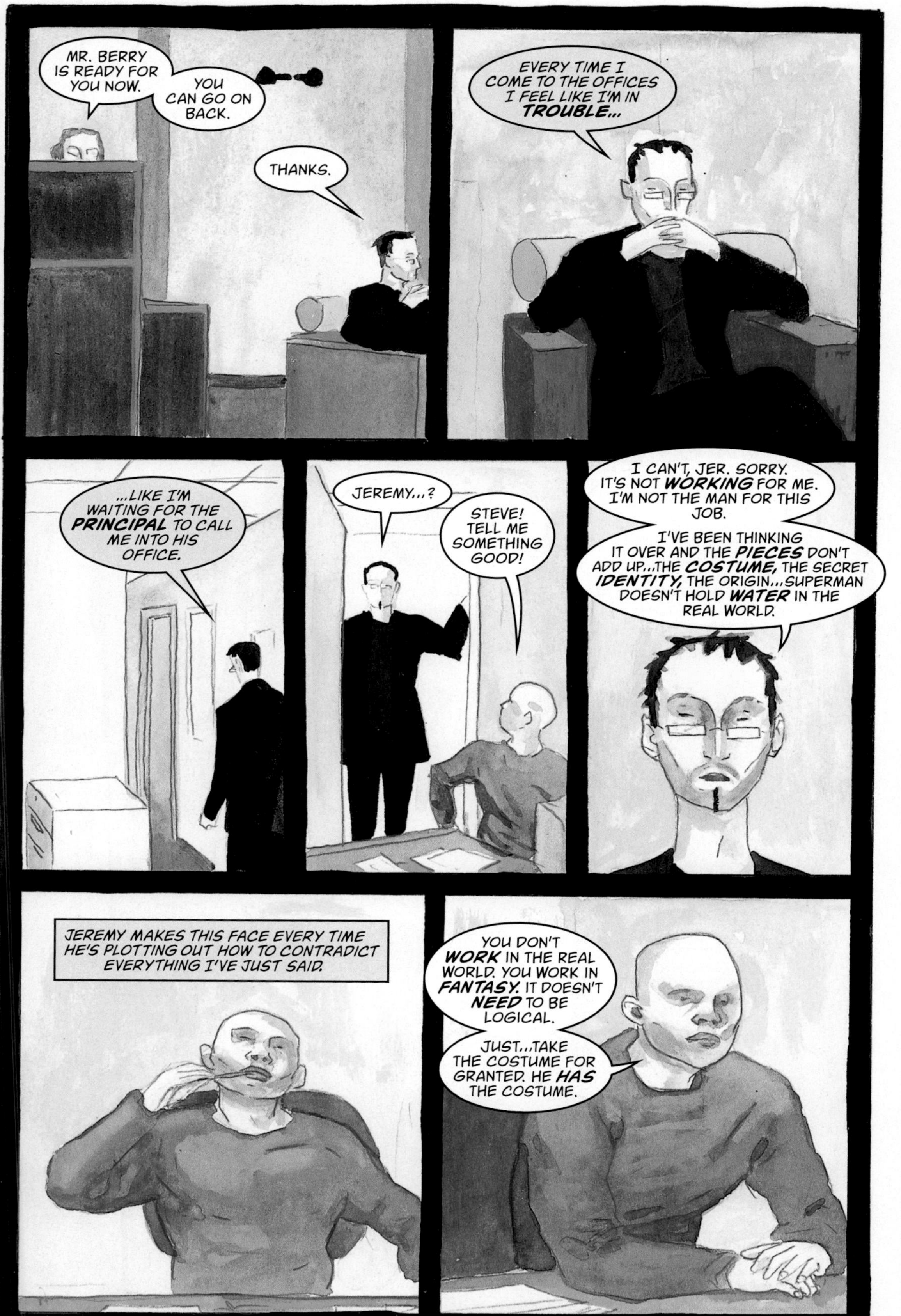
MR. BERRY IS READY FOR YOU NOW.
YOU CAN GO ON BACK.
THANKS.
EVERY TIME I COME TO THE OFFICES I FEEL LIKE I'M IN TROUBLE...
...LIKE I'M WAITING FOR THE PRINCIPAL TO CALL ME INTO HIS OFFICE.
JEREMY...?
STEVE! TELL ME SOMETHING GOOD!
I CAN'T, JER. SORRY. IT'S NOT WORKING FOR ME. I'M NOT THE MAN FOR THIS JOB.
I'VE BEEN THINKING IT OVER AND THE PIECES DON'T ADD UP...THE COSTUME, THE SECRET IDENTITY, THE ORIGIN...SUPERMAN DOESN'T HOLD WATER IN THE REAL WORLD.
JEREMY MAKES THIS FACE EVERY TIME HE'S PLOTTING OUT HOW TO CONTRADICT EVERYTHING I'VE JUST SAID.
YOU DON'T WORK IN THE REAL WORLD. YOU WORK IN FANTASY. IT DOESN'T NEED TO BE LOGICAL.
JUST...TAKE THE COSTUME FOR GRANTED. HE HAS THE COSTUME.

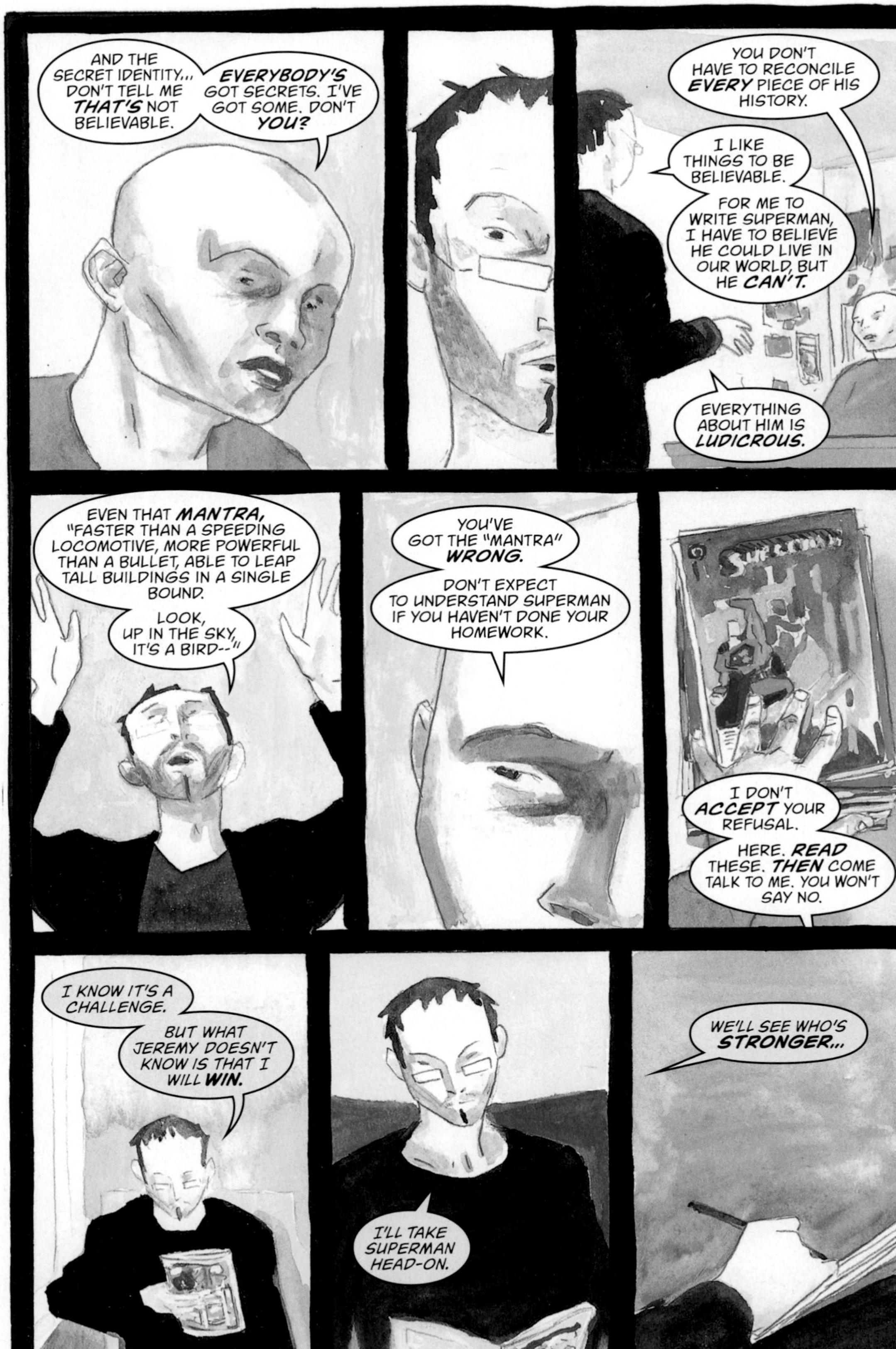
AND THE SECRET IDENTITY... DON'T TELL ME THAT'S NOT BELIEVABLE.
EVERYBODY'S GOT SECRETS. I'VE GOT SOME. DON'T YOU?
YOU DON'T HAVE TO RECONCILE EVERY PIECE OF HIS HISTORY.
I LIKE THINGS TO BE BELIEVABLE.
FOR ME TO WRITE SUPERMAN, I HAVE TO BELIEVE HE COULD LIVE IN OUR WORLD, BUT HE CAN'T.
EVERYTHING ABOUT HIM IS LUDICROUS.
EVEN THAT MANTRA, "FASTER THAN A SPEEDING LOCOMOTIVE, MORE POWERFUL THAN A BULLET, ABLE TO LEAP TALL BUILDINGS IN A SINGLE BOUND.
LOOK, UP IN THE SKY, IT'S A BIRD--"
YOU'VE GOT THE "MANTRA" WRONG.
DON'T EXPECT TO UNDERSTAND SUPERMAN IF YOU HAVEN'T DONE YOUR HOMEWORK.
I DON'T ACCEPT YOUR REFUSAL.
HERE. READ THESE. THEN COME TALK TO ME. YOU WON'T SAY NO.
I KNOW IT'S A CHALLENGE.
BUT WHAT JEREMY DOESN'T KNOW IS THAT I WILL WIN.
I'LL TAKE SUPERMAN HEAD-ON.
WE'LL SEE WHO'S STRONGER...

INVULNERABLE

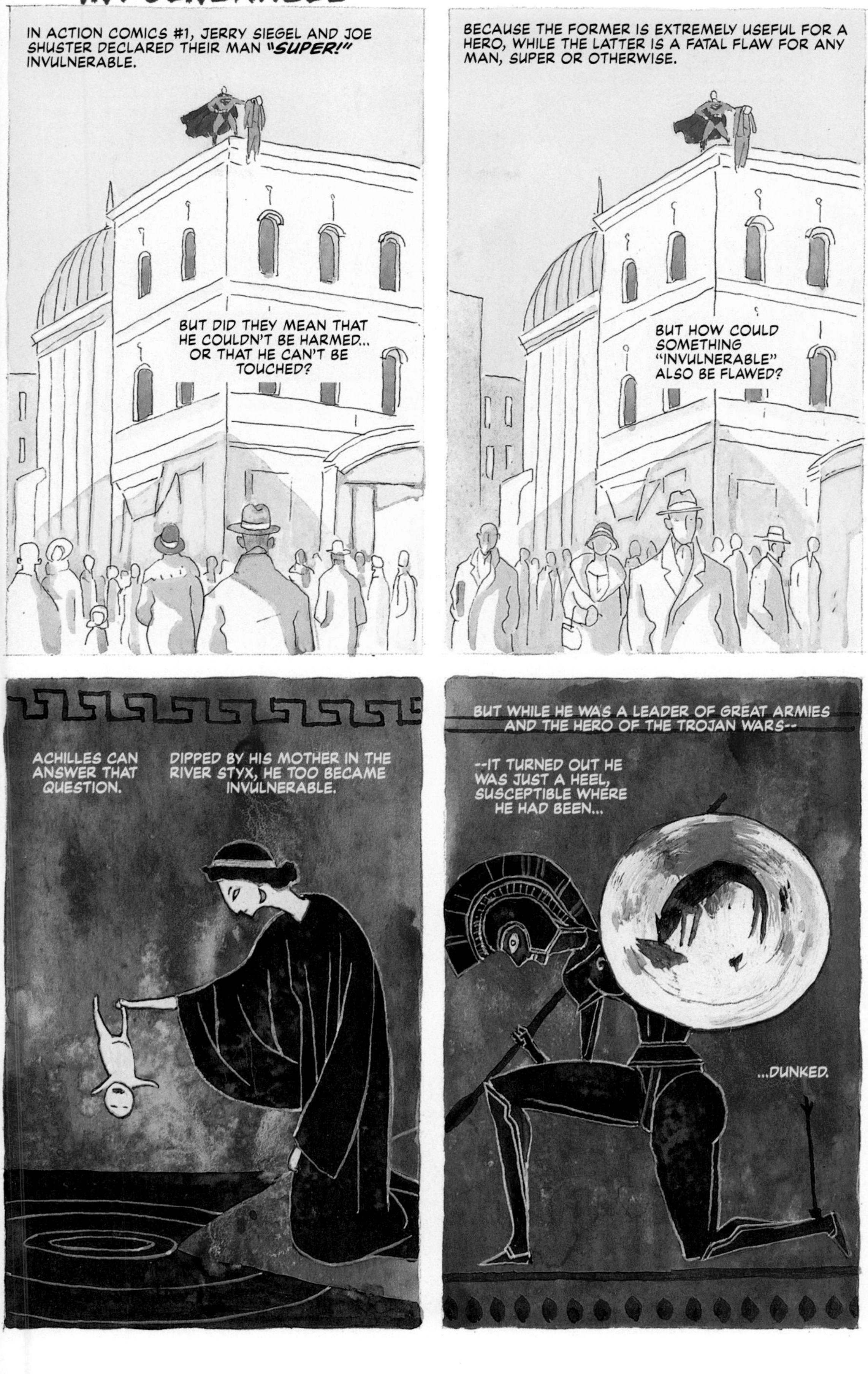
IN ACTION COMICS #1, JERRY SIEGEL AND JOE SHUSTER DECLARED THEIR MAN "SUPER!" INVULNERABLE.
BUT DID THEY MEAN THAT HE COULDN'T BE HARMED... OR THAT HE CAN'T BE TOUCHED?
BECAUSE THE FORMER IS EXTREMELY USEFUL FOR A HERO, WHILE THE LATTER IS A FATAL FLAW FOR ANY MAN, SUPER OR OTHERWISE.
BUT HOW COULD SOMETHING "INVULNERABLE" ALSO BE FLAWED?
ACHILLES CAN ANSWER THAT QUESTION.
DIPPED BY HIS MOTHER IN THE RIVER STYX, HE TOO BECAME INVULNERABLE.
BUT WHILE HE WAS A LEADER OF GREAT ARMIES AND THE HERO OF THE TROJAN WARS--
--IT TURNED OUT HE WAS JUST A HEEL, SUSCEPTIBLE WHERE HE HAD BEEN...
...DUNKED.

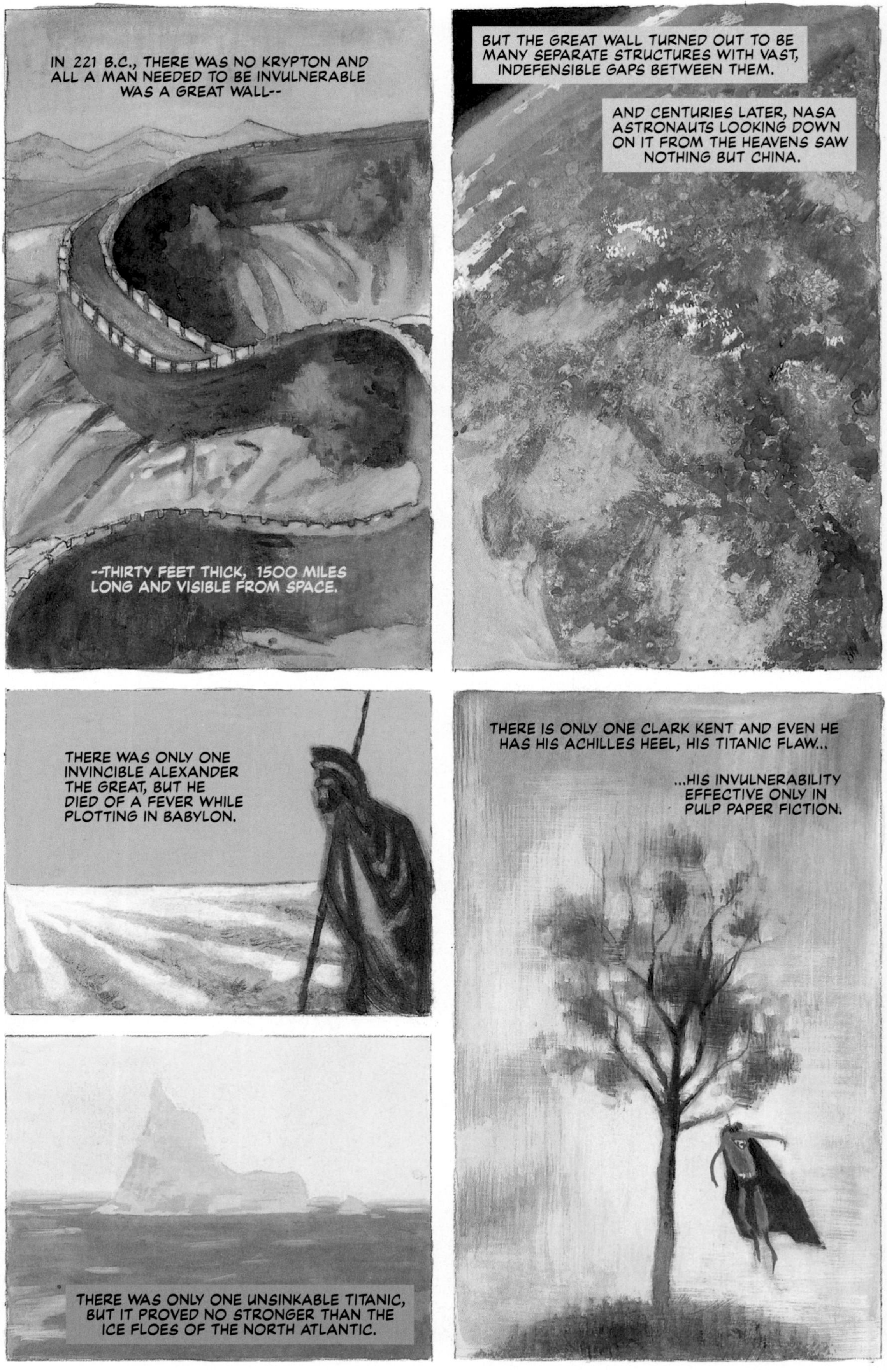
IN 221 B.C., THERE WAS NO KRYPTON AND ALL A MAN NEEDED TO BE INVULNERABLE WAS A GREAT WALL--
--THIRTY FEET THICK, 1500 MILES LONG AND VISIBLE FROM SPACE.
BUT THE GREAT WALL TURNED OUT TO BE MANY SEPARATE STRUCTURES WITH VAST, INDEFENSIBLE GAPS BETWEEN THEM.
AND CENTURIES LATER, NASA ASTRONAUTS LOOKING DOWN ON IT FROM THE HEAVENS SAW NOTHING BUT CHINA.
THERE WAS ONLY ONE INVINCIBLE ALEXANDER THE GREAT, BUT HE DIED OF A FEVER WHILE PLOTTING IN BABYLON.
THERE WAS ONLY ONE UNSINKABLE TITANIC, BUT IT PROVED NO STRONGER THAN THE ICE FLOES OF THE NORTH ATLANTIC.
THERE IS ONLY ONE CLARK KENT AND EVEN HE HAS HIS ACHILLES HEEL, HIS TITANIC FLAW...
...HIS INVULNERABILITY EFFECTIVE ONLY IN PULP PAPER FICTION.

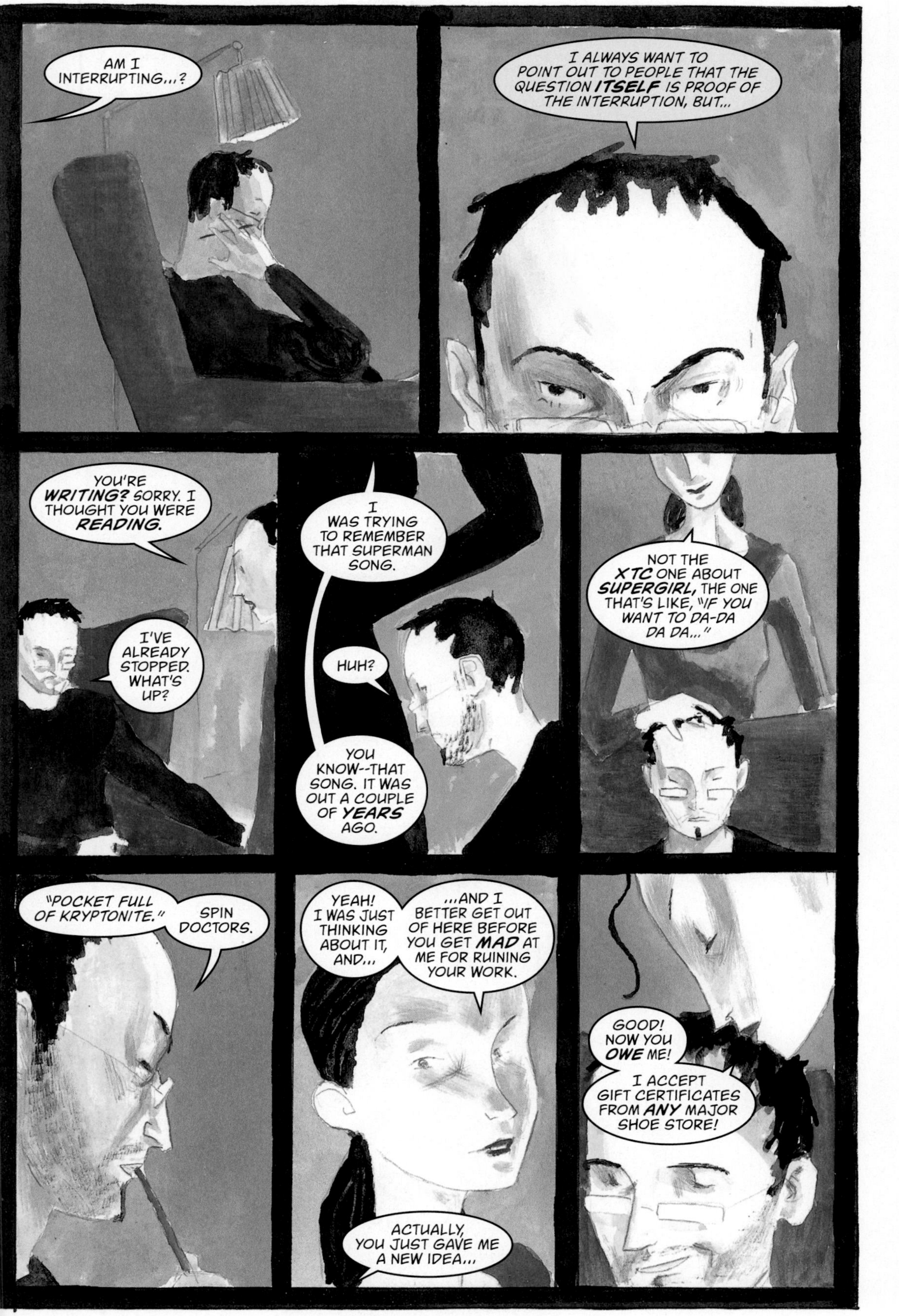
AM I INTERRUPTING...?
I ALWAYS WANT TO POINT OUT TO PEOPLE THAT THE QUESTION ITSELF IS PROOF OF THE INTERRUPTION, BUT...
YOU'RE WRITING? SORRY. I THOUGHT YOU WERE READING.
I'VE ALREADY STOPPED. WHAT'S UP?
I WAS TRYING TO REMEMBER THAT SUPERMAN SONG.
HUH?
YOU KNOW--THAT SONG. IT WAS OUT A COUPLE OF YEARS AGO.
NOT THE XTC ONE ABOUT SUPERGIRL, THE ONE THAT'S LIKE, "IF YOU WANT TO DA-DA DA DA..."
"POCKET FULL OF KRYPTONITE."
SPIN DOCTORS.
YEAH! I WAS JUST THINKING ABOUT IT, AND...
...AND I BETTER GET OUT OF HERE BEFORE YOU GET MAD AT ME FOR RUINING YOUR WORK.
ACTUALLY, YOU JUST GAVE ME A NEW IDEA...
GOOD! NOW YOU OWE ME!
I ACCEPT GIFT CERTIFICATES FROM ANY MAJOR SHOE STORE!

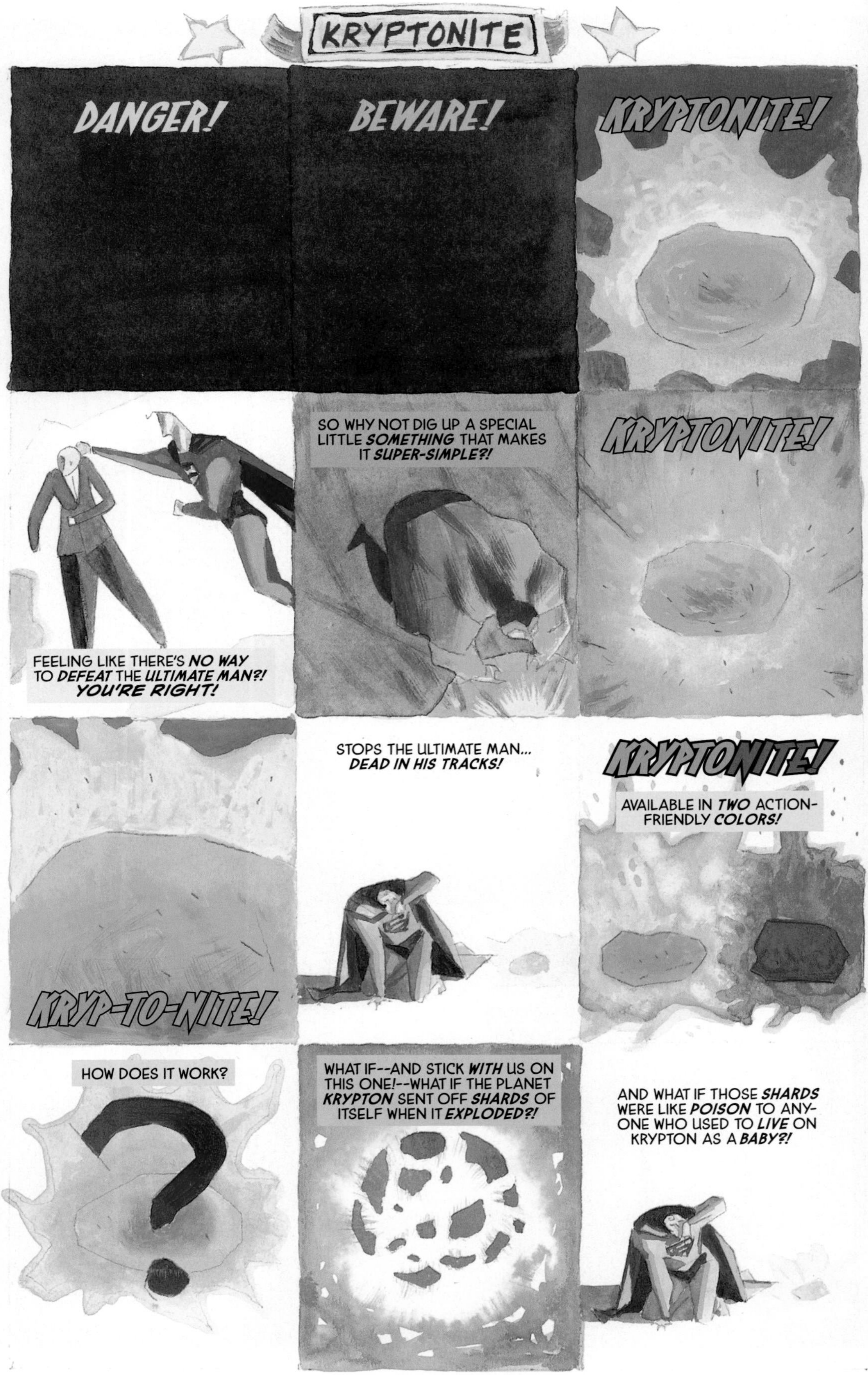
KRYPTONITE
DANGER!
BEWARE!
KRYPTONITE!
FEELING LIKE THERE'S NO WAY TO DEFEAT THE ULTIMATE MAN?! YOU'RE RIGHT!
SO WHY NOT DIG UP A SPECIAL LITTLE SOMETHING THAT MAKES IT SUPER-SIMPLE?!
KRYPTONITE!
KRYP-TO-NITE!
STOPS THE ULTIMATE MAN... DEAD IN HIS TRACKS!
KRYPTONITE!
AVAILABLE IN TWO ACTION-FRIENDLY COLORS!
HOW DOES IT WORK?
WHAT IF--AND STICK WITH US ON THIS ONE!--WHAT IF THE PLANET KRYPTON SENT OFF SHARDS OF ITSELF WHEN IT EXPLODED?!
AND WHAT IF THOSE SHARDS WERE LIKE POISON TO ANY-ONE WHO USED TO LIVE ON KRYPTON AS A BABY?!

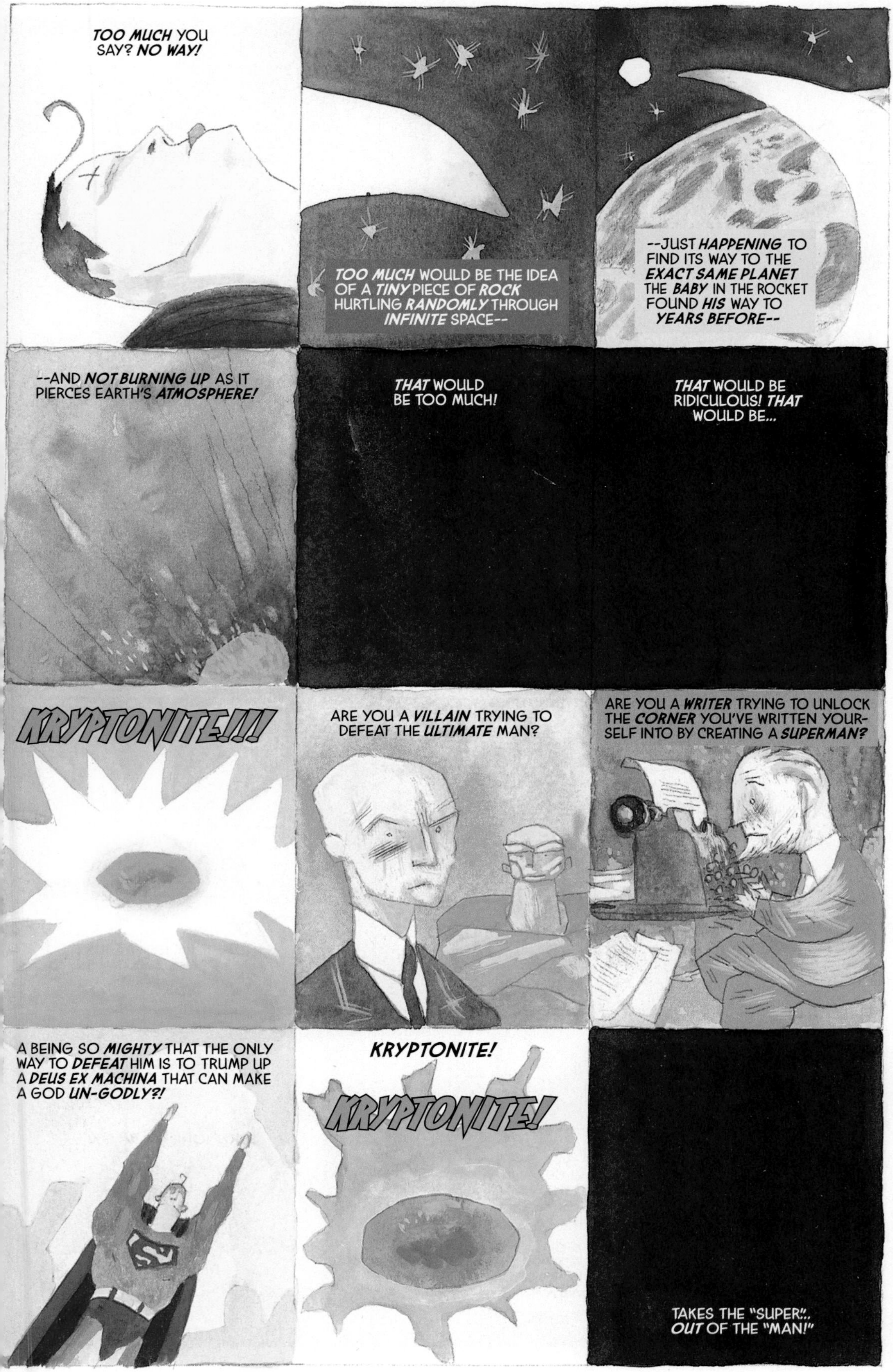
TOO MUCH YOU SAY? NO WAY!
TOO MUCH WOULD BE THE IDEA OF A TINY PIECE OF ROCK HURTLING RANDOMLY THROUGH INFINITE SPACE--
--JUST HAPPENING TO FIND ITS WAY TO THE EXACT SAME PLANET THE BABY IN THE ROCKET FOUND HIS WAY TO YEARS BEFORE--
--AND NOT BURNING UP AS IT PIERCES EARTH'S ATMOSPHERE!
THAT WOULD BE TOO MUCH!
THAT WOULD BE RIDICULOUS! THAT WOULD BE...
KRYPTONITE!!!
ARE YOU A VILLAIN TRYING TO DEFEAT THE ULTIMATE MAN?
ARE YOU A WRITER TRYING TO UNLOCK THE CORNER YOU'VE WRITTEN YOURSELF INTO BY CREATING A SUPERMAN?
A BEING SO MIGHTY THAT THE ONLY WAY TO DEFEAT HIM IS TO TRUMP UP A DEUS EX MACHINA THAT CAN MAKE A GOD UN-GODLY?!
KRYPTONITE!
KRYPTONITE!
TAKES THE "SUPER" OUT OF THE "MAN!"

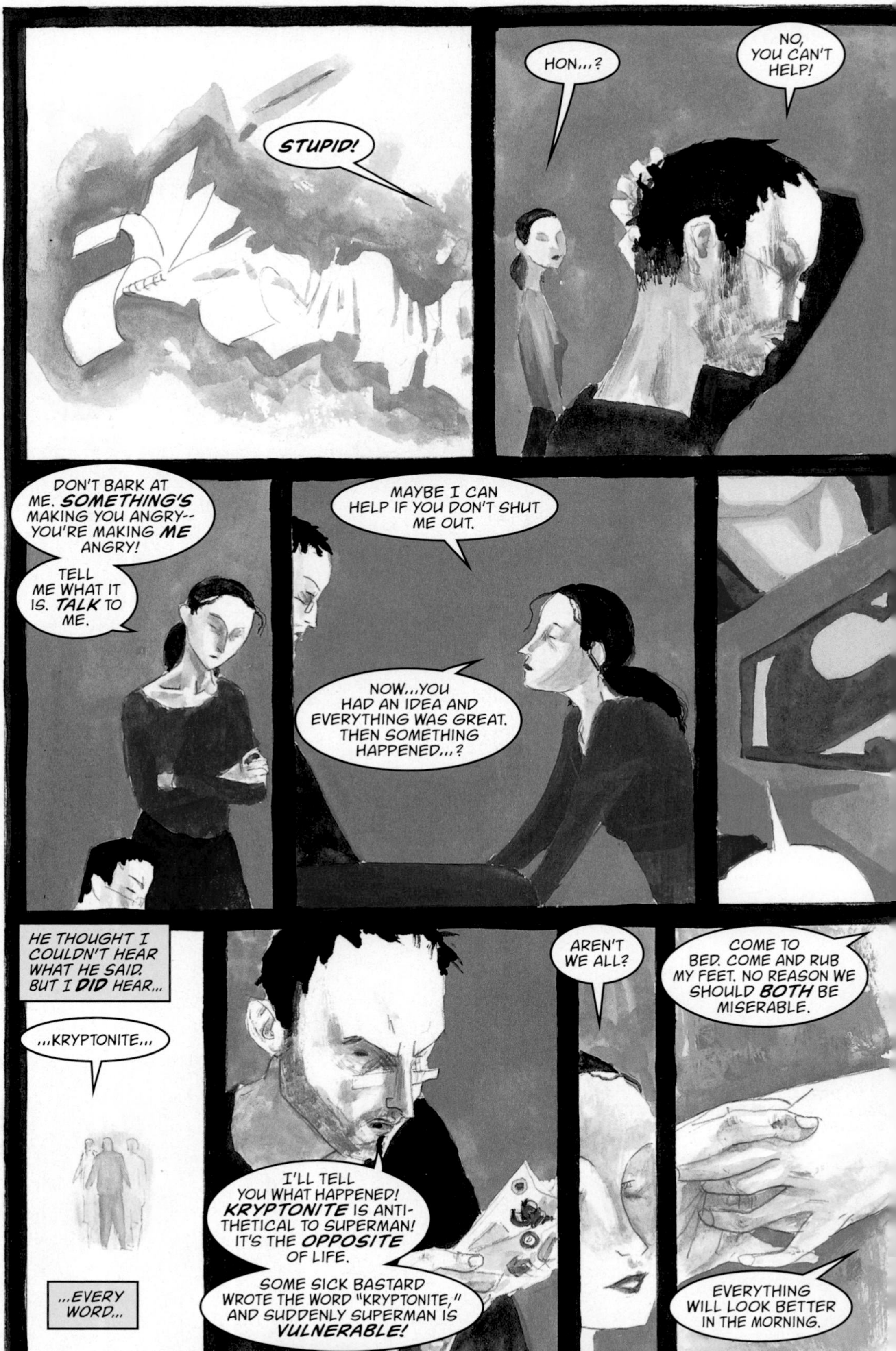
STUPID!
HON...?
NO, YOU CAN'T HELP!
DON'T BARK AT ME. SOMETHING'S MAKING YOU ANGRY-- YOU'RE MAKING ME ANGRY!
TELL ME WHAT IT IS. TALK TO ME.
MAYBE I CAN HELP IF YOU DON'T SHUT ME OUT.
NOW...YOU HAD AN IDEA AND EVERYTHING WAS GREAT. THEN SOMETHING HAPPENED...?
HE THOUGHT I COULDN'T HEAR WHAT HE SAID. BUT I DID HEAR...
...KRYPTONITE...
...EVERY WORD...
I'LL TELL YOU WHAT HAPPENED! KRYPTONITE IS ANTI-THETICAL TO SUPERMAN! IT'S THE OPPOSITE OF LIFE.
SOME SICK BASTARD WROTE THE WORD "KRYPTONITE," AND SUDDENLY SUPERMAN IS VULNERABLE!
AREN'T WE ALL?
COME TO BED. COME AND RUB MY FEET. NO REASON WE SHOULD BOTH BE MISERABLE.
EVERYTHING WILL LOOK BETTER IN THE MORNING.

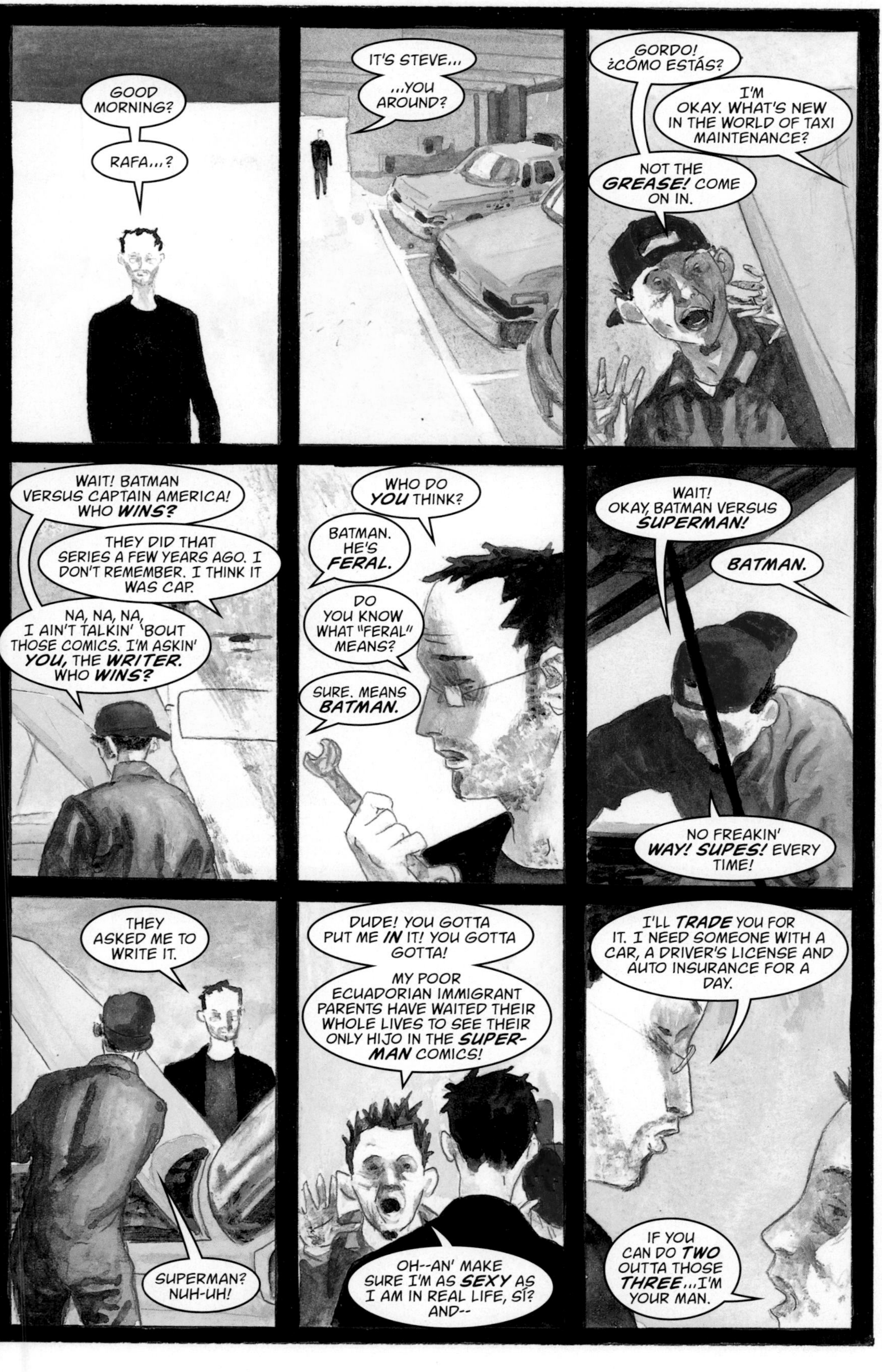
GOOD MORNING?
RAFA...?
IT'S STEVE...
...YOU AROUND?
GORDO! ¿CÓMO ESTÁS?
I'M OKAY. WHAT'S NEW IN THE WORLD OF TAXI MAINTENANCE?
NOT THE GREASE! COME ON IN.
WAIT! BATMAN VERSUS CAPTAIN AMERICA! WHO WINS?
THEY DID THAT SERIES A FEW YEARS AGO. I DON'T REMEMBER. I THINK IT WAS CAP.
NA, NA, NA, I AIN'T TALKIN' 'BOUT THOSE COMICS. I'M ASKIN' YOU, THE WRITER. WHO WINS?
WHO DO YOU THINK?
BATMAN. HE'S FERAL.
DO YOU KNOW WHAT "FERAL" MEANS?
SURE. MEANS BATMAN.
WAIT! OKAY, BATMAN VERSUS SUPERMAN!
BATMAN.
NO FREAKIN' WAY! SUPES! EVERY TIME!
THEY ASKED ME TO WRITE IT.
SUPERMAN? NUH-UH!
DUDE! YOU GOTTA PUT ME IN IT! YOU GOTTA GOTTA!
MY POOR ECUADORIAN IMMIGRANT PARENTS HAVE WAITED THEIR WHOLE LIVES TO SEE THEIR ONLY HIJO IN THE SUPER-MAN COMICS!
OH--AN' MAKE SURE I'M AS SEXY AS I AM IN REAL LIFE, SÍ? AND--
I'LL TRADE YOU FOR IT. I NEED SOMEONE WITH A CAR, A DRIVER'S LICENSE AND AUTO INSURANCE FOR A DAY.
IF YOU CAN DO TWO OUTTA THOSE THREE...I'M YOUR MAN.

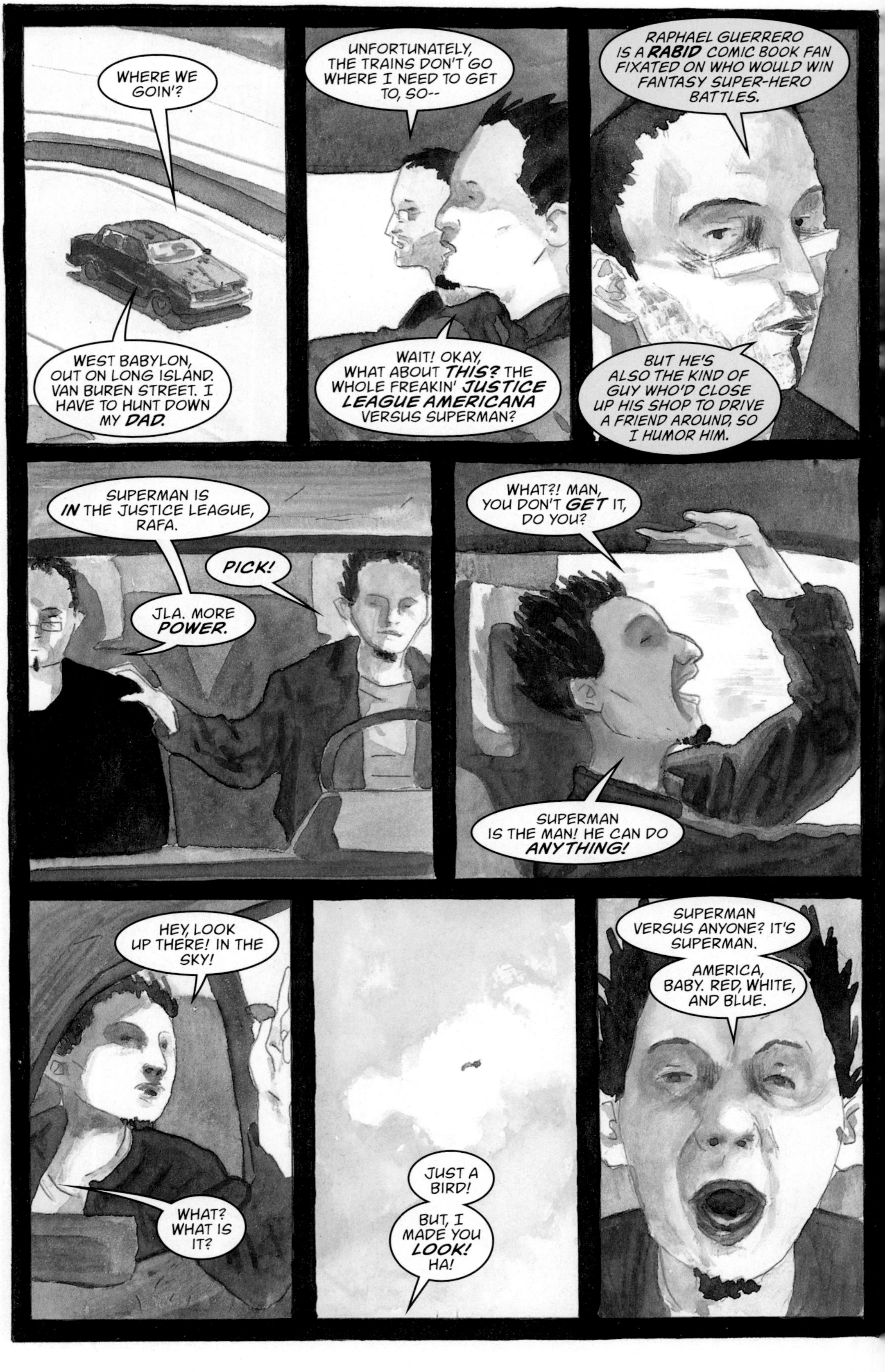
WHERE WE GOIN'?
WEST BABYLON, OUT ON LONG ISLAND. VAN BUREN STREET. I HAVE TO HUNT DOWN MY DAD.
UNFORTUNATELY, THE TRAINS DON'T GO WHERE I NEED TO GET TO, SO--
WAIT! OKAY, WHAT ABOUT THIS? THE WHOLE FREAKIN' JUSTICE LEAGUE AMERICANA VERSUS SUPERMAN?
RAPHAEL GUERRERO IS A RABID COMIC BOOK FAN FIXATED ON WHO WOULD WIN FANTASY SUPER-HERO BATTLES.
BUT HE'S ALSO THE KIND OF GUY WHO'D CLOSE UP HIS SHOP TO DRIVE A FRIEND AROUND, SO I HUMOR HIM.
SUPERMAN IS IN THE JUSTICE LEAGUE, RAFA.
PICK!
JLA. MORE POWER.
WHAT?! MAN, YOU DON'T GET IT, DO YOU?
SUPERMAN IS THE MAN! HE CAN DO ANYTHING!
HEY, LOOK UP THERE! IN THE SKY!
WHAT? WHAT IS IT?
JUST A BIRD!
BUT, I MADE YOU LOOK! HA!
SUPERMAN VERSUS ANYONE? IT'S SUPERMAN.
AMERICA, BABY. RED, WHITE, AND BLUE.

RED, YELLOW, BLUE

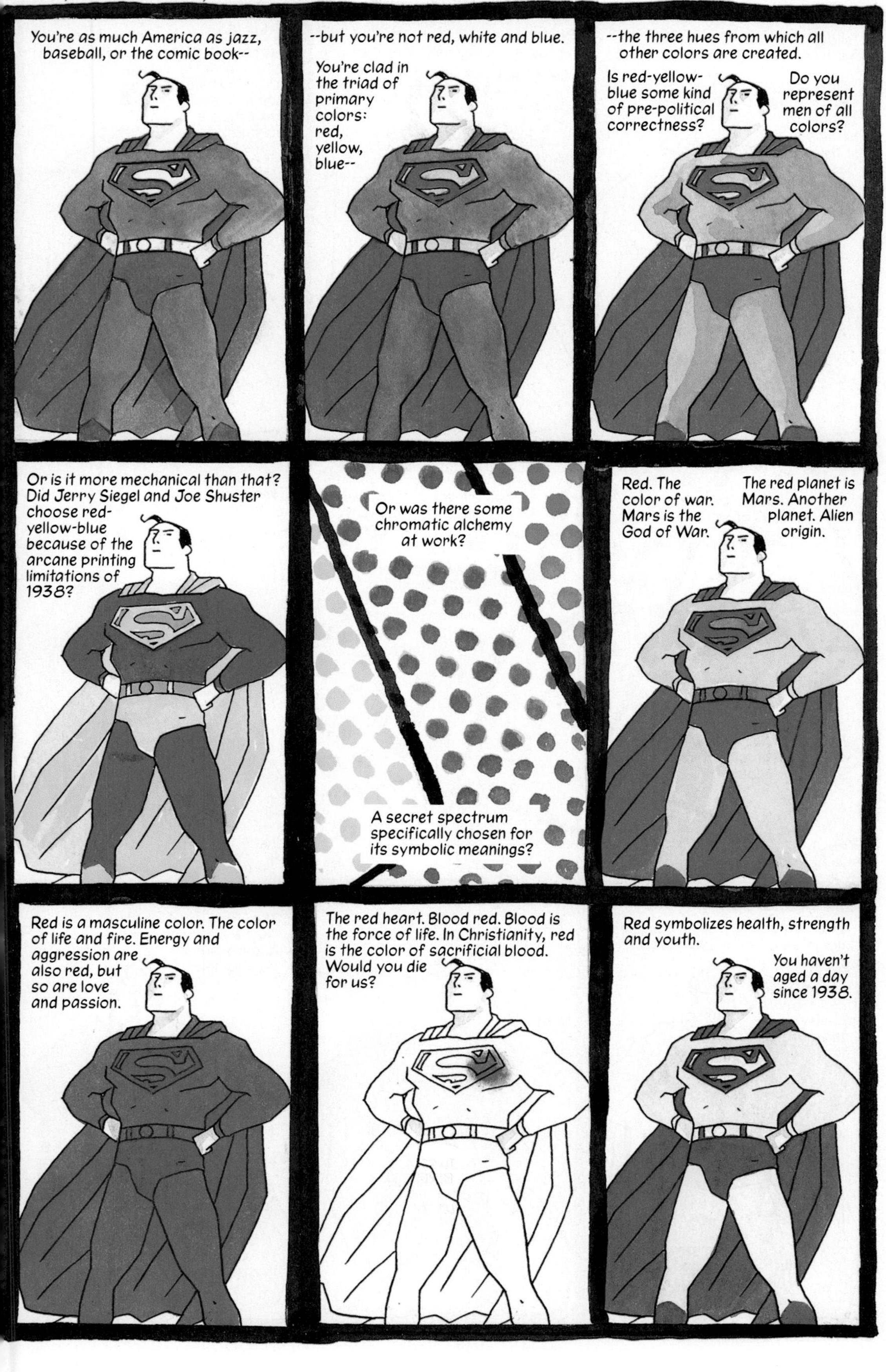

You're as much America as jazz, baseball, or the comic book--
--but you're not red, white and blue.
You're clad in the triad of primary colors: red, yellow, blue--
--the three hues from which all other colors are created.
Is red-yellow-blue some kind of pre-political correctness?
Do you represent men of all colors?
Or is it more mechanical than that? Did Jerry Siegel and Joe Shuster choose red-yellow-blue because of the arcane printing limitations of 1938?
Or was there some chromatic alchemy at work?
A secret spectrum specifically chosen for its symbolic meanings?
Red. The color of war. Mars is the God of War.
The red planet is Mars. Another planet. Alien origin.
Red is a masculine color. The color of life and fire. Energy and aggression are also red, but so are love and passion.
The red heart. Blood red. Blood is the force of life. In Christianity, red is the color of sacrificial blood. Would you die for us?
Red symbolizes health, strength and youth.
You haven't aged a day since 1938.

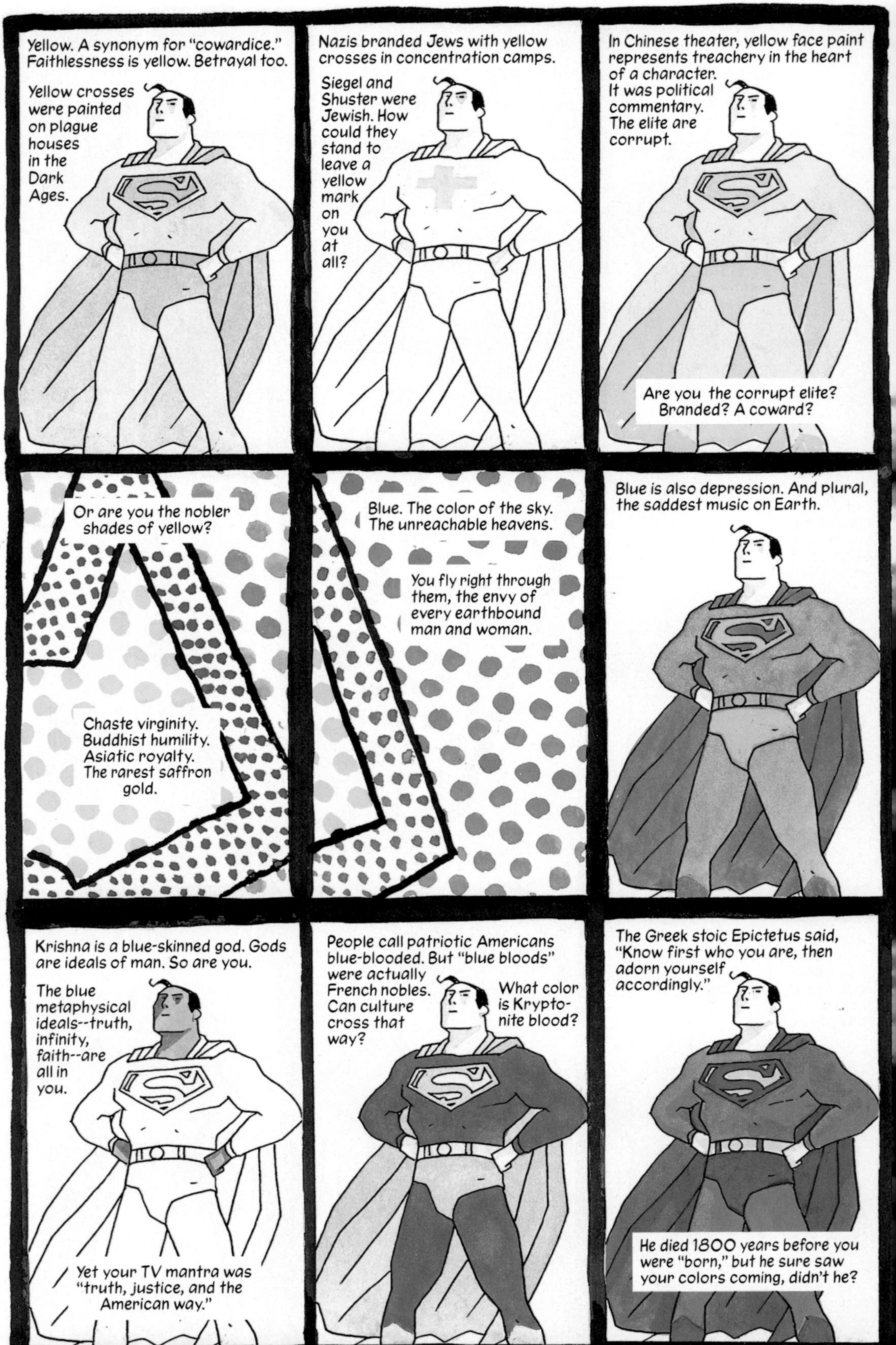
Yellow. A synonym for "cowardice." Faithlessness is yellow. Betrayal too.
Yellow crosses were painted on plague houses in the Dark Ages.
Nazis branded Jews with yellow crosses in concentration camps.
Siegel and Shuster were Jewish. How could they stand to leave a yellow mark on you at all?
In Chinese theater, yellow face paint represents treachery in the heart of a character.
It was political commentary. The elite are corrupt.
Are you the corrupt elite? Branded? A coward?
Or are you the nobler shades of yellow?
Chaste virginity. Buddhist humility. Asiatic royalty. The rarest saffron gold.
Blue. The color of the sky. The unreachable heavens.
You fly right through them, the envy of every earthbound man and woman.
Blue is also depression. And plural, the saddest music on Earth.
Krishna is a blue-skinned god. Gods are ideals of man. So are you.
The blue metaphysical ideals--truth, infinity, faith--are all in you.
Yet your TV mantra was "truth, justice, and the American way."
People call patriotic Americans blue-blooded. But "blue bloods" were actually French nobles. Can culture cross that way?
What color is Krypto-nite blood?
The Greek stoic Epictetus said, "Know first who you are, then adorn yourself accordingly."
He died 1800 years before you were "born," but he sure saw your colors coming, didn't he?

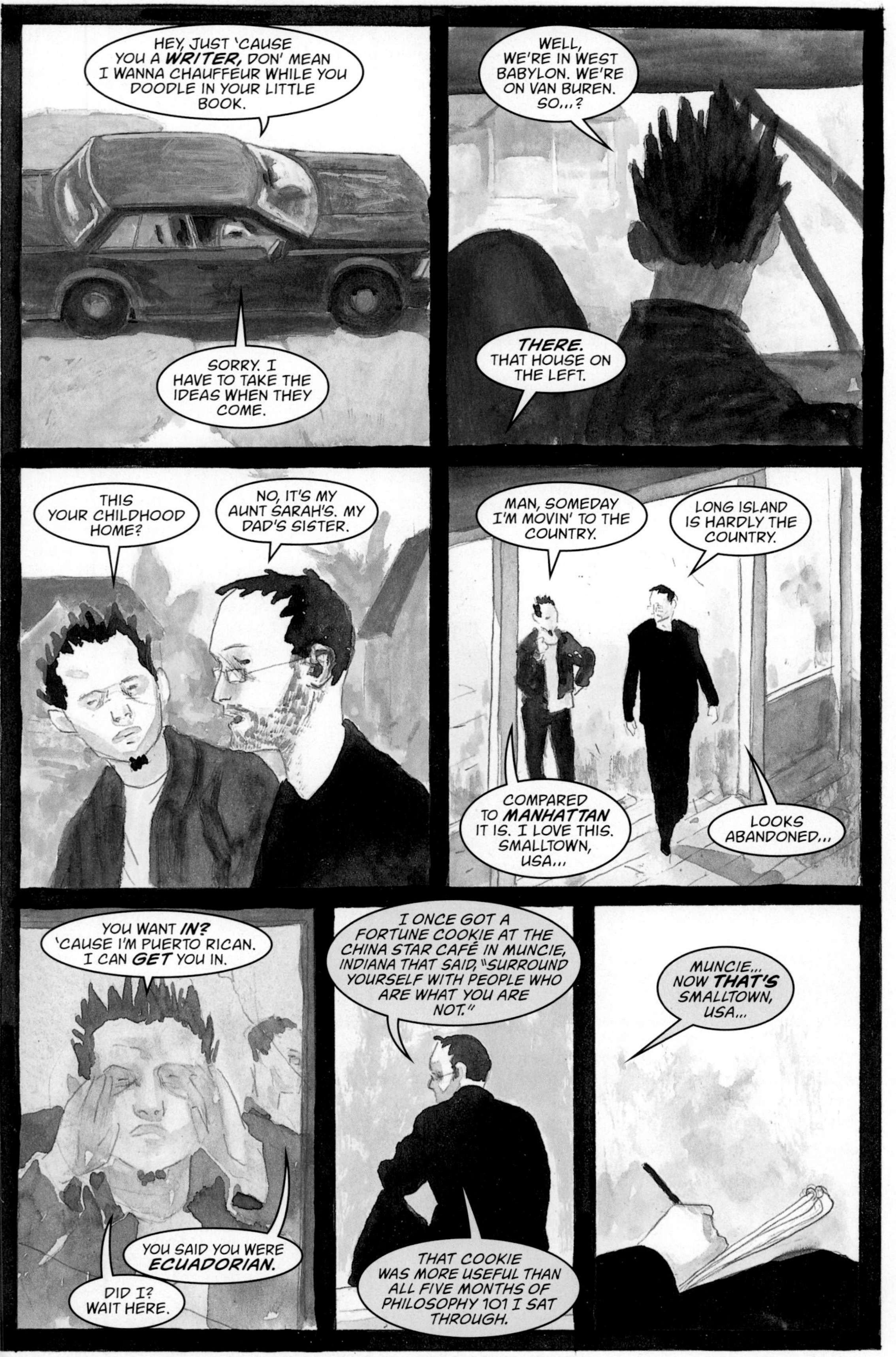
HEY, JUST 'CAUSE YOU A WRITER, DON' MEAN I WANNA CHAUFFEUR WHILE YOU DOODLE IN YOUR LITTLE BOOK.
SORRY. I HAVE TO TAKE THE IDEAS WHEN THEY COME.
WELL, WE'RE IN WEST BABYLON. WE'RE ON VAN BUREN. SO...?
THERE. THAT HOUSE ON THE LEFT.
THIS YOUR CHILDHOOD HOME?
NO, IT'S MY AUNT SARAH'S. MY DAD'S SISTER.
MAN, SOMEDAY I'M MOVIN' TO THE COUNTRY.
LONG ISLAND IS HARDLY THE COUNTRY.
COMPARED TO MANHATTAN IT IS. I LOVE THIS. SMALLTOWN, USA...
LOOKS ABANDONED...
YOU WANT IN? 'CAUSE I'M PUERTO RICAN. I CAN GET YOU IN.
YOU SAID YOU WERE ECUADORIAN.
DID I? WAIT HERE.
I ONCE GOT A FORTUNE COOKIE AT THE CHINA STAR CAFÉ IN MUNCIE, INDIANA THAT SAID, "SURROUND YOURSELF WITH PEOPLE WHO ARE WHAT YOU ARE NOT."
THAT COOKIE WAS MORE USEFUL THAN ALL FIVE MONTHS OF PHILOSOPHY 101 I SAT THROUGH.
MUNCIE... NOW THAT'S SMALLTOWN, USA...

SMALLVILLE

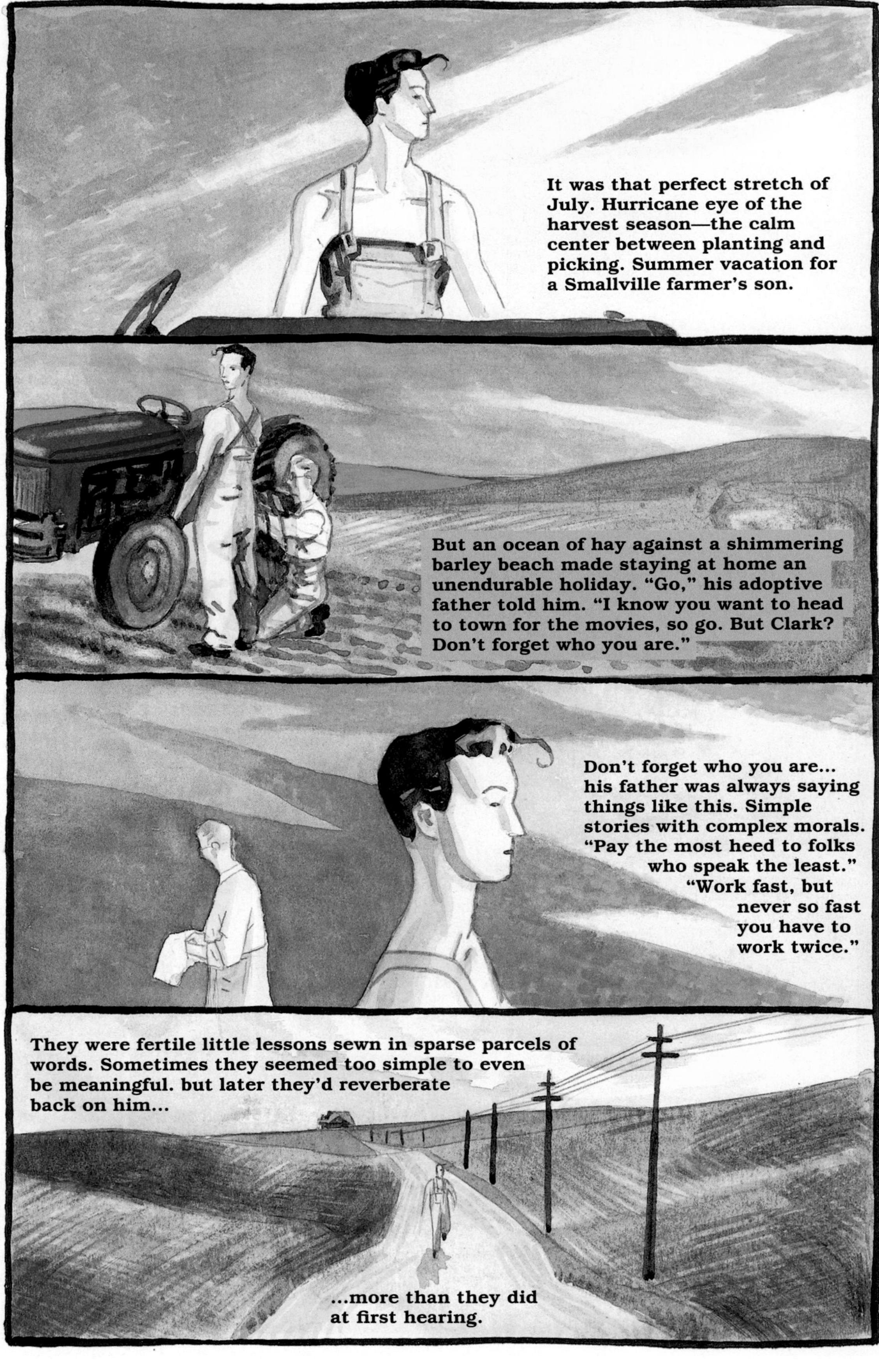
It was that perfect stretch of July. Hurricane eye of the harvest season—the calm center between planting and picking. Summer vacation for a Smallville farmer's son.
But an ocean of hay against a shimmering barley beach made staying at home an unendurable holiday. "Go," his adoptive father told him. "I know you want to head to town for the movies, so go. But Clark? Don't forget who you are."
Don't forget who you are... his father was always saying things like this. Simple stories with complex morals. "Pay the most heed to folks who speak the least." "Work fast, but never so fast you have to work twice."
They were fertile little lessons sewn in sparse parcels of words. Sometimes they seemed too simple to even be meaningful. but later they'd reverberate back on him...
...more than they did at first hearing.

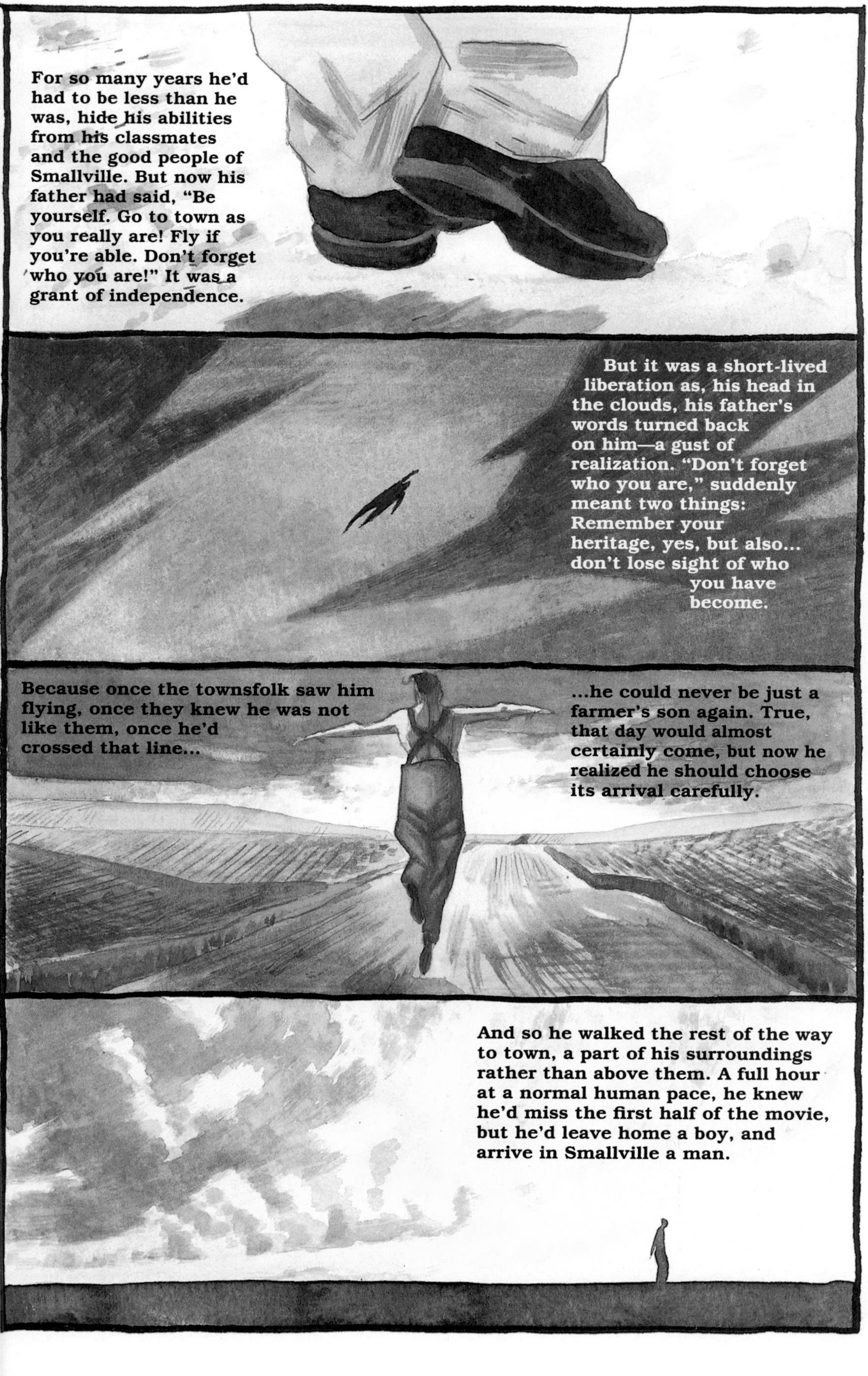
For so many years he'd had to be less than he was, hide his abilities from his classmates and the good people of Smallville. But now his father had said, "Be yourself. Go to town as you really are! Fly if you're able. Don't forget who you are!" It was a grant of independence.
But it was a short-lived liberation as, his head in the clouds, his father's words turned back on him—a gust of realization. "Don't forget who you are," suddenly meant two things: Remember your heritage, yes, but also... don't lose sight of who you have become.
Because once the townsfolk saw him flying, once they knew he was not like them, once he'd crossed that line...
...he could never be just a farmer's son again. True, that day would almost certainly come, but now he realized he should choose its arrival carefully.
And so he walked the rest of the way to town, a part of his surroundings rather than above them. A full hour at a normal human pace, he knew he'd miss the first half of the movie, but he'd leave home a boy, and arrive in Smallville a man.

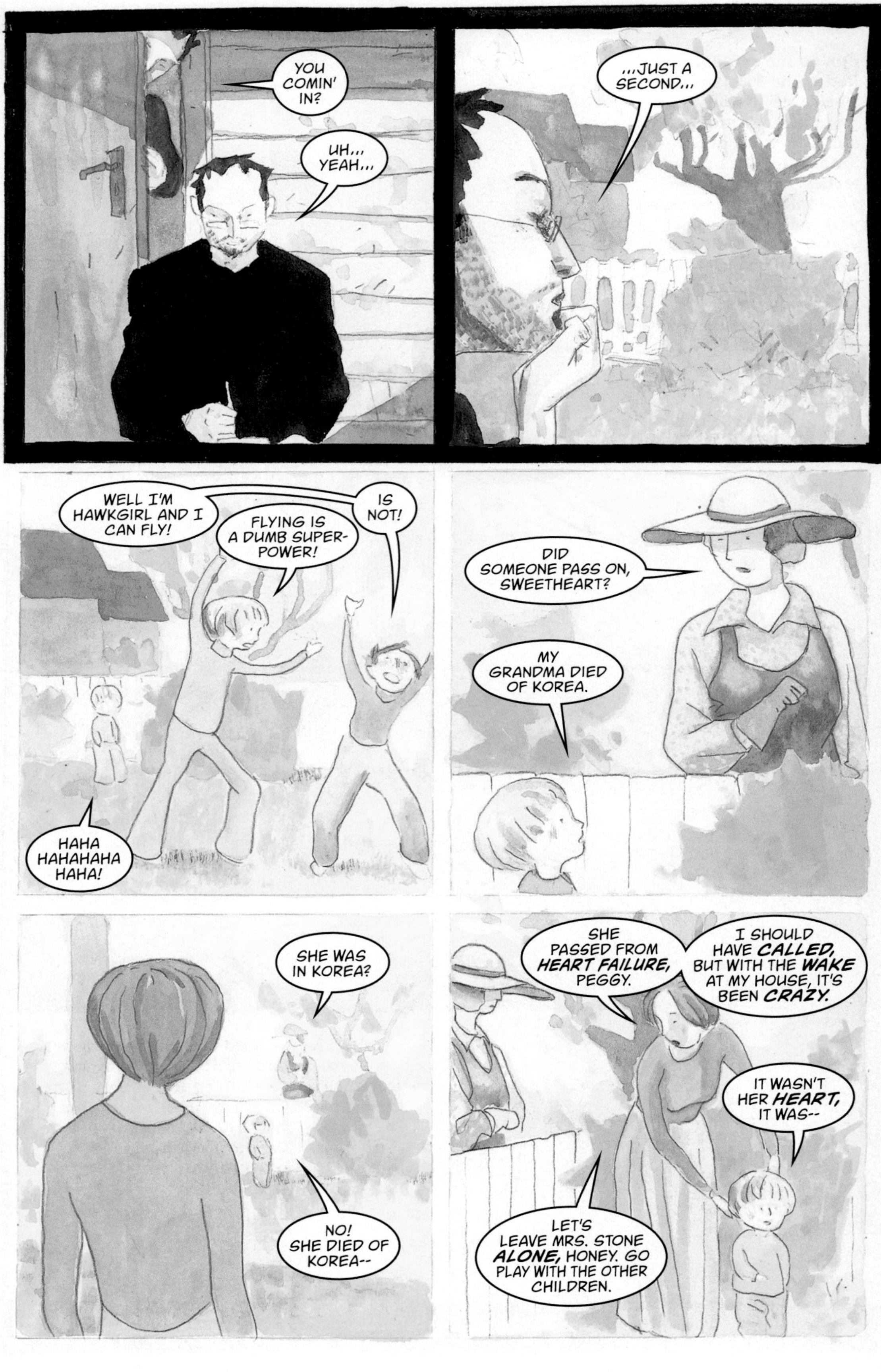
YOU COMIN' IN?
UH... YEAH...
...JUST A SECOND...
WELL I'M HAWKGIRL AND I CAN FLY!
FLYING IS A DUMB SUPER-POWER!
IS NOT!
HAHA HAHAHAHA HAHA!
DID SOMEONE PASS ON, SWEETHEART?
MY GRANDMA DIED OF KOREA.
SHE WAS IN KOREA?
NO! SHE DIED OF KOREA--
SHE PASSED FROM HEART FAILURE, PEGGY.
I SHOULD HAVE CALLED, BUT WITH THE WAKE AT MY HOUSE, IT'S BEEN CRAZY.
IT WASN'T HER HEART, IT WAS--
LET'S LEAVE MRS. STONE ALONE, HONEY. GO PLAY WITH THE OTHER CHILDREN.

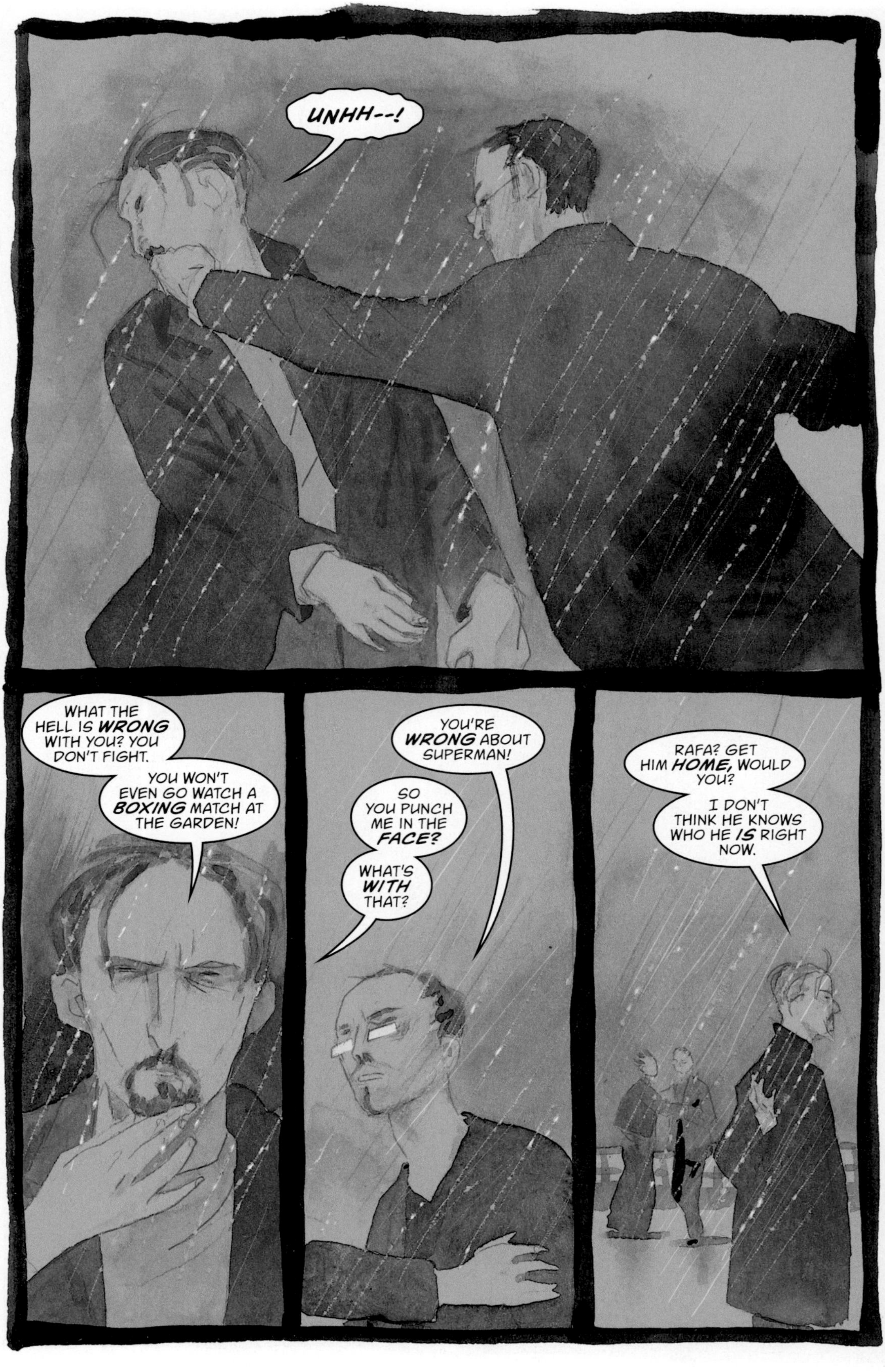
UNHH--!
WHAT THE HELL IS WRONG WITH YOU? YOU DON'T FIGHT.
YOU WON'T EVEN GO WATCH A BOXING MATCH AT THE GARDEN!
YOU'RE WRONG ABOUT SUPERMAN!
SO YOU PUNCH ME IN THE FACE?
WHAT'S WITH THAT?
RAFA? GET HIM HOME, WOULD YOU?
I DON'T THINK HE KNOWS WHO HE IS RIGHT NOW.

SECRET IDENTITY

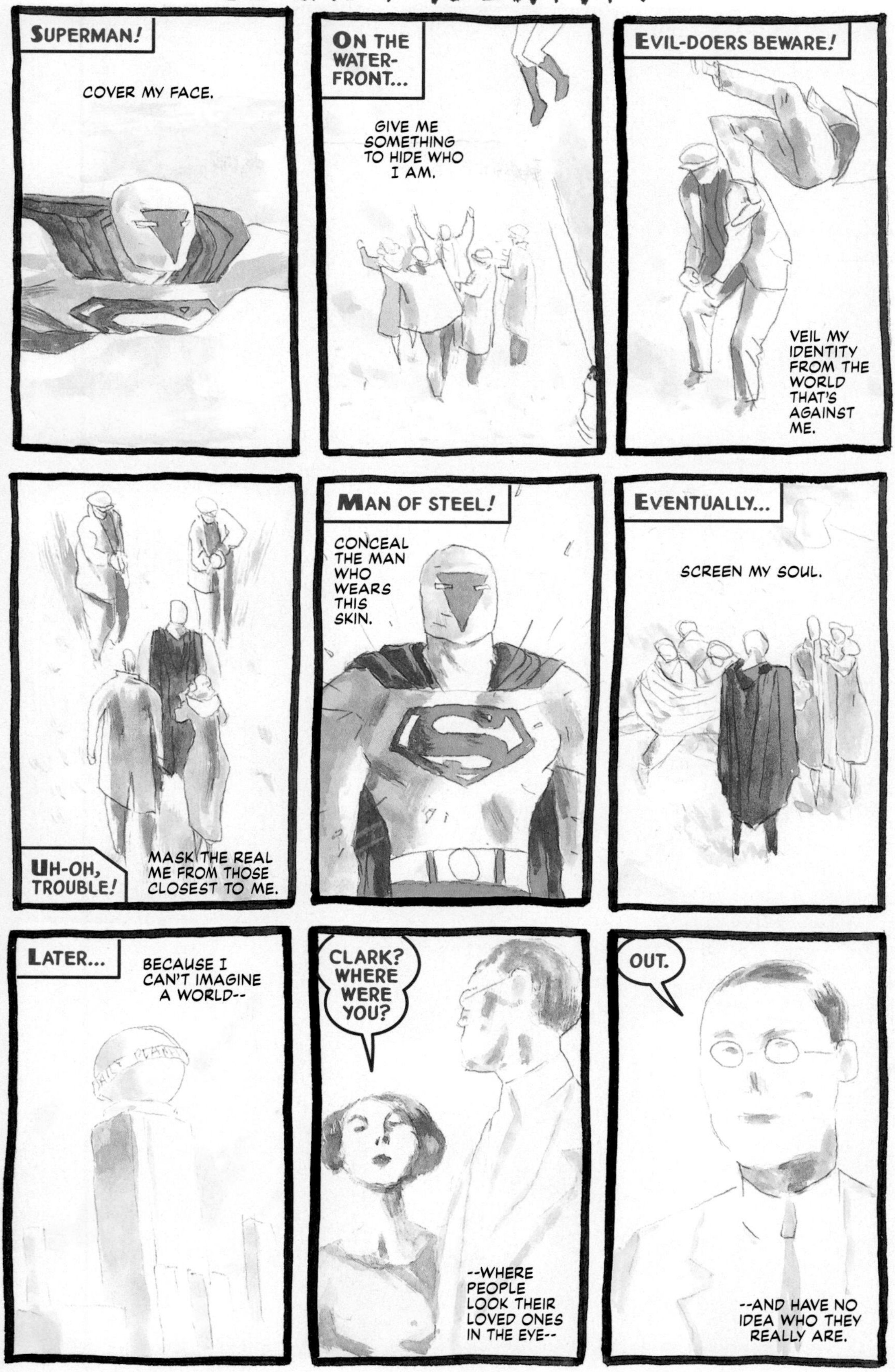

SUPERMAN!
COVER MY FACE.
ON THE WATER-FRONT...
GIVE ME SOMETHING TO HIDE WHO I AM.
EVIL-DOERS BEWARE!
VEIL MY IDENTITY FROM THE WORLD THAT'S AGAINST ME.
UH-OH, TROUBLE!
MASK THE REAL ME FROM THOSE CLOSEST TO ME.
MAN OF STEEL!
CONCEAL THE MAN WHO WEARS THIS SKIN.
EVENTUALLY...
SCREEN MY SOUL.
LATER...
BECAUSE I CAN'T IMAGINE A WORLD--
CLARK? WHERE WERE YOU?
--WHERE PEOPLE LOOK THEIR LOVED ONES IN THE EYE--
OUT.
--AND HAVE NO IDEA WHO THEY REALLY ARE.

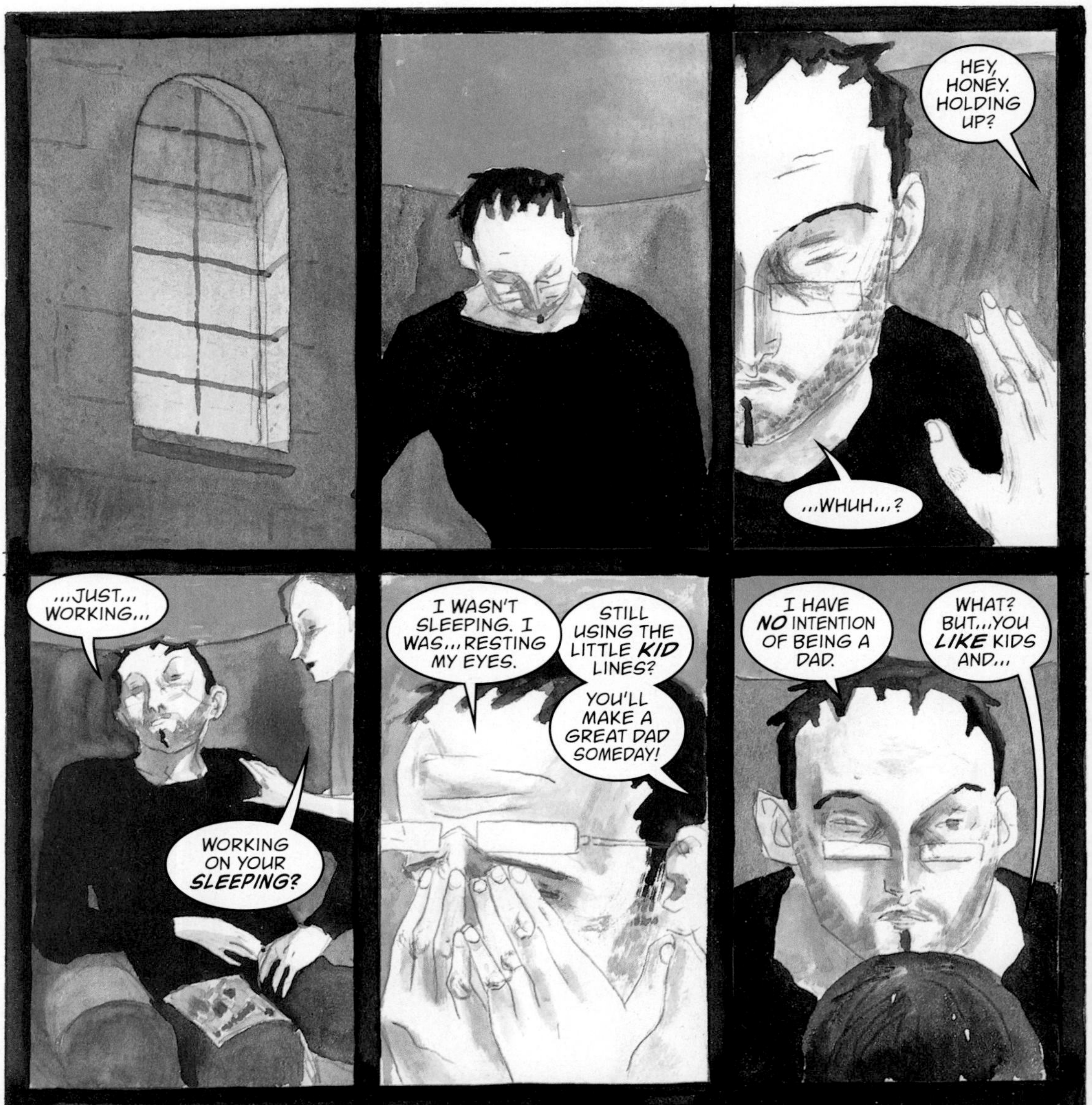
HEY, HONEY. HOLDING UP?
...WHUH...?
...JUST... WORKING...
WORKING ON YOUR SLEEPING?
I WASN'T SLEEPING. I WAS...RESTING MY EYES.
STILL USING THE LITTLE KID LINES?
YOU'LL MAKE A GREAT DAD SOMEDAY!
I HAVE NO INTENTION OF BEING A DAD.
WHAT? BUT...YOU LIKE KIDS AND...
WAIT A MINUTE. YOU DON'T WANT KIDS EVER?
WHY?

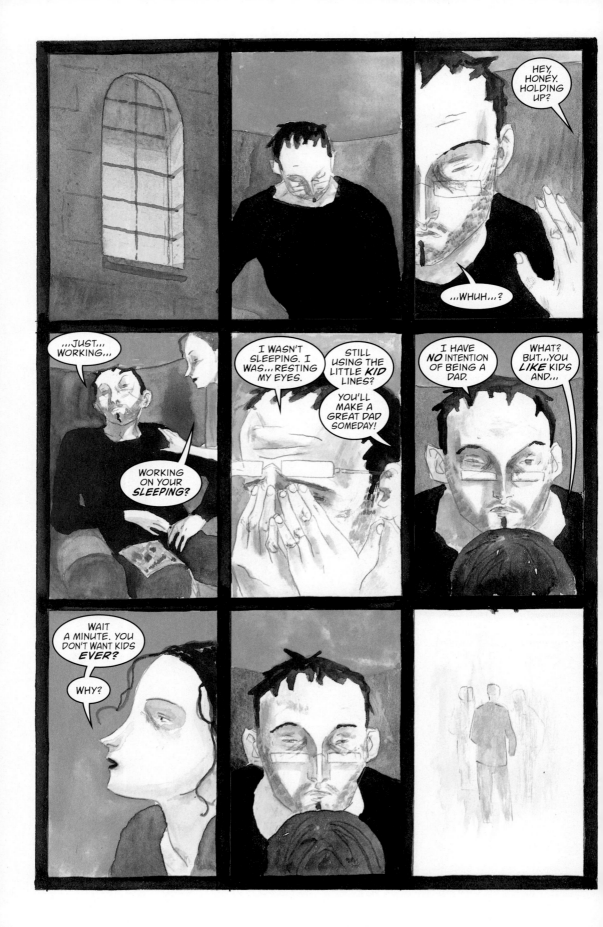

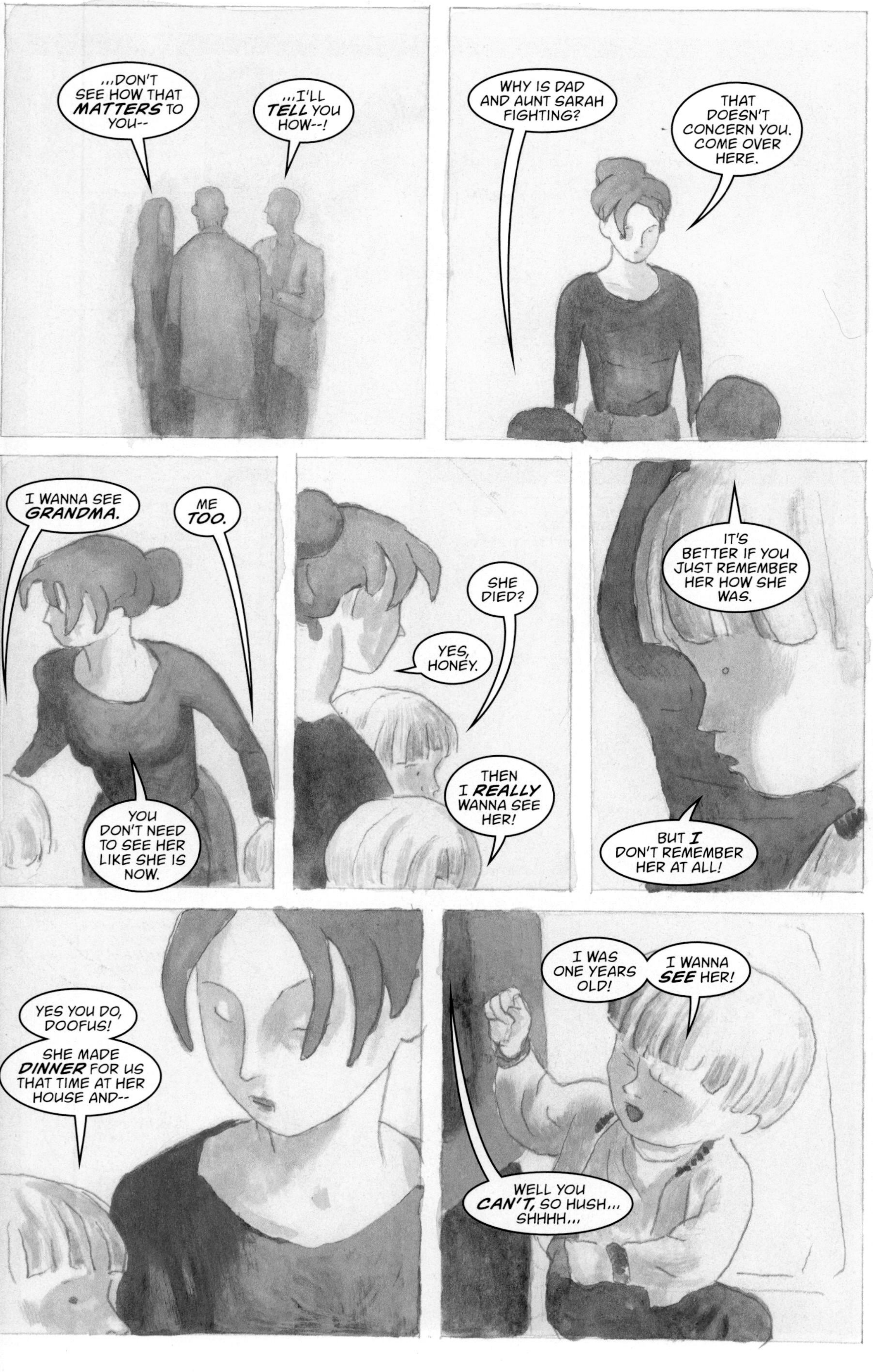
...DON'T SEE HOW THAT MATTERS TO YOU--
...I'LL TELL YOU HOW--!
WHY IS DAD AND AUNT SARAH FIGHTING?
THAT DOESN'T CONCERN YOU. COME OVER HERE.
I WANNA SEE GRANDMA.
ME TOO.
YOU DON'T NEED TO SEE HER LIKE SHE IS NOW.
SHE DIED?
YES, HONEY.
THEN I REALLY WANNA SEE HER!
IT'S BETTER IF YOU JUST REMEMBER HER HOW SHE WAS.
BUT I DON'T REMEMBER HER AT ALL!
YES YOU DO, DOOFUS!
SHE MADE DINNER FOR US THAT TIME AT HER HOUSE AND--
I WAS ONE YEARS OLD!
I WANNA SEE HER!
WELL YOU CAN'T, SO HUSH... SHHHH...

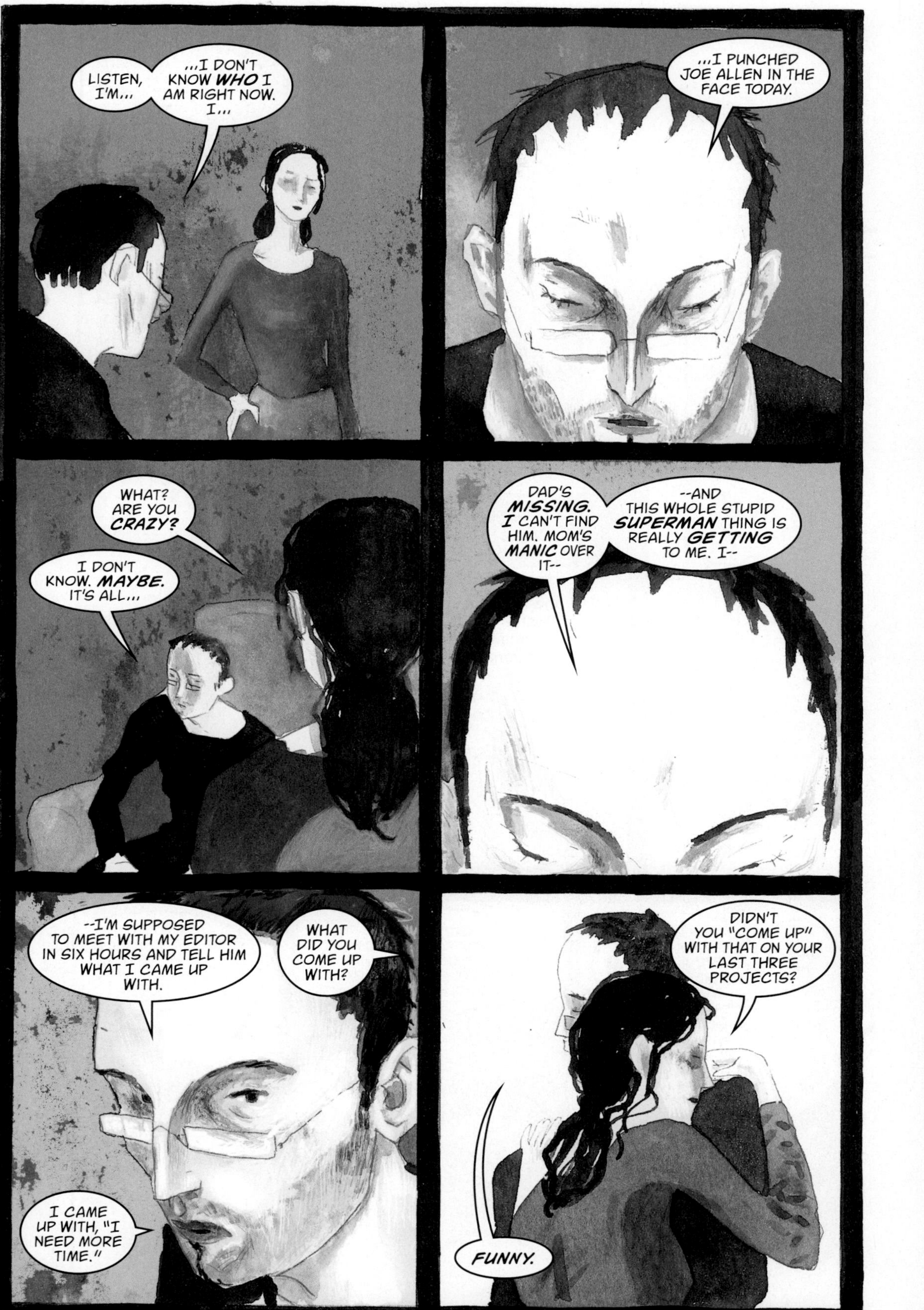
LISTEN, I'M...
...I DON'T KNOW WHO I AM RIGHT NOW. I...
...I PUNCHED JOE ALLEN IN THE FACE TODAY.
WHAT? ARE YOU CRAZY?
I DON'T KNOW. MAYBE. IT'S ALL...
DAD'S MISSING. I CAN'T FIND HIM. MOM'S MANIC OVER IT--
--AND THIS WHOLE STUPID SUPERMAN THING IS REALLY GETTING TO ME. I--
--I'M SUPPOSED TO MEET WITH MY EDITOR IN SIX HOURS AND TELL HIM WHAT I CAME UP WITH.
WHAT DID YOU COME UP WITH?
I CAME UP WITH, "I NEED MORE TIME."
DIDN'T YOU "COME UP" WITH THAT ON YOUR LAST THREE PROJECTS?
FUNNY.

POWER

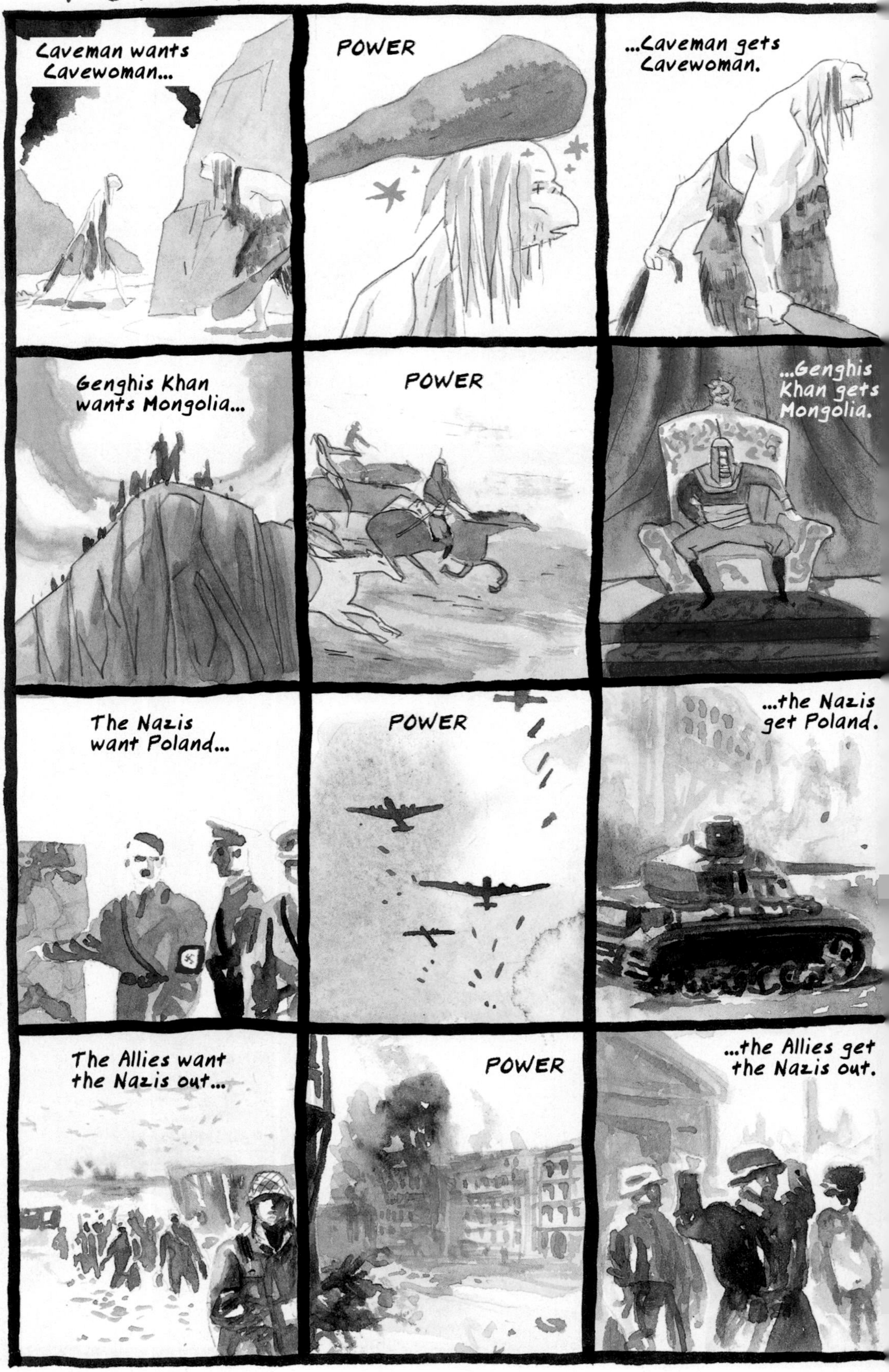

Caveman wants Cavewoman...
POWER
...Caveman gets Cavewoman.
Genghis Khan wants Mongolia...
POWER
...Genghis Khan gets Mongolia.
The Nazis want Poland...
POWER
...the Nazis get Poland.
The Allies want the Nazis out...
POWER
...the Allies get the Nazis out.

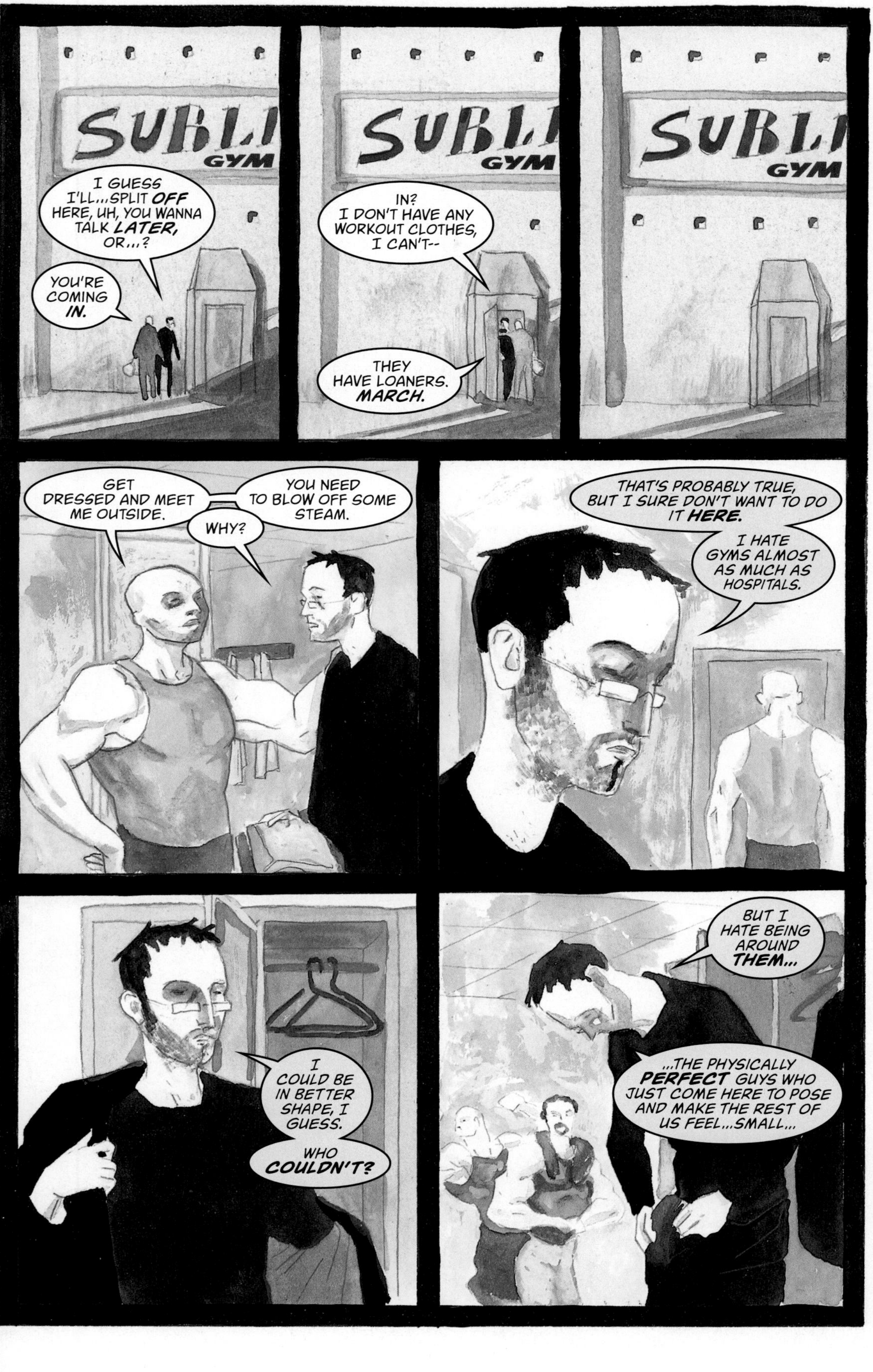
SUBLI
GYM
I GUESS I'LL...SPLIT OFF HERE, UH, YOU WANNA TALK LATER, OR...?
YOU'RE COMING IN.
SUBLI
GYM
IN? I DON'T HAVE ANY WORKOUT CLOTHES, I CAN'T--
THEY HAVE LOANERS. MARCH.
SUBLI
GYM
GET DRESSED AND MEET ME OUTSIDE.
YOU NEED TO BLOW OFF SOME STEAM.
WHY?
THAT'S PROBABLY TRUE, BUT I SURE DON'T WANT TO DO IT HERE.
I HATE GYMS ALMOST AS MUCH AS HOSPITALS.
I COULD BE IN BETTER SHAPE, I GUESS.
WHO COULDN'T?
BUT I HATE BEING AROUND THEM...
...THE PHYSICALLY PERFECT GUYS WHO JUST COME HERE TO POSE AND MAKE THE REST OF US FEEL...SMALL...

PERFECT

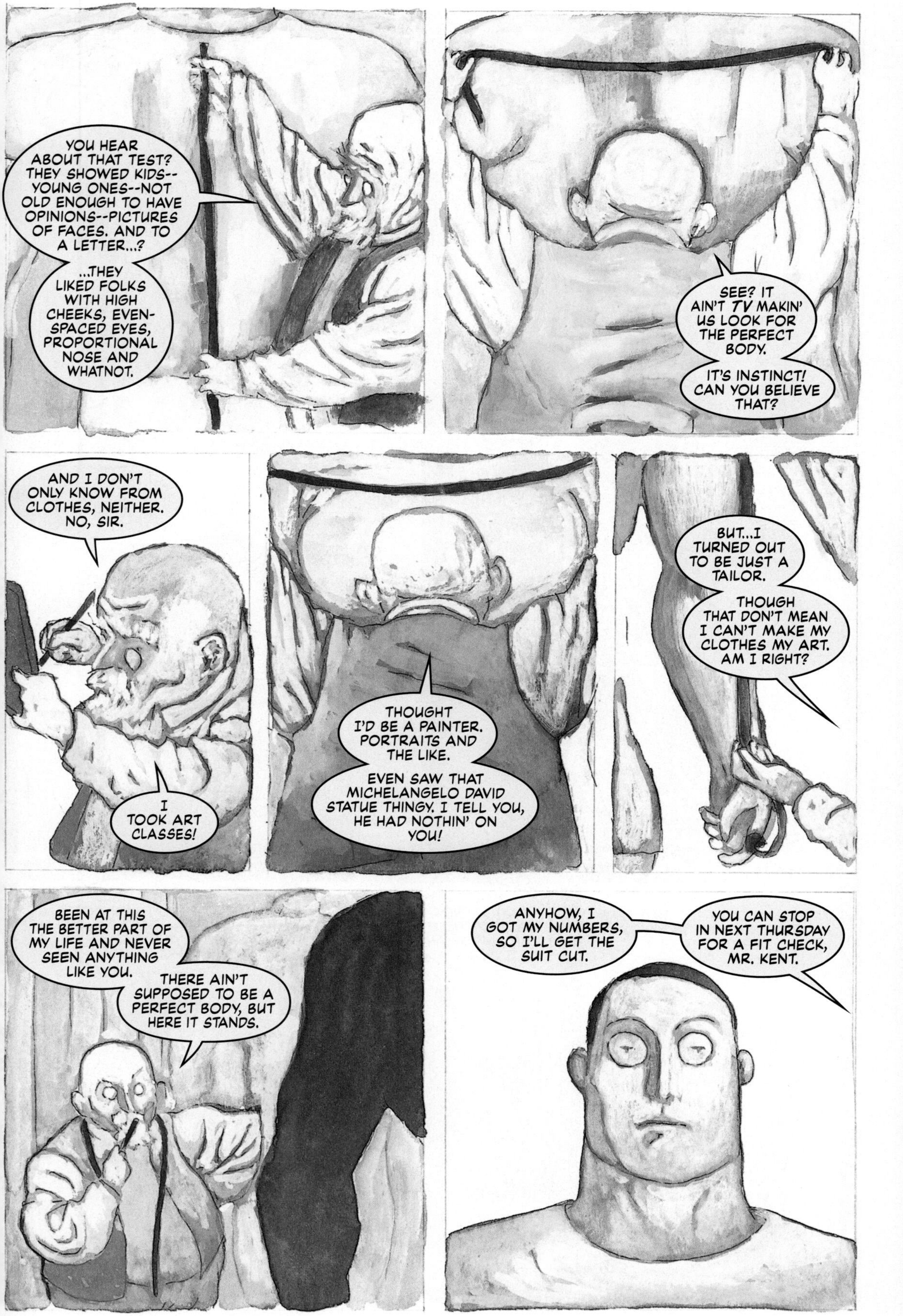
YOU HEAR ABOUT THAT TEST? THEY SHOWED KIDS--YOUNG ONES--NOT OLD ENOUGH TO HAVE OPINIONS--PICTURES OF FACES. AND TO A LETTER...?
...THEY LIKED FOLKS WITH HIGH CHEEKS, EVEN-SPACED EYES, PROPORTIONAL NOSE AND WHATNOT.
SEE? IT AIN'T TV MAKIN' US LOOK FOR THE PERFECT BODY.
IT'S INSTINCT! CAN YOU BELIEVE THAT?
AND I DON'T ONLY KNOW FROM CLOTHES, NEITHER. NO, SIR.
I TOOK ART CLASSES!
THOUGHT I'D BE A PAINTER. PORTRAITS AND THE LIKE.
EVEN SAW THAT MICHELANGELO DAVID STATUE THINGY. I TELL YOU, HE HAD NOTHIN' ON YOU!
BUT...I TURNED OUT TO BE JUST A TAILOR.
THOUGH THAT DON'T MEAN I CAN'T MAKE MY CLOTHES MY ART. AM I RIGHT?
BEEN AT THIS THE BETTER PART OF MY LIFE AND NEVER SEEN ANYTHING LIKE YOU.
THERE AIN'T SUPPOSED TO BE A PERFECT BODY, BUT HERE IT STANDS.
ANYHOW, I GOT MY NUMBERS, SO I'LL GET THE SUIT CUT.
YOU CAN STOP IN NEXT THURSDAY FOR A FIT CHECK, MR. KENT.

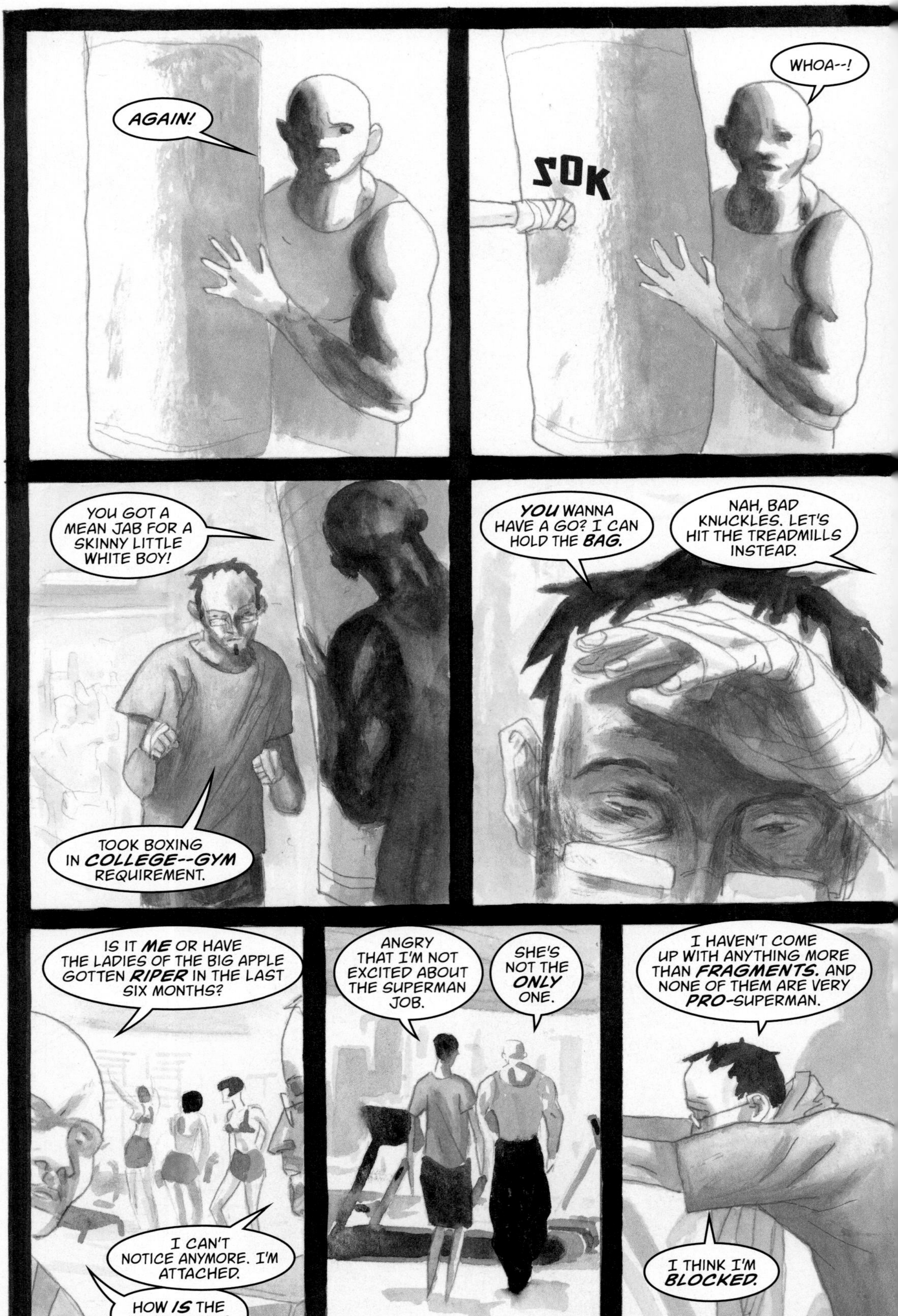
AGAIN!
SOK
WHOA--!
YOU GOT A MEAN JAB FOR A SKINNY LITTLE WHITE BOY!
TOOK BOXING IN COLLEGE--GYM REQUIREMENT.
YOU WANNA HAVE A GO? I CAN HOLD THE BAG.
NAH, BAD KNUCKLES. LET'S HIT THE TREADMILLS INSTEAD.
IS IT ME OR HAVE THE LADIES OF THE BIG APPLE GOTTEN RIPER IN THE LAST SIX MONTHS?
I CAN'T NOTICE ANYMORE. I'M ATTACHED.
HOW IS THE LOVELY LISA?
ANGRY THAT I'M NOT EXCITED ABOUT THE SUPERMAN JOB.
SHE'S NOT THE ONLY ONE.
I HAVEN'T COME UP WITH ANYTHING MORE THAN FRAGMENTS. AND NONE OF THEM ARE VERY PRO-SUPERMAN.
I THINK I'M BLOCKED.

HIDDEN

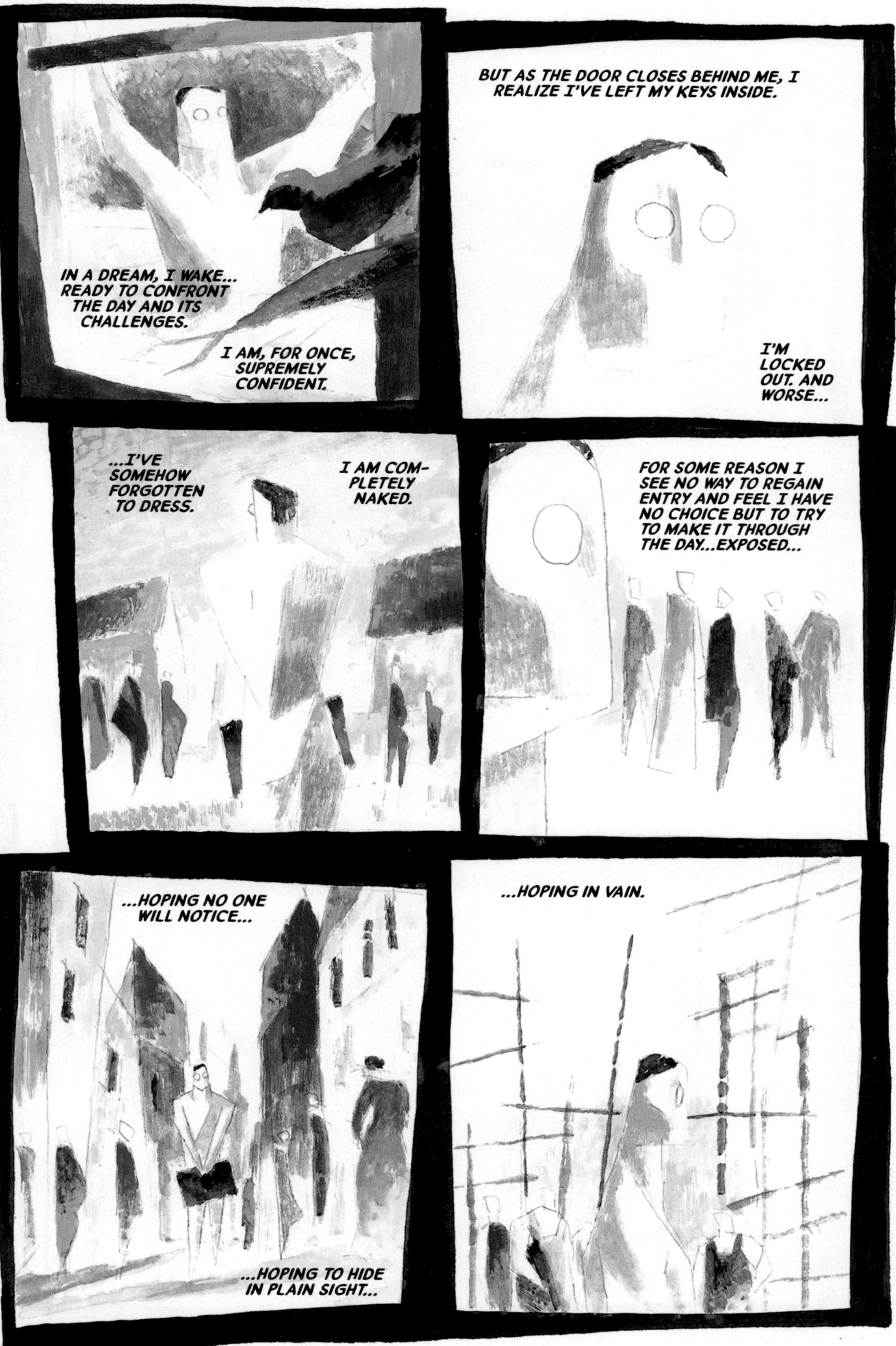
IN A DREAM, I WAKE... READY TO CONFRONT THE DAY AND ITS CHALLENGES.
I AM, FOR ONCE, SUPREMELY CONFIDENT.
BUT AS THE DOOR CLOSES BEHIND ME, I REALIZE I'VE LEFT MY KEYS INSIDE.
I'M LOCKED OUT. AND WORSE...
...I'VE SOMEHOW FORGOTTEN TO DRESS.
I AM COM- PLETELY NAKED.
FOR SOME REASON I SEE NO WAY TO REGAIN ENTRY AND FEEL I HAVE NO CHOICE BUT TO TRY TO MAKE IT THROUGH THE DAY...EXPOSED...
...HOPING NO ONE WILL NOTICE...
...HOPING TO HIDE IN PLAIN SIGHT...
...HOPING IN VAIN.

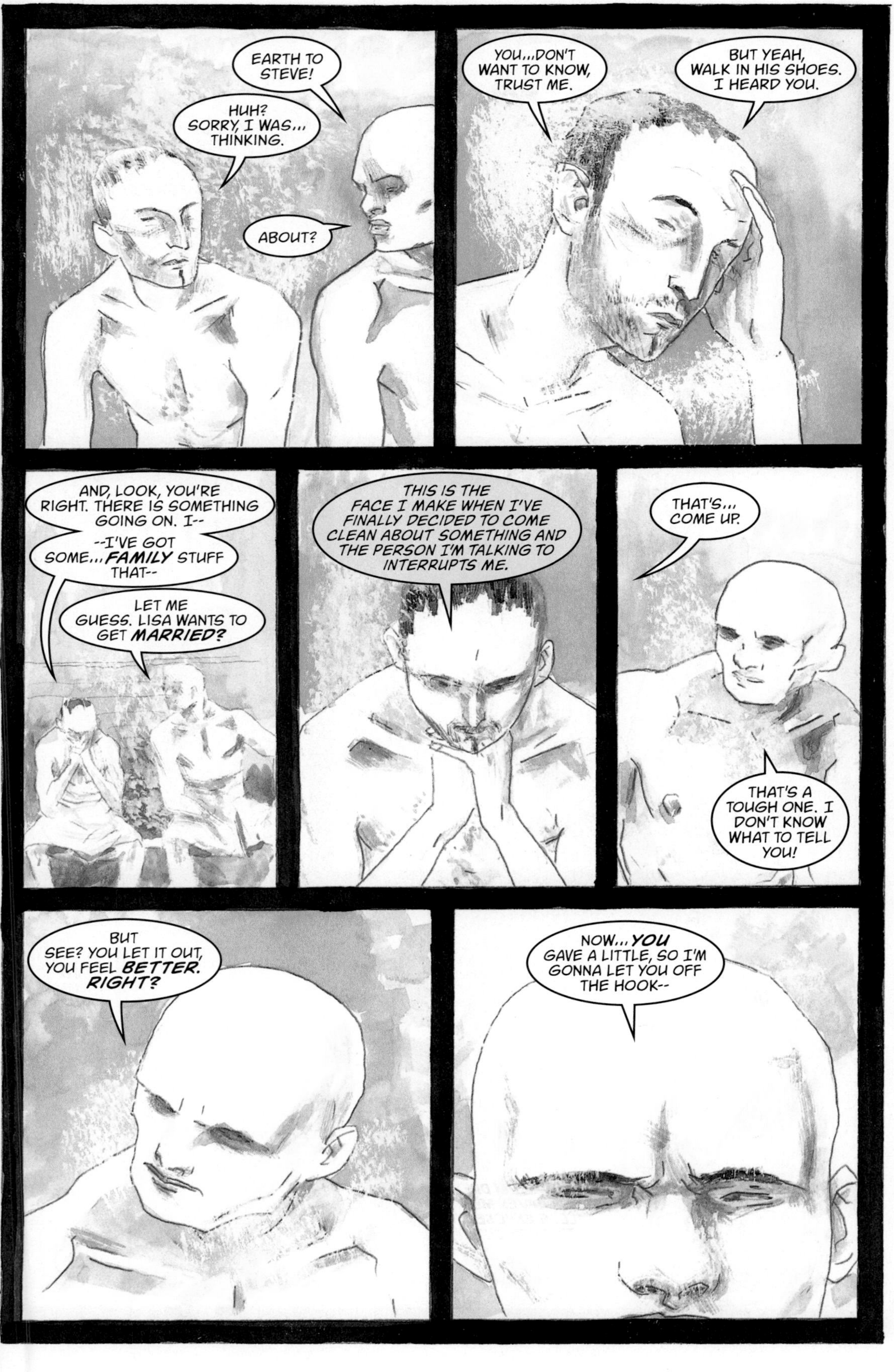
EARTH TO STEVE!
HUH? SORRY, I WAS... THINKING.
ABOUT?
YOU...DON'T WANT TO KNOW, TRUST ME.
BUT YEAH, WALK IN HIS SHOES. I HEARD YOU.
AND, LOOK, YOU'RE RIGHT. THERE IS SOMETHING GOING ON. I--
--I'VE GOT SOME...**FAMILY** STUFF THAT--
LET ME GUESS. LISA WANTS TO GET **MARRIED?**
THIS IS THE FACE I MAKE WHEN I'VE FINALLY DECIDED TO COME CLEAN ABOUT SOMETHING AND THE PERSON I'M TALKING TO INTERRUPTS ME.
THAT'S... COME UP.
THAT'S A TOUGH ONE. I DON'T KNOW WHAT TO TELL YOU!
BUT SEE? YOU LET IT OUT, YOU FEEL **BETTER. RIGHT?**
NOW...**YOU** GAVE A LITTLE, SO I'M GONNA LET YOU OFF THE HOOK--

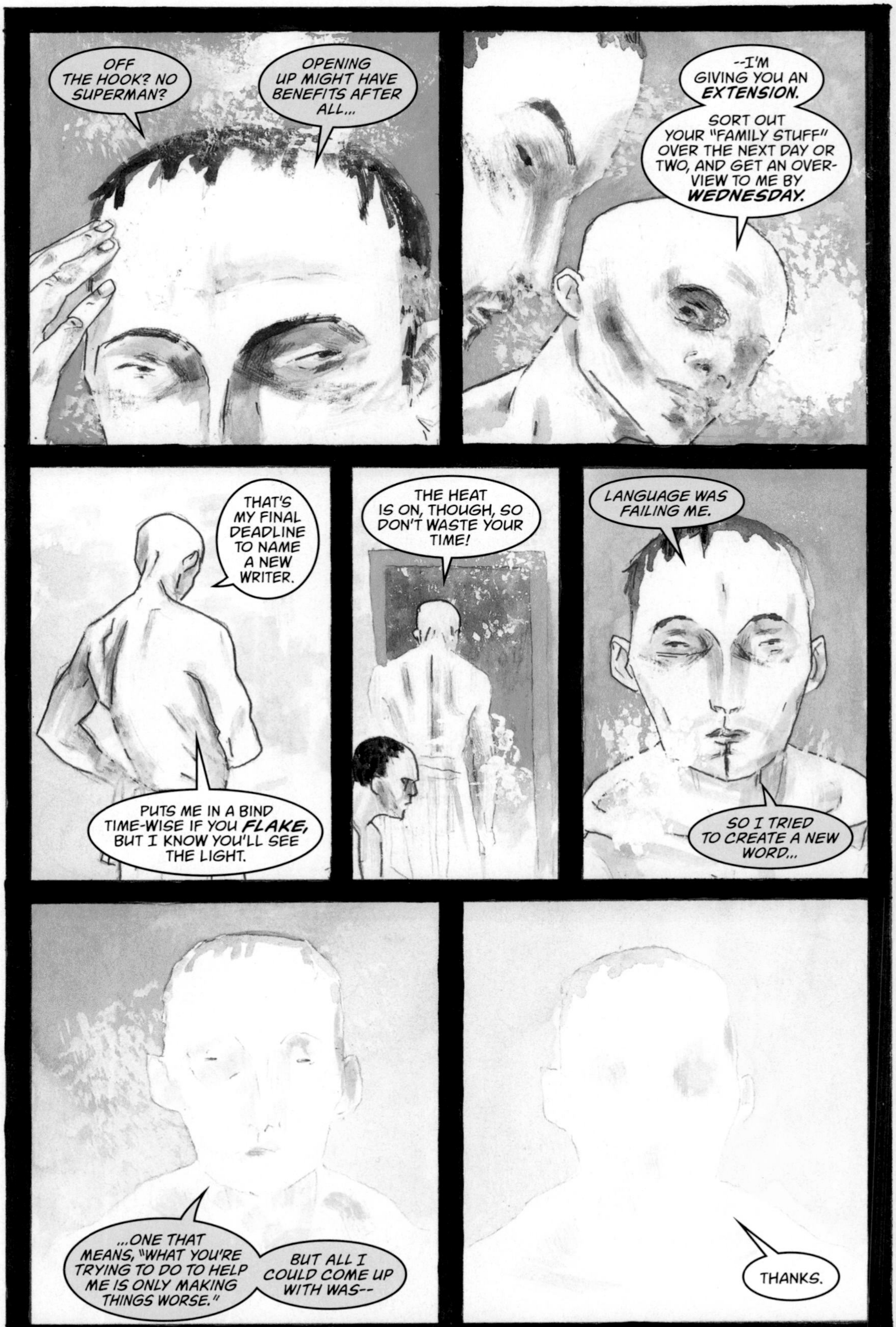
OFF THE HOOK? NO SUPERMAN?
OPENING UP MIGHT HAVE BENEFITS AFTER ALL...
--I'M GIVING YOU AN EXTENSION.
SORT OUT YOUR "FAMILY STUFF" OVER THE NEXT DAY OR TWO, AND GET AN OVER-VIEW TO ME BY WEDNESDAY.
THAT'S MY FINAL DEADLINE TO NAME A NEW WRITER.
PUTS ME IN A BIND TIME-WISE IF YOU FLAKE, BUT I KNOW YOU'LL SEE THE LIGHT.
THE HEAT IS ON, THOUGH, SO DON'T WASTE YOUR TIME!
LANGUAGE WAS FAILING ME.
SO I TRIED TO CREATE A NEW WORD...
...ONE THAT MEANS, "WHAT YOU'RE TRYING TO DO TO HELP ME IS ONLY MAKING THINGS WORSE."
BUT ALL I COULD COME UP WITH WAS--
THANKS.

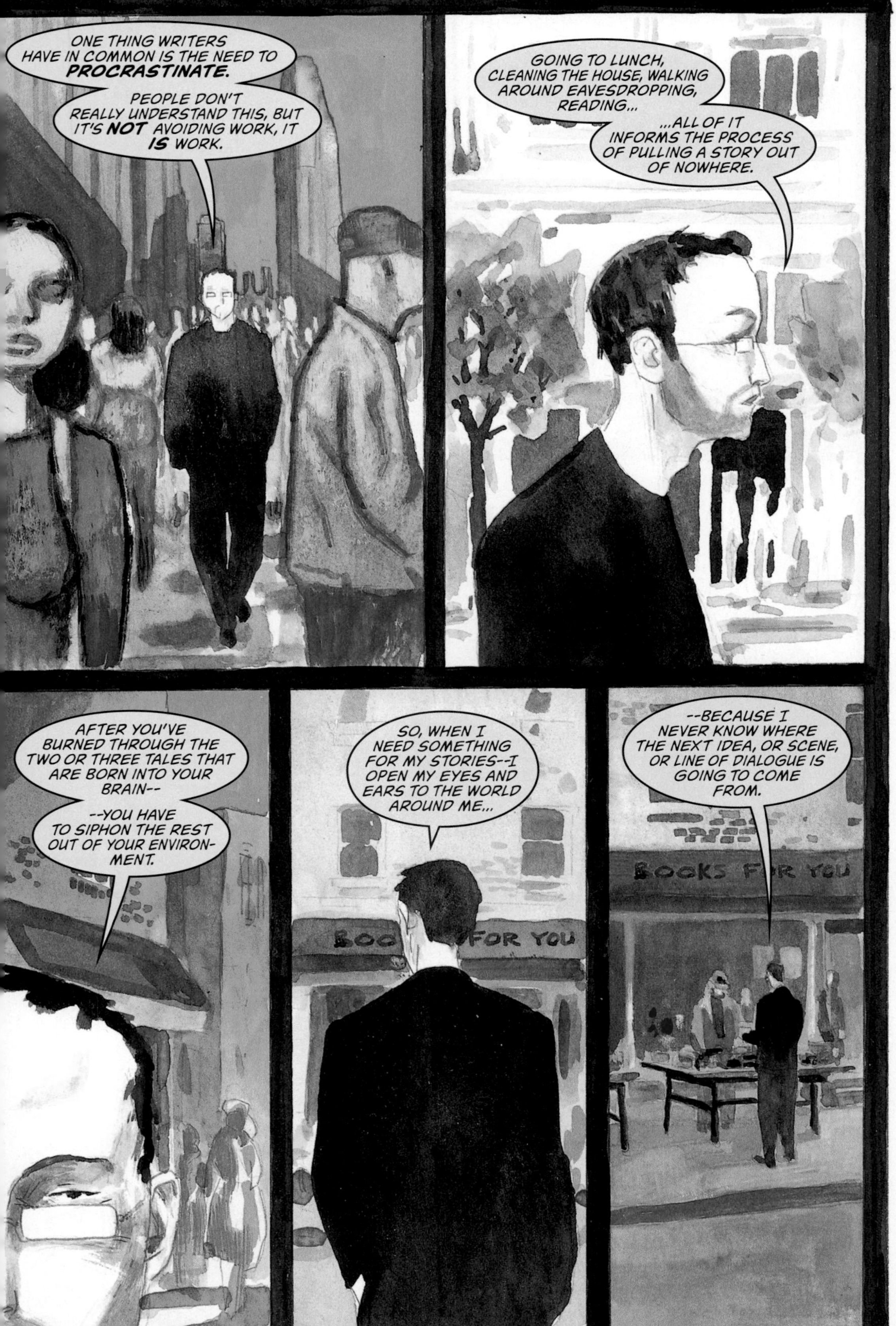
ONE THING WRITERS HAVE IN COMMON IS THE NEED TO **PROCRASTINATE.**
PEOPLE DON'T REALLY UNDERSTAND THIS, BUT IT'S **NOT** AVOIDING WORK, IT **IS** WORK.
GOING TO LUNCH, CLEANING THE HOUSE, WALKING AROUND EAVESDROPPING, READING...
...ALL OF IT INFORMS THE PROCESS OF PULLING A STORY OUT OF NOWHERE.
AFTER YOU'VE BURNED THROUGH THE TWO OR THREE TALES THAT ARE BORN INTO YOUR BRAIN--
--YOU HAVE TO SIPHON THE REST OUT OF YOUR ENVIRON-MENT.
SO, WHEN I NEED SOMETHING FOR MY STORIES--I OPEN MY EYES AND EARS TO THE WORLD AROUND ME...
--BECAUSE I NEVER KNOW WHERE THE NEXT IDEA, OR SCENE, OR LINE OF DIALOGUE IS GOING TO COME FROM.
BOOKS FOR YOU

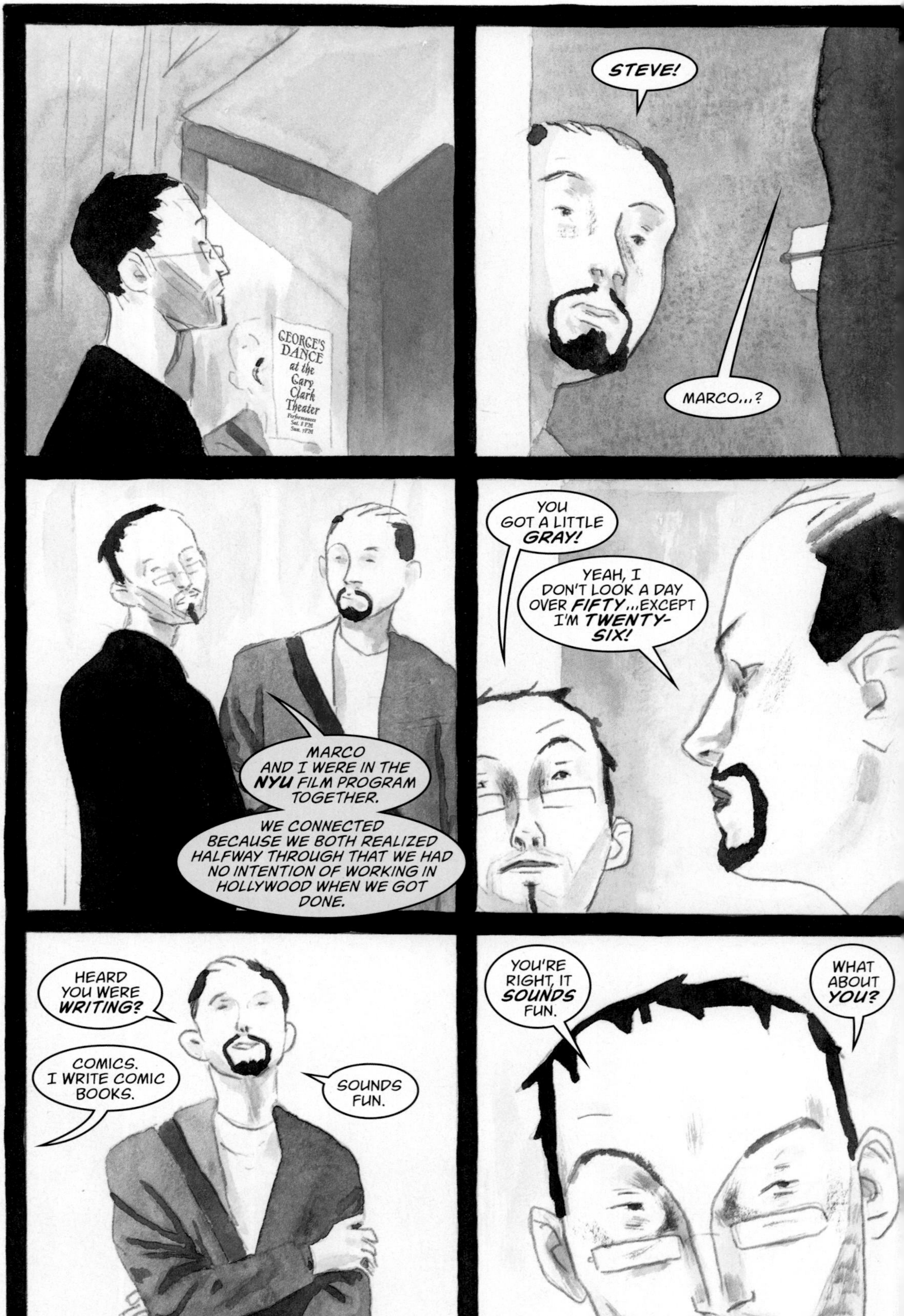

GEORGE'S DANCE at the Gary Clark Theater
STEVE!
MARCO...?
MARCO AND I WERE IN THE NYU FILM PROGRAM TOGETHER.
WE CONNECTED BECAUSE WE BOTH REALIZED HALFWAY THROUGH THAT WE HAD NO INTENTION OF WORKING IN HOLLYWOOD WHEN WE GOT DONE.
YOU GOT A LITTLE GRAY!
YEAH, I DON'T LOOK A DAY OVER FIFTY...EXCEPT I'M TWENTY-SIX!
HEARD YOU WERE WRITING?
COMICS. I WRITE COMIC BOOKS.
SOUNDS FUN.
YOU'RE RIGHT, IT SOUNDS FUN.
WHAT ABOUT YOU?

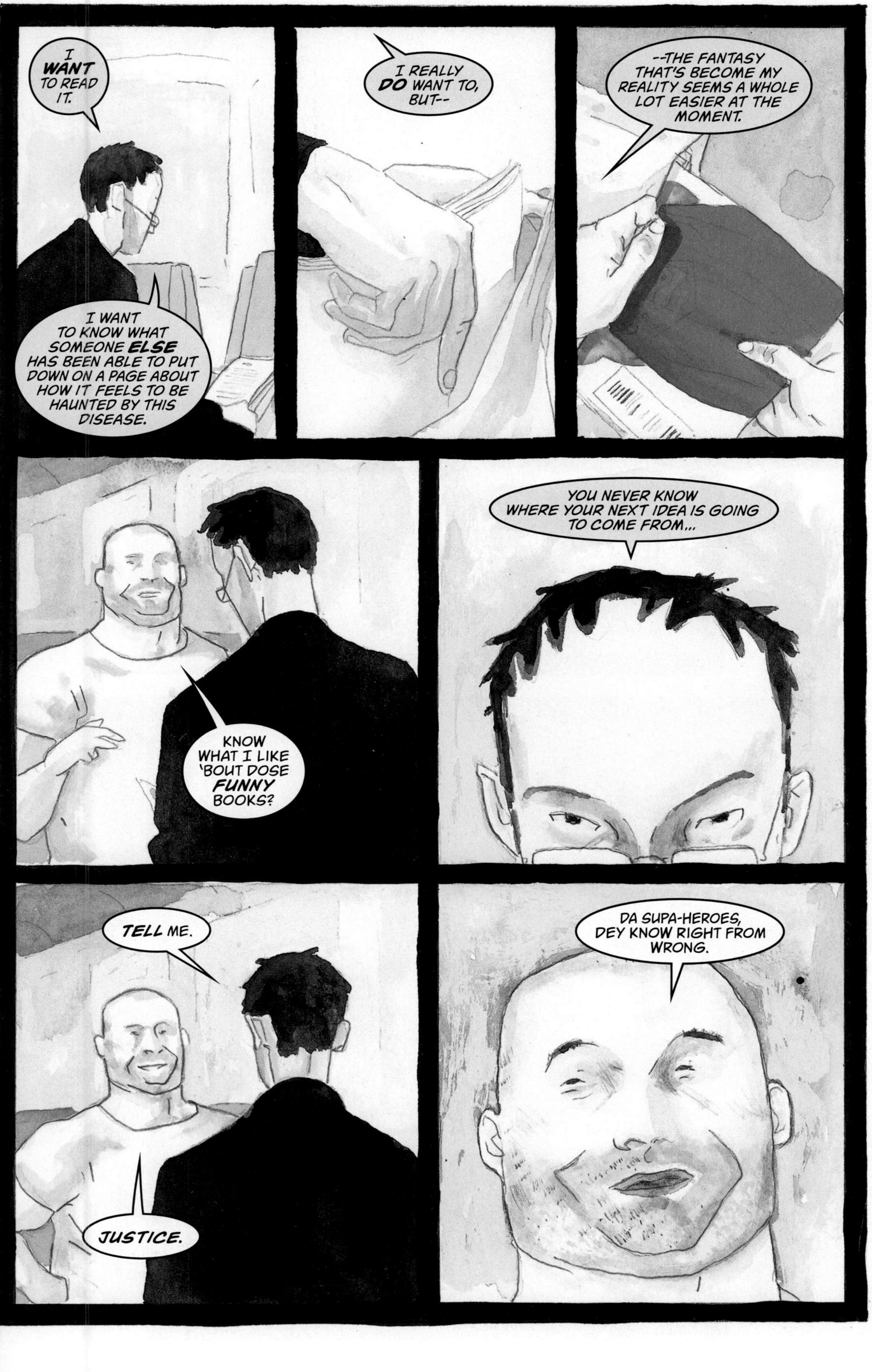
I WANT TO READ IT.
I WANT TO KNOW WHAT SOMEONE ELSE HAS BEEN ABLE TO PUT DOWN ON A PAGE ABOUT HOW IT FEELS TO BE HAUNTED BY THIS DISEASE.
I REALLY DO WANT TO, BUT--
--THE FANTASY THAT'S BECOME MY REALITY SEEMS A WHOLE LOT EASIER AT THE MOMENT.
KNOW WHAT I LIKE 'BOUT DOSE FUNNY BOOKS?
YOU NEVER KNOW WHERE YOUR NEXT IDEA IS GOING TO COME FROM...
TELL ME.
JUSTICE.
DA SUPA-HEROES, DEY KNOW RIGHT FROM WRONG.

JUSTICE

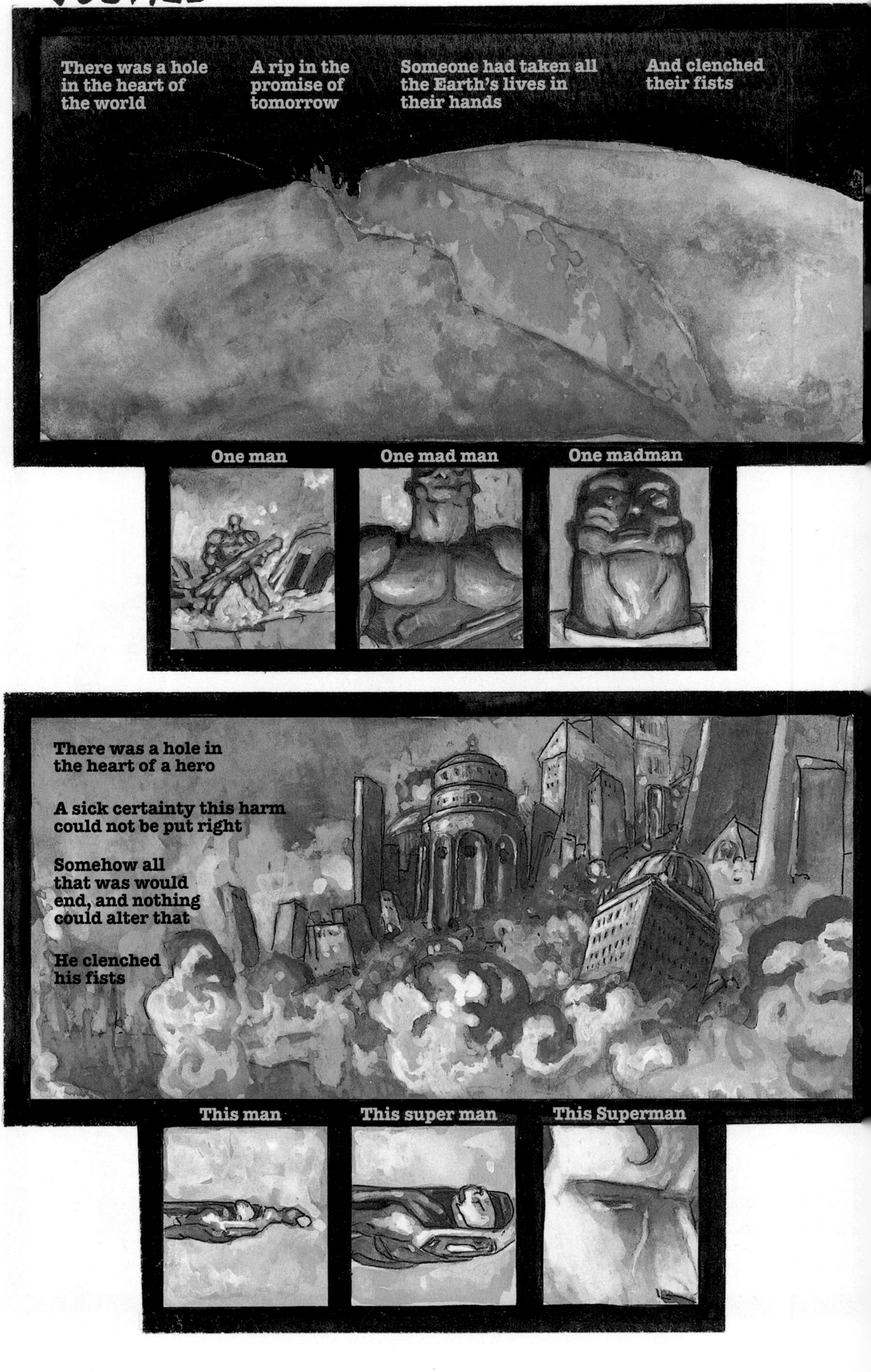

There was a hole in the heart of the world

A rip in the promise of tomorrow

Someone had taken all the Earth's lives in their hands

And clenched their fists

One man

One mad man

One madman

There was a hole in the heart of a hero

A sick certainty this harm could not be put right

Somehow all that was would end, and nothing could alter that

He clenched his fists

This man

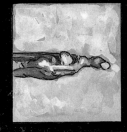

This super man

This Superman

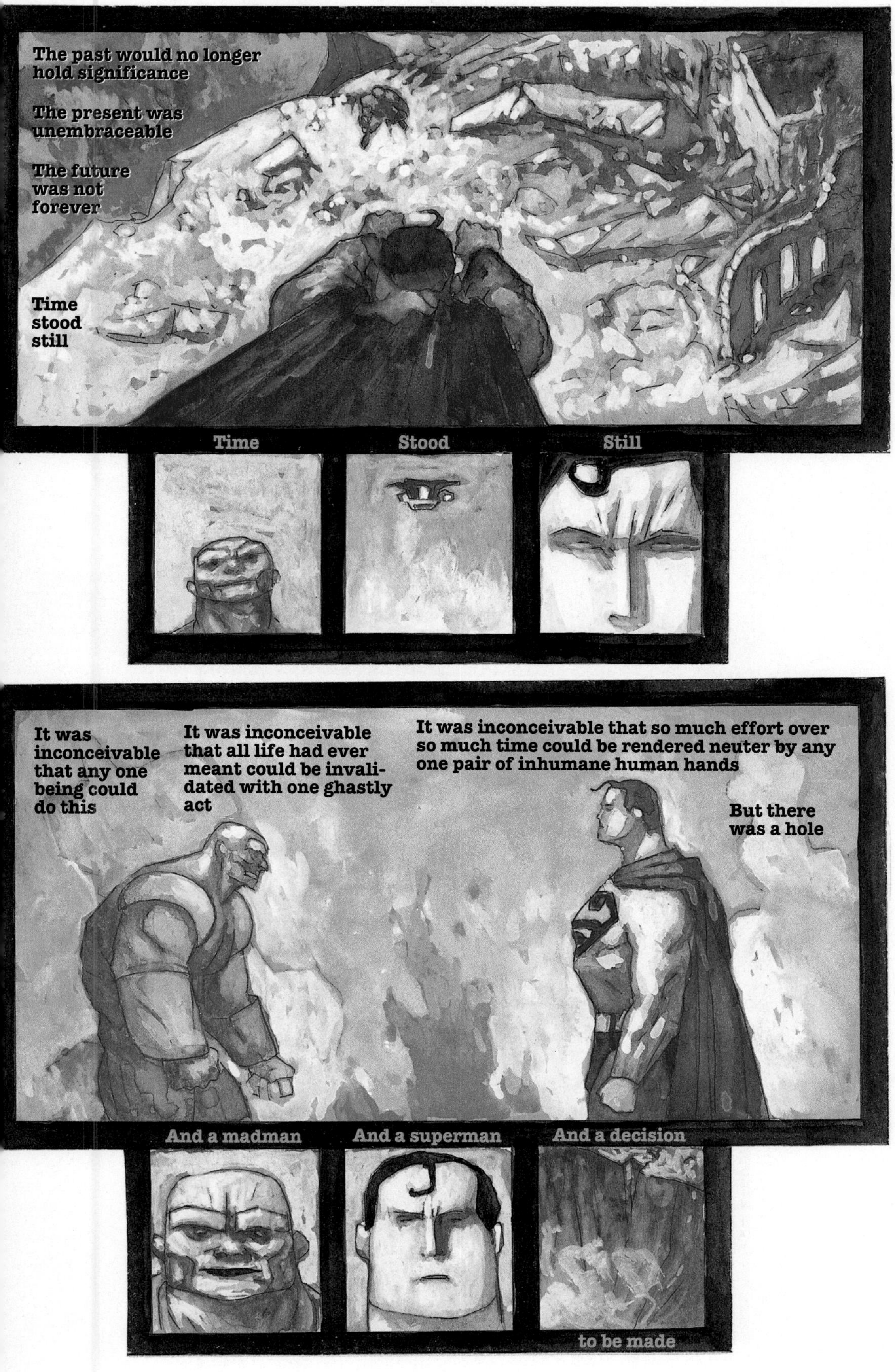
The past would no longer hold significance
The present was unembraceable
The future was not forever
Time stood still
Time
Stood
Still
It was inconceivable that any one being could do this
It was inconceivable that all life had ever meant could be invali-dated with one ghastly act
It was inconceivable that so much effort over so much time could be rendered neuter by any one pair of inhumane human hands
But there was a hole
And a madman
And a superman
And a decision
to be made

At the end of the day   At the end of the world   What is justice?

The superman could hurl the madman into the abyss he had opened

Is justice the fierce pair of flesh scalded from bone by sulfuric steam?

Is justice the coarse collision of meat and bone with magma and base rock?

The superman could force the madman to witness the final days of the planet he had crippled

Is justice the realization that one has brought doom to that which gave him life?

Is justice living out the life sentence he has condemned others to serve?

Or is justice nothing more than an ideal?   Which, after a point, becomes purely

  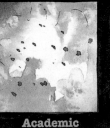

Academic

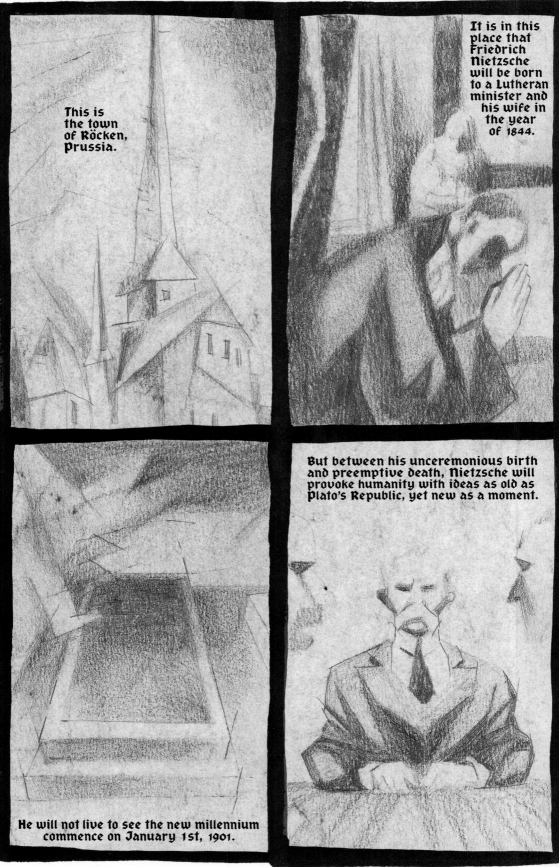

This is the town of Röcken, Prussia.

It is in this place that Friedrich Nietzsche will be born to a Lutheran minister and his wife in the year of 1844.

He will not live to see the new millennium commence on January 1st, 1901.

But between his unceremonious birth and preemptive death, Nietzsche will provoke humanity with ideas as old as Plato's Republic, yet new as a moment.

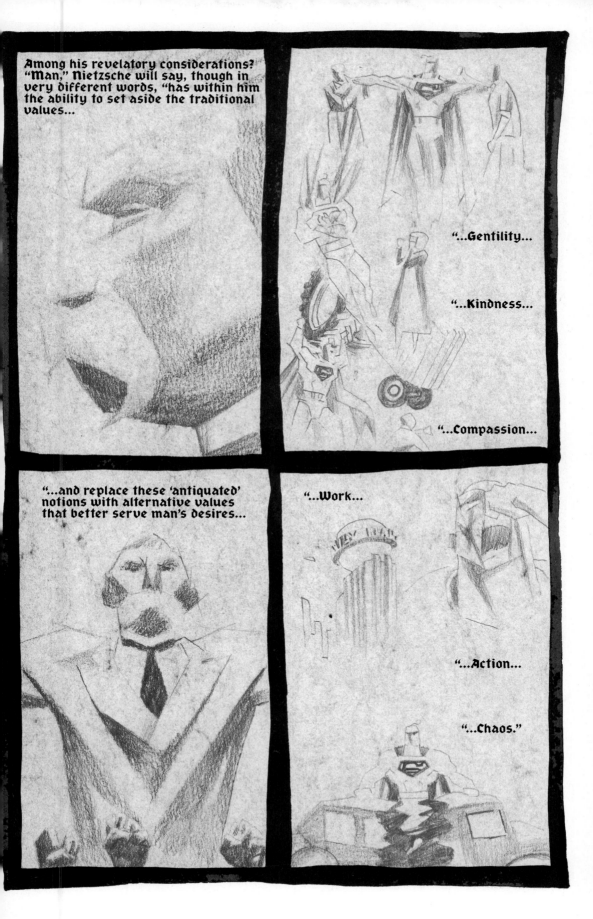

Among his revelatory considerations? "Man," Nietzsche will say, though in very different words, "has within him the ability to set aside the traditional values...

"...Gentility...

"...Kindness...

"...Compassion...

"...and replace these 'antiquated' notions with alternative values that better serve man's desires...

"...Work...

"...Action...

"...Chaos."

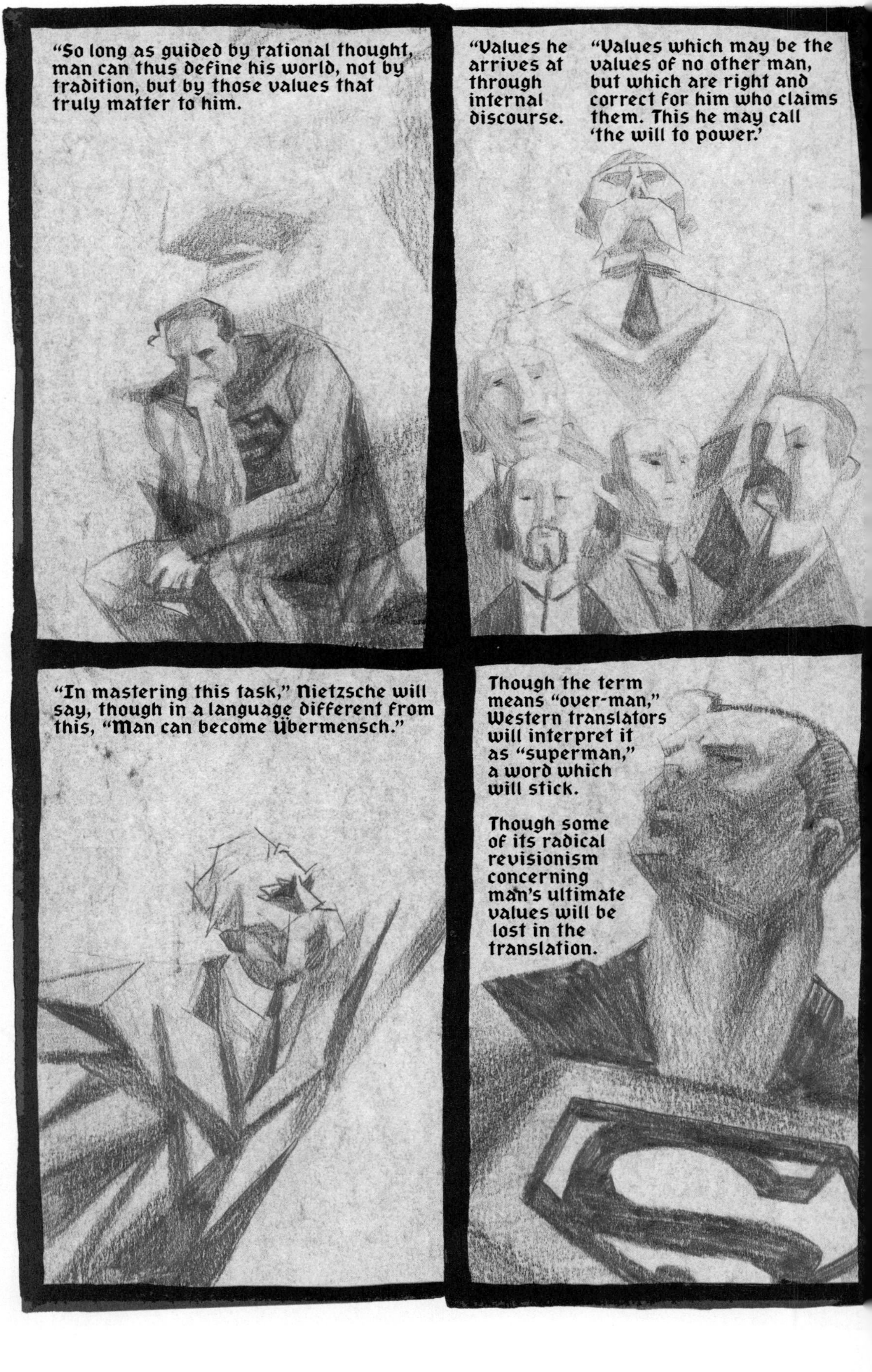
"So long as guided by rational thought, man can thus define his world, not by tradition, but by those values that truly matter to him.
"Values he arrives at through internal discourse.
"Values which may be the values of no other man, but which are right and correct for him who claims them. This he may call 'the will to power.'
"In mastering this task," Nietzsche will say, though in a language different from this, "Man can become Übermensch."
Though the term means "over-man," Western translators will interpret it as "superman," a word which will stick.
Though some of its radical revisionism concerning man's ultimate values will be lost in the translation.

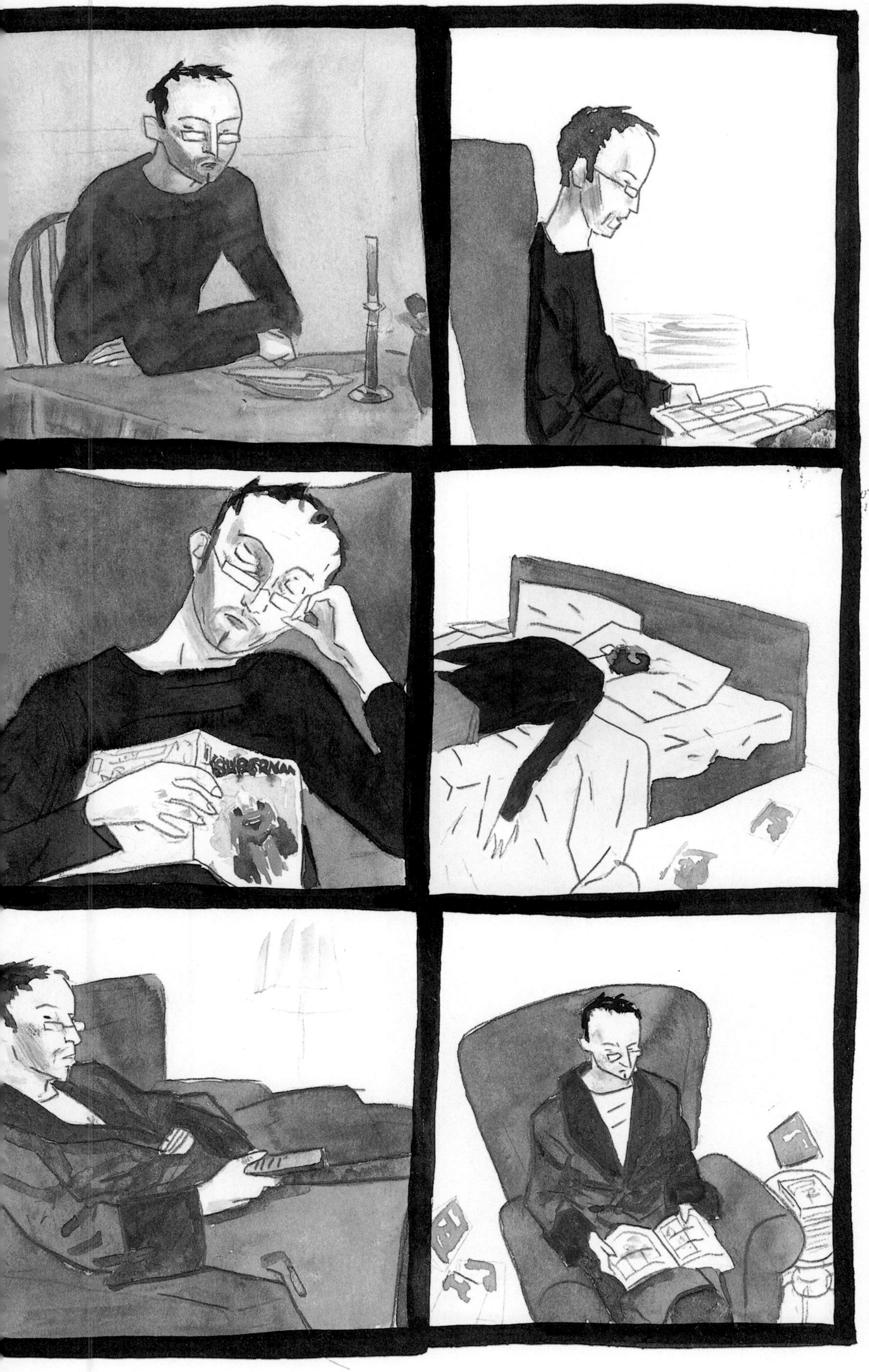
SUPERMAN

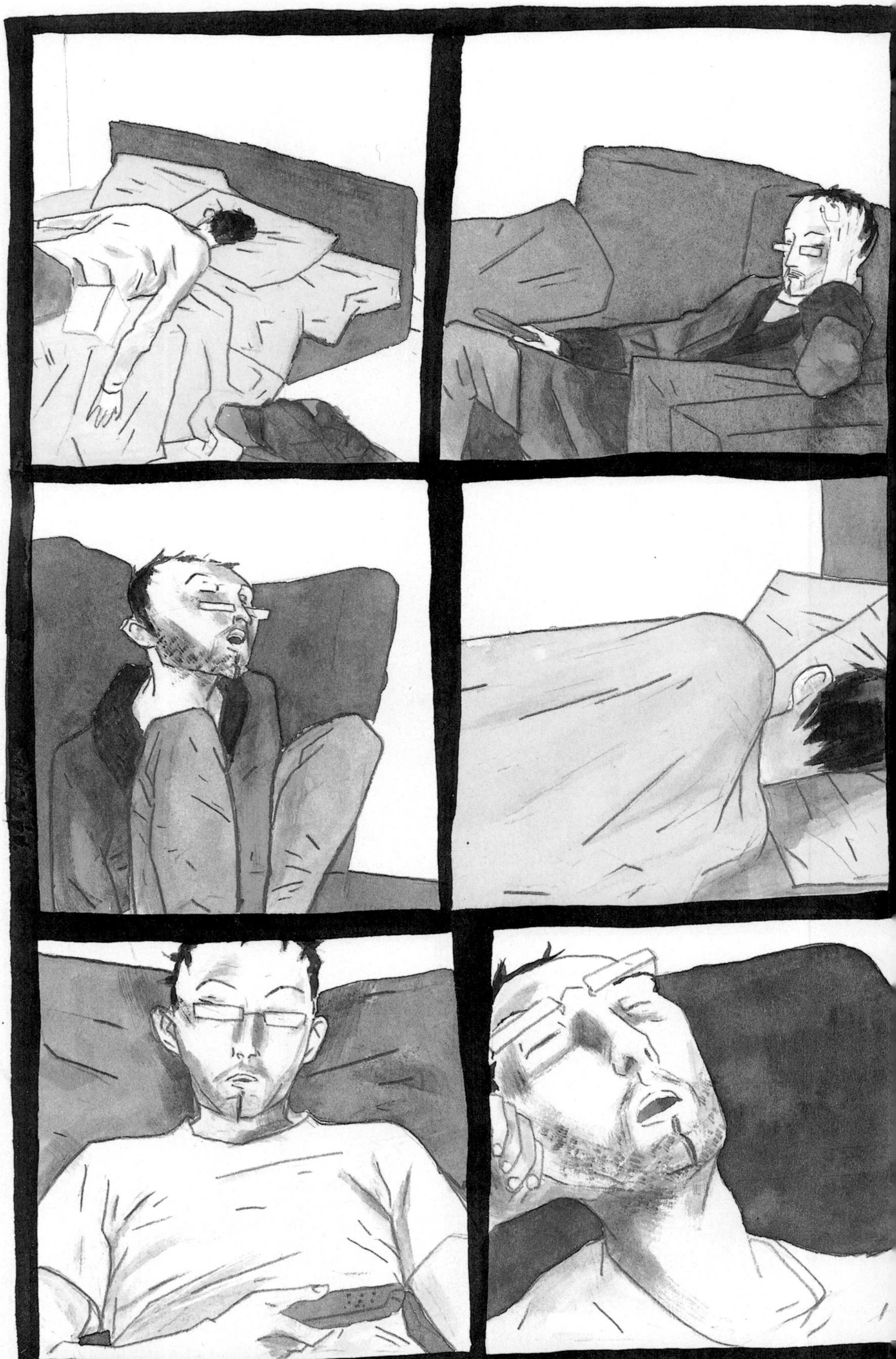

What the old man most desired was solitude.

He yearned to commit himself wholly to consideration of the great philosophical questions of his modern times.

But the world of his construction--wife Lotte, children Ernst and Gretl-- were of great distraction to his ruminations.

He took a menial job and earned money enough to subsist on while completing his metaphysical considerations.

But as his fellow workers came to know him, they began to speak pleasantries and invite him to social gatherings.

And so the old man moved far away, without telling family or friends that he was leaving.

Angered, the old man relocated to a cramped, windowless storage room in the rear of the facility.

Far from the others, he was content once more...until a janitor found his hidden workplace and began to service it.

Troubled by this minor intrusion, the old man quit his job altogether.

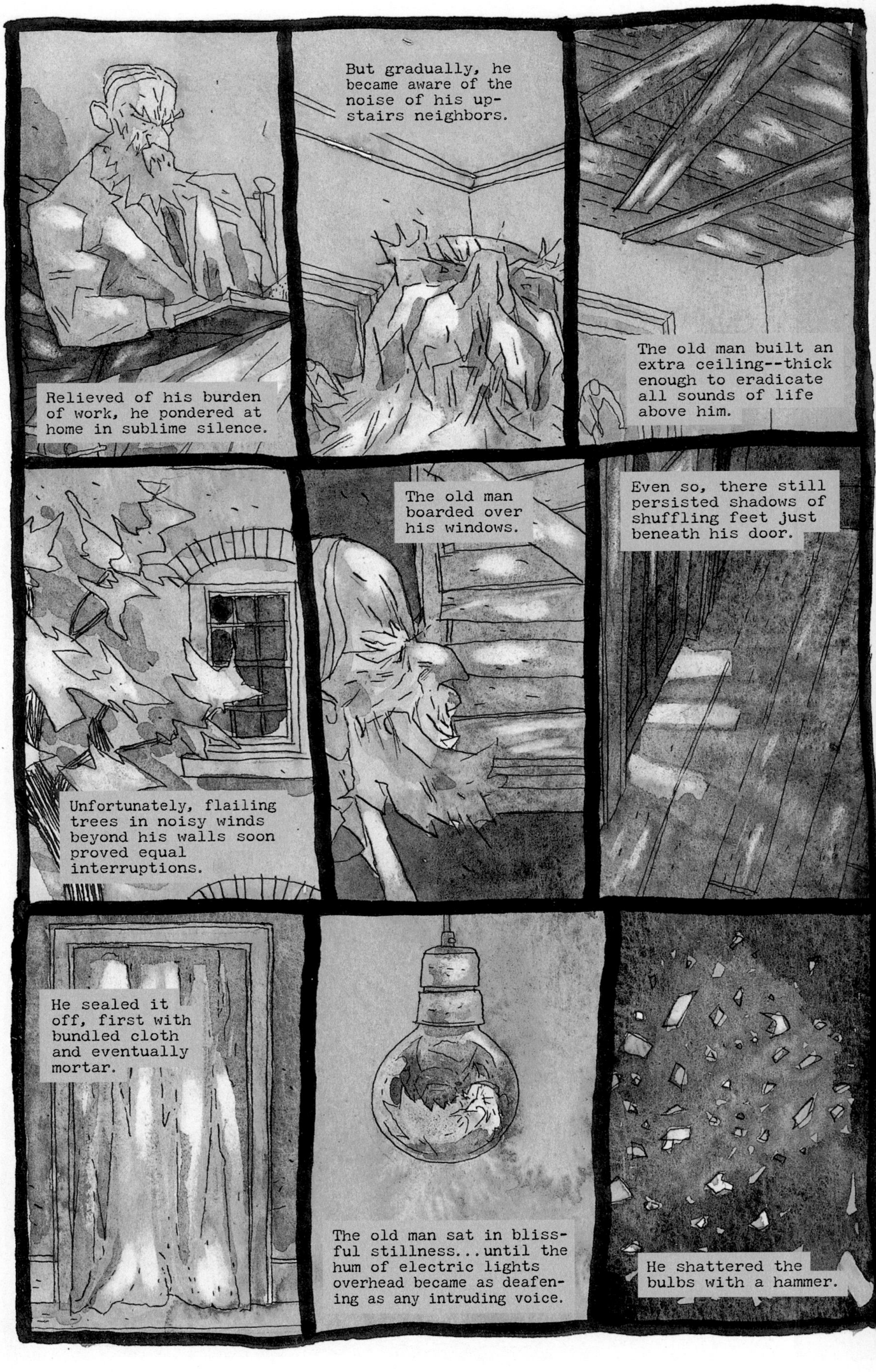
Relieved of his burden of work, he pondered at home in sublime silence.
But gradually, he became aware of the noise of his up-stairs neighbors.
The old man built an extra ceiling--thick enough to eradicate all sounds of life above him.
Unfortunately, flailing trees in noisy winds beyond his walls soon proved equal interruptions.
The old man boarded over his windows.
Even so, there still persisted shadows of shuffling feet just beneath his door.
He sealed it off, first with bundled cloth and eventually mortar.
The old man sat in bliss-ful stillness...until the hum of electric lights overhead became as deafen-ing as any intruding voice.
He shattered the bulbs with a hammer.

The old man fumigated with a poison he found in his pantry.

The sealed apartment retained the fumes at full potency for many, many days and the insects eventually died.

Lying in his bed, there arose the chirps of crickets in the walls.

Finally...silence, but the old man could no longer hear, see, read, or even think clearly.

A man without human contact is a man without aid, without hope, without life.

But a great notion did occur to him in this moment.

He could no longer be heard, but he had finally found what he had so long sought...

The old man called for those around him, but the fortress of his own making swallowed all sound.

...perfect lasting solitude.

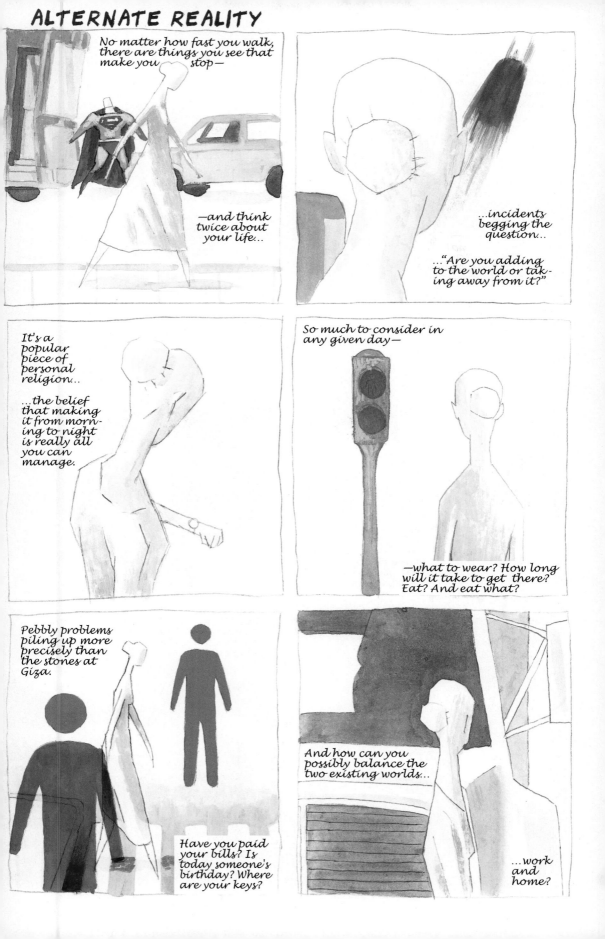

But there are more worlds than just the little one that's fractaling around you faster than you care to notice...

..."alternative universes" where people pick through trash cans to decide what to wear or eat...

...townships where there are no bills because there is nothing to buy...

...cities where keys are as moot as the doors they might unlock.

...villages where children don't consider their births the least bit worth celebrating...

These things remind us that it is not people from another planet who are supermen...

...it is any individual able to see past their own little world...and reach out to the alternate ones beyond their limited scope of existence.

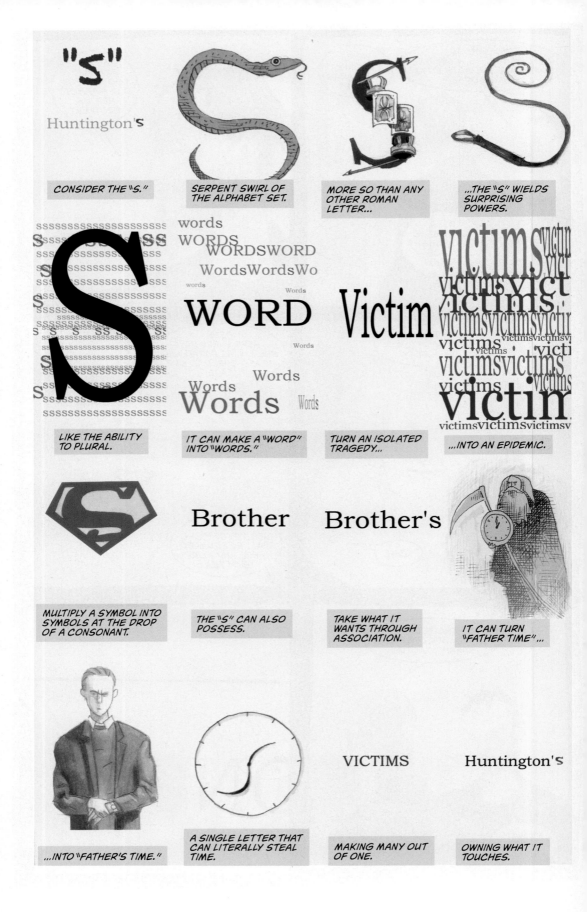

"S"

Huntington's

CONSIDER THE "S."

SERPENT SWIRL OF THE ALPHABET SET.

MORE SO THAN ANY OTHER ROMAN LETTER...

...THE "S" WIELDS SURPRISING POWERS.

sssssssssssssssssss
S ssssssssssss ss sss
ssssssssssssss sss
ssssss ss ss sss
sssssssssss ssss
ssssssssssss ssss
S sssssssssss sss
ss sssssss ssss
S ssssssss ssss
sssssssssssssssss

words
WORDS
WORDSWORD
WordsWordsWo
words · Words

WORD

Words

Words
Words
Words · Words

victims
victims
victims
victimsvictimsvictim
victims · victi
victimsvictims
victims
victim
victimsvictimsvictimsv

LIKE THE ABILITY TO PLURAL.

IT CAN MAKE A "WORD" INTO "WORDS."

TURN AN ISOLATED TRAGEDY...

...INTO AN EPIDEMIC.

Brother

Brother's

MULTIPLY A SYMBOL INTO SYMBOLS AT THE DROP OF A CONSONANT.

THE "S" CAN ALSO POSSESS.

TAKE WHAT IT WANTS THROUGH ASSOCIATION.

IT CAN TURN "FATHER TIME"...

VICTIMS

Huntington's

...INTO "FATHER'S TIME."

A SINGLE LETTER THAT CAN LITERALLY STEAL TIME.

MAKING MANY OUT OF ONE.

OWNING WHAT IT TOUCHES.

THE ALIEN

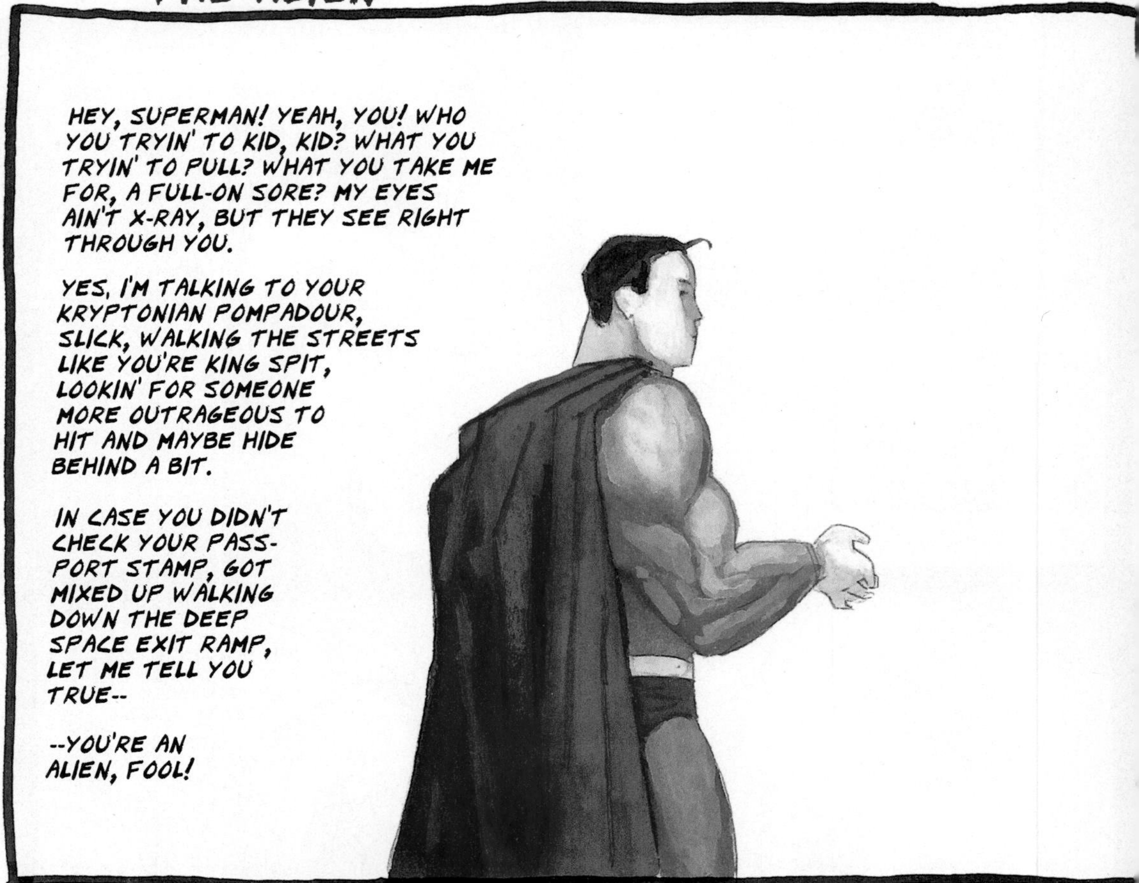
HEY, SUPERMAN! YEAH, YOU! WHO YOU TRYIN' TO KID, KID? WHAT YOU TRYIN' TO PULL? WHAT YOU TAKE ME FOR, A FULL-ON SORE? MY EYES AIN'T X-RAY, BUT THEY SEE RIGHT THROUGH YOU.
YES, I'M TALKING TO YOUR KRYPTONIAN POMPADOUR, SLICK, WALKING THE STREETS LIKE YOU'RE KING SPIT, LOOKIN' FOR SOMEONE MORE OUTRAGEOUS TO HIT AND MAYBE HIDE BEHIND A BIT.
IN CASE YOU DIDN'T CHECK YOUR PASS-PORT STAMP, GOT MIXED UP WALKING DOWN THE DEEP SPACE EXIT RAMP, LET ME TELL YOU TRUE--
--YOU'RE AN ALIEN, FOOL!

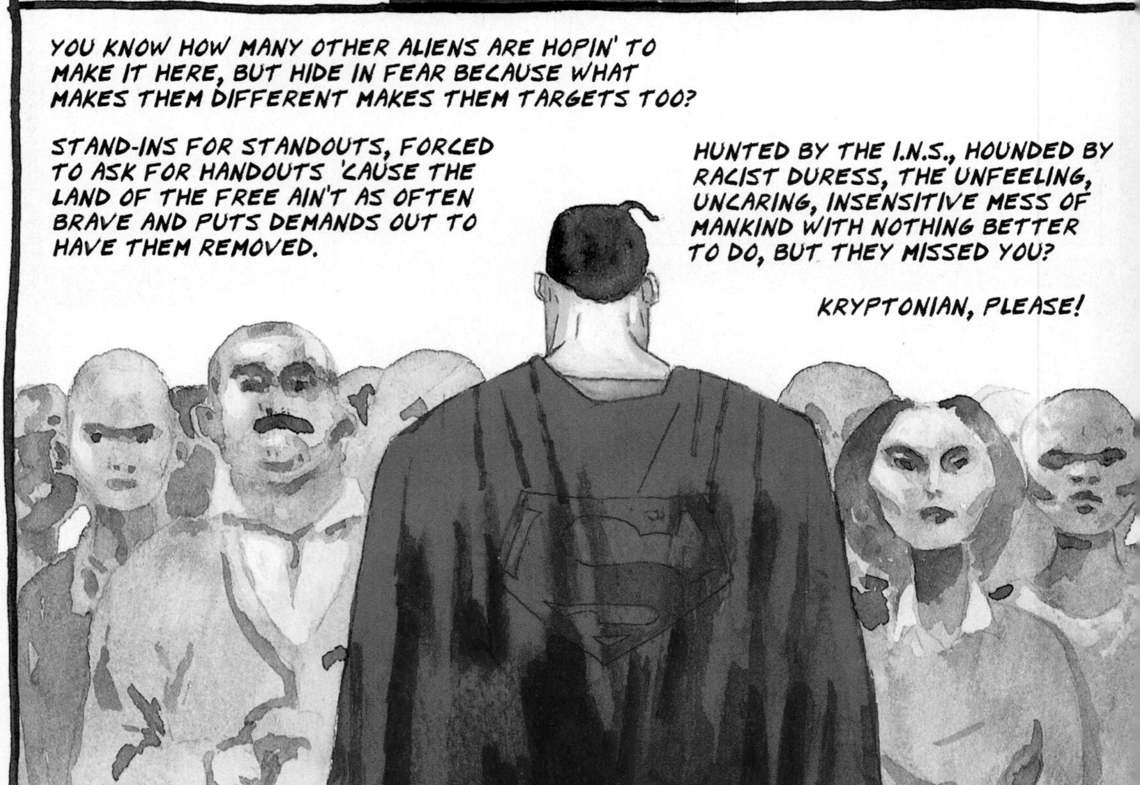
YOU KNOW HOW MANY OTHER ALIENS ARE HOPIN' TO MAKE IT HERE, BUT HIDE IN FEAR BECAUSE WHAT MAKES THEM DIFFERENT MAKES THEM TARGETS TOO?
STAND-INS FOR STANDOUTS, FORCED TO ASK FOR HANDOUTS 'CAUSE THE LAND OF THE FREE AIN'T AS OFTEN BRAVE AND PUTS DEMANDS OUT TO HAVE THEM REMOVED.
HUNTED BY THE I.N.S., HOUNDED BY RACIST DURESS, THE UNFEELING, UNCARING, INSENSITIVE MESS OF MANKIND WITH NOTHING BETTER TO DO, BUT THEY MISSED YOU?
KRYPTONIAN, PLEASE!

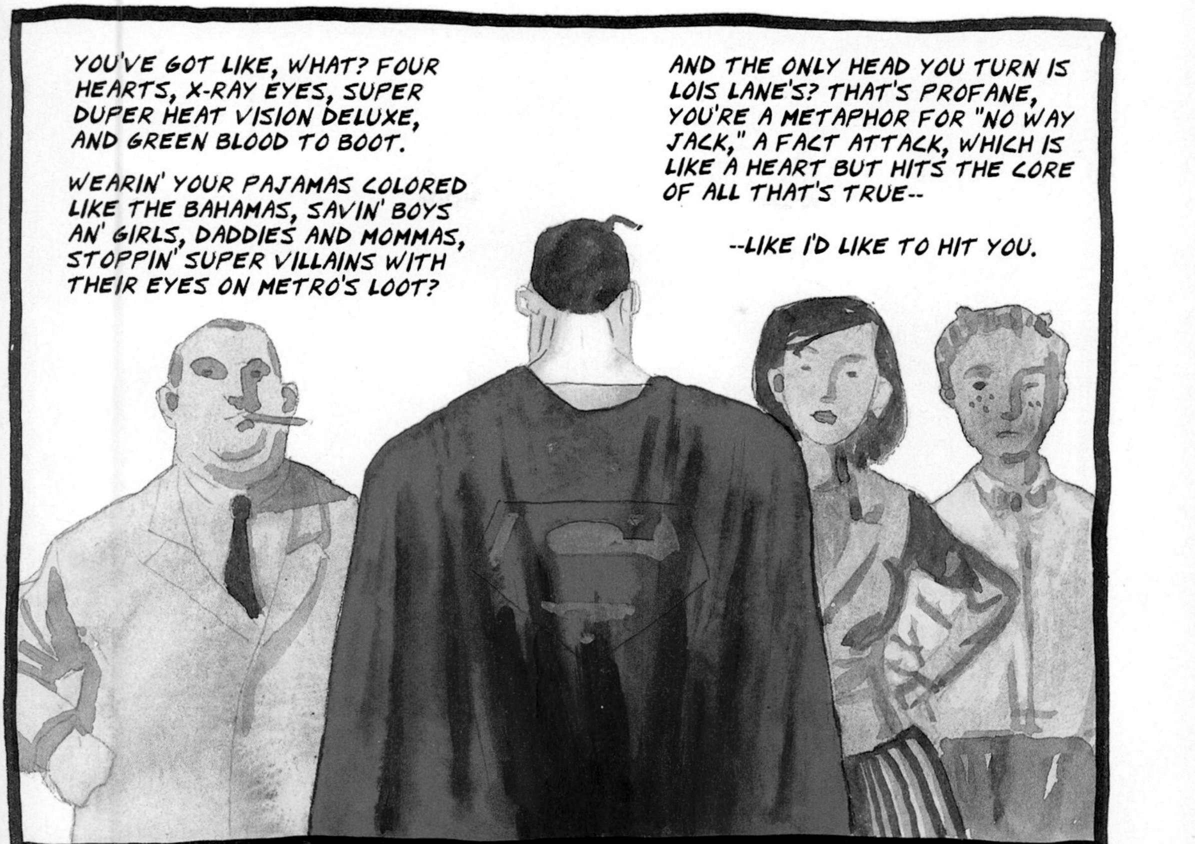
YOU'VE GOT LIKE, WHAT? FOUR HEARTS, X-RAY EYES, SUPER DUPER HEAT VISION DELUXE, AND GREEN BLOOD TO BOOT.
WEARIN' YOUR PAJAMAS COLORED LIKE THE BAHAMAS, SAVIN' BOYS AN' GIRLS, DADDIES AND MOMMAS, STOPPIN' SUPER VILLAINS WITH THEIR EYES ON METRO'S LOOT?
AND THE ONLY HEAD YOU TURN IS LOIS LANE'S? THAT'S PROFANE, YOU'RE A METAPHOR FOR "NO WAY JACK," A FACT ATTACK, WHICH IS LIKE A HEART BUT HITS THE CORE OF ALL THAT'S TRUE--
--LIKE I'D LIKE TO HIT YOU.

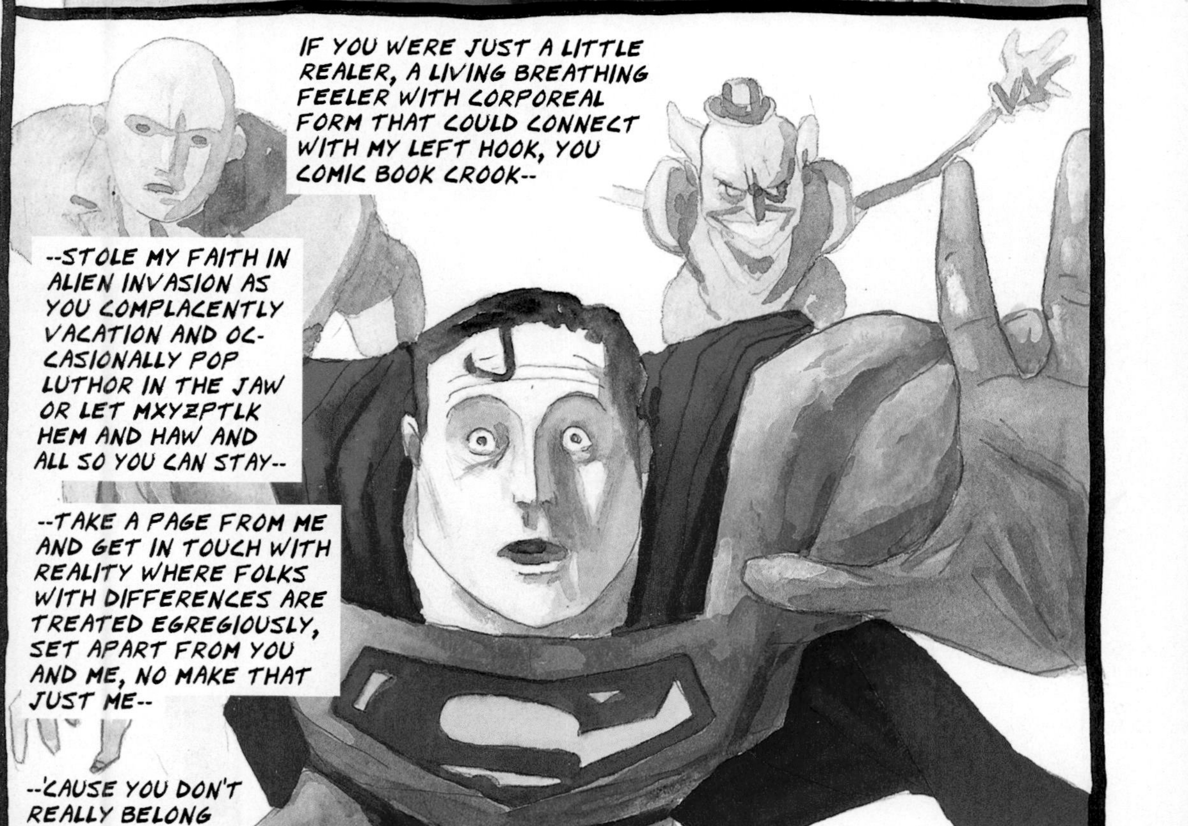
IF YOU WERE JUST A LITTLE REALER, A LIVING BREATHING FEELER WITH CORPOREAL FORM THAT COULD CONNECT WITH MY LEFT HOOK, YOU COMIC BOOK CROOK--
--STOLE MY FAITH IN ALIEN INVASION AS YOU COMPLACENTLY VACATION AND OC-CASIONALLY POP LUTHOR IN THE JAW OR LET MXYZPTLK HEM AND HAW AND ALL SO YOU CAN STAY--
--TAKE A PAGE FROM ME AND GET IN TOUCH WITH REALITY WHERE FOLKS WITH DIFFERENCES ARE TREATED EGREGIOUSLY, SET APART FROM YOU AND ME, NO MAKE THAT JUST ME--
--'CAUSE YOU DON'T REALLY BELONG HERE, SEE?

ESCAPE

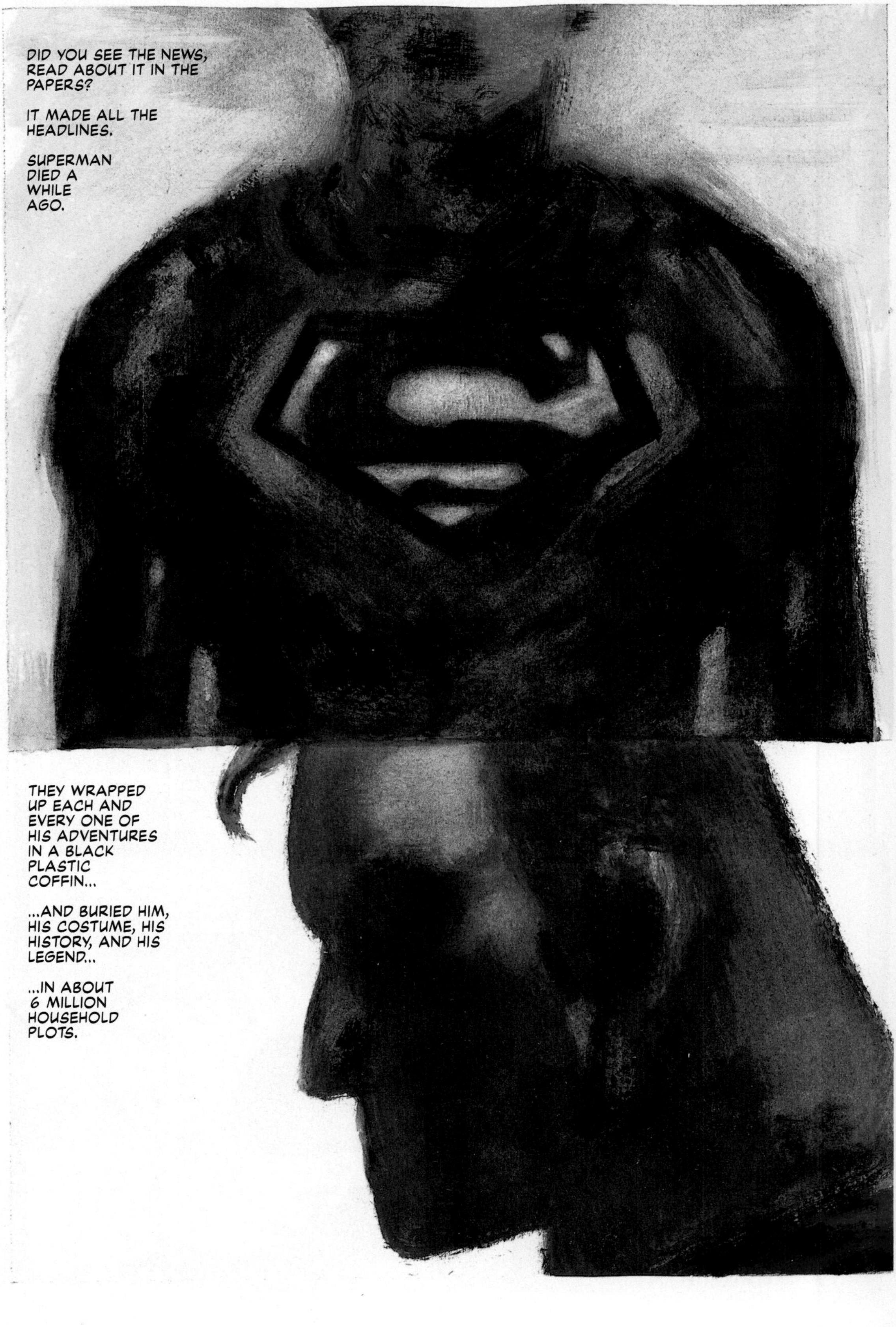
DID YOU SEE THE NEWS, READ ABOUT IT IN THE PAPERS?
IT MADE ALL THE HEADLINES.
SUPERMAN DIED A WHILE AGO.
THEY WRAPPED UP EACH AND EVERY ONE OF HIS ADVENTURES IN A BLACK PLASTIC COFFIN...
...AND BURIED HIM, HIS COSTUME, HIS HISTORY, AND HIS LEGEND...
...IN ABOUT 6 MILLION HOUSEHOLD PLOTS.

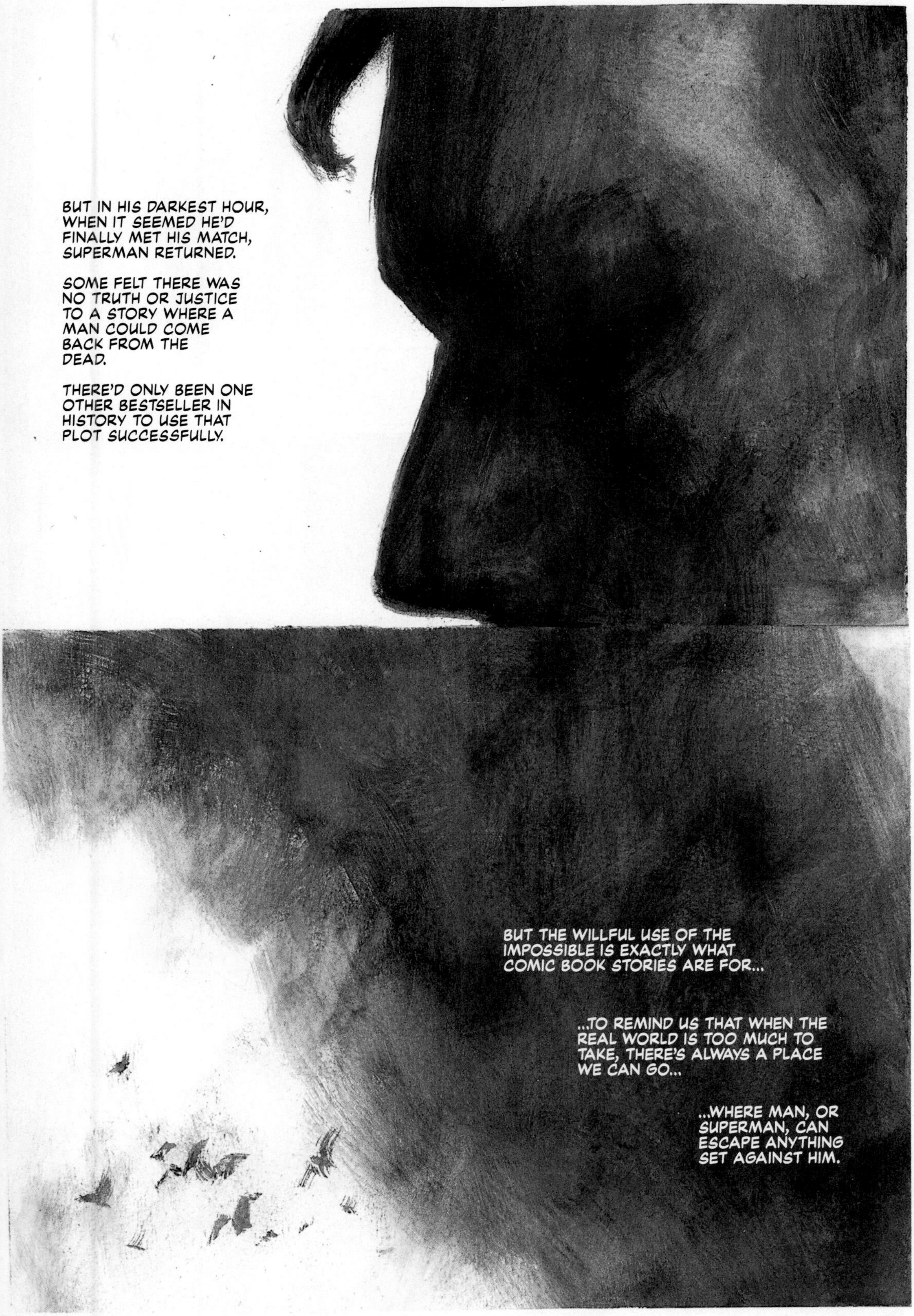
BUT IN HIS DARKEST HOUR, WHEN IT SEEMED HE'D FINALLY MET HIS MATCH, SUPERMAN RETURNED.
SOME FELT THERE WAS NO TRUTH OR JUSTICE TO A STORY WHERE A MAN COULD COME BACK FROM THE DEAD.
THERE'D ONLY BEEN ONE OTHER BESTSELLER IN HISTORY TO USE THAT PLOT SUCCESSFULLY.
BUT THE WILLFUL USE OF THE IMPOSSIBLE IS EXACTLY WHAT COMIC BOOK STORIES ARE FOR...
...TO REMIND US THAT WHEN THE REAL WORLD IS TOO MUCH TO TAKE, THERE'S ALWAYS A PLACE WE CAN GO...
...WHERE MAN, OR SUPERMAN, CAN ESCAPE ANYTHING SET AGAINST HIM.

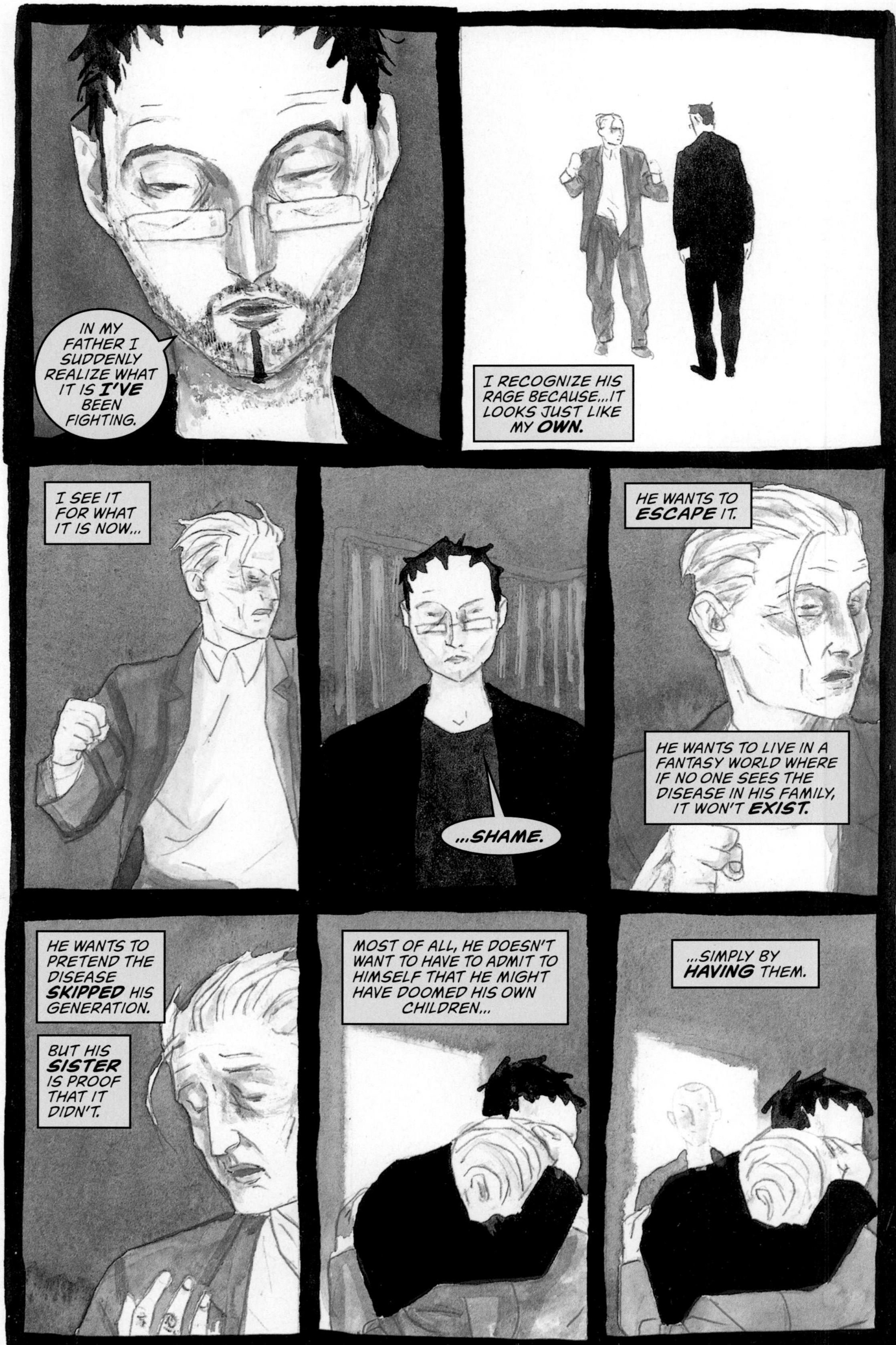
IN MY FATHER I SUDDENLY REALIZE WHAT IT IS I'VE BEEN FIGHTING.
I RECOGNIZE HIS RAGE BECAUSE...IT LOOKS JUST LIKE MY OWN.
I SEE IT FOR WHAT IT IS NOW...
...SHAME.
HE WANTS TO ESCAPE IT.
HE WANTS TO LIVE IN A FANTASY WORLD WHERE IF NO ONE SEES THE DISEASE IN HIS FAMILY, IT WON'T EXIST.
HE WANTS TO PRETEND THE DISEASE SKIPPED HIS GENERATION.
BUT HIS SISTER IS PROOF THAT IT DIDN'T.
MOST OF ALL, HE DOESN'T WANT TO HAVE TO ADMIT TO HIMSELF THAT HE MIGHT HAVE DOOMED HIS OWN CHILDREN...
...SIMPLY BY HAVING THEM.

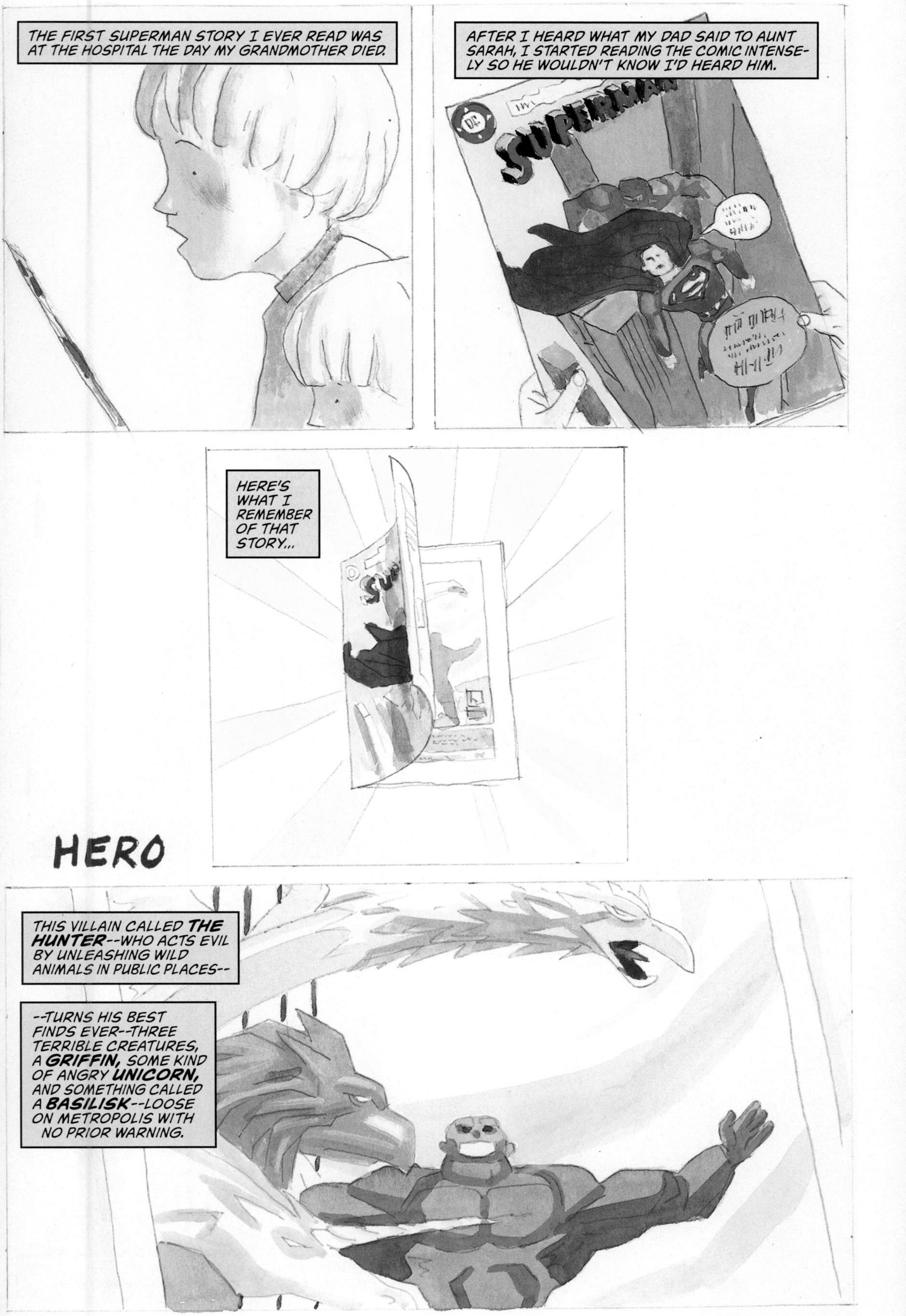

THE FIRST SUPERMAN STORY I EVER READ WAS AT THE HOSPITAL THE DAY MY GRANDMOTHER DIED.
AFTER I HEARD WHAT MY DAD SAID TO AUNT SARAH, I STARTED READING THE COMIC INTENSE-LY SO HE WOULDN'T KNOW I'D HEARD HIM.
SUPERMAN
HERE'S WHAT I REMEMBER OF THAT STORY...
HERO
THIS VILLAIN CALLED **THE HUNTER**--WHO ACTS EVIL BY UNLEASHING WILD ANIMALS IN PUBLIC PLACES--
--TURNS HIS BEST FINDS EVER--THREE TERRIBLE CREATURES, A **GRIFFIN,** SOME KIND OF ANGRY **UNICORN,** AND SOMETHING CALLED A **BASILISK**--LOOSE ON METROPOLIS WITH NO PRIOR WARNING.

Look! Up in the sky!

TON'S

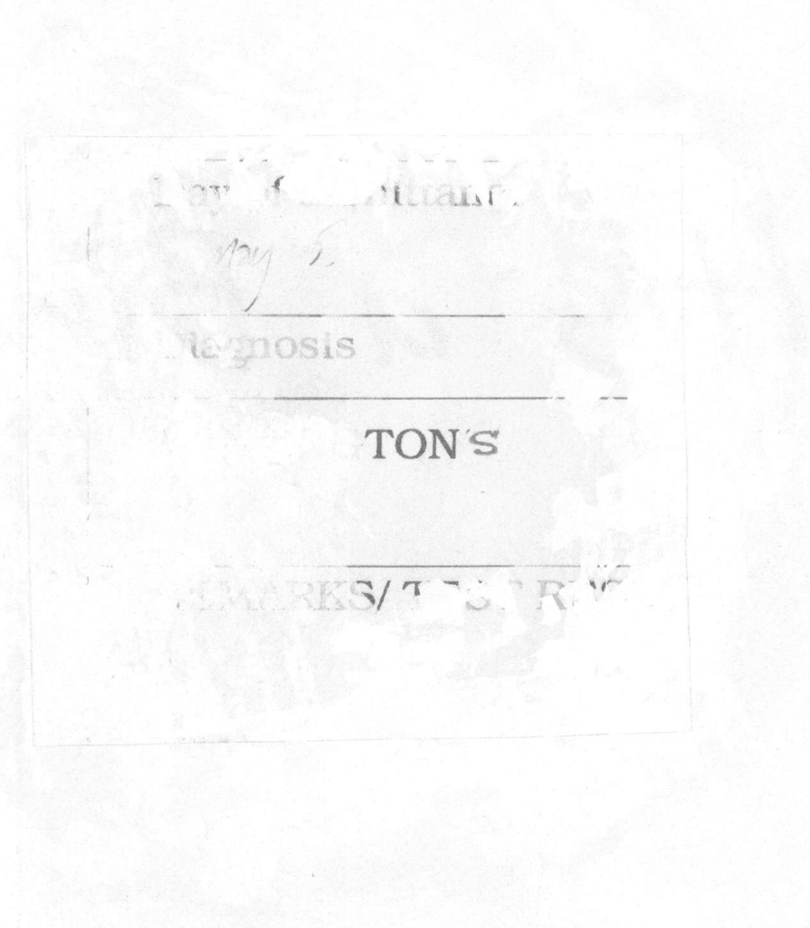

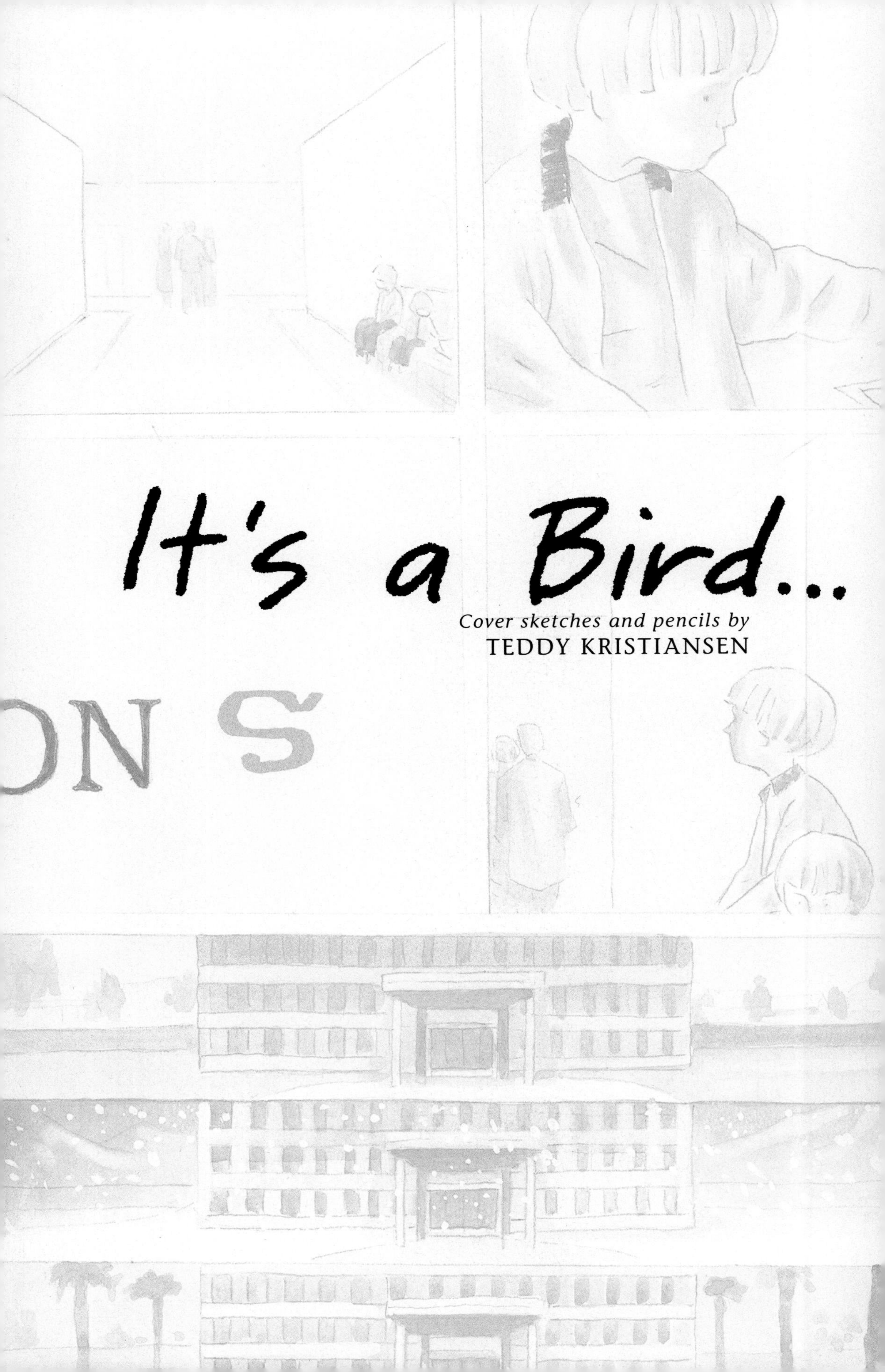

It's a Bird...

Cover sketches and pencils by
TEDDY KRISTIANSEN

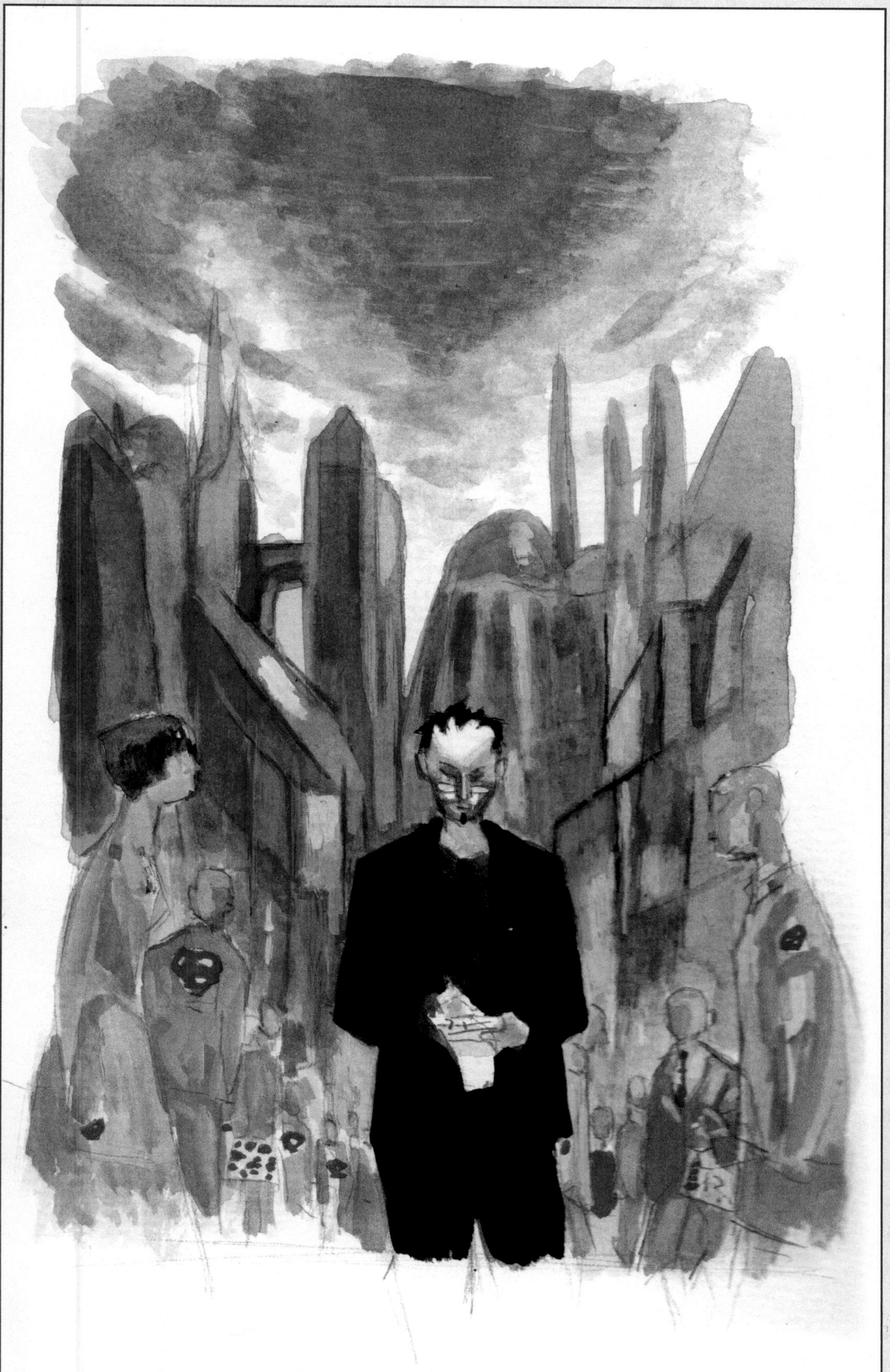

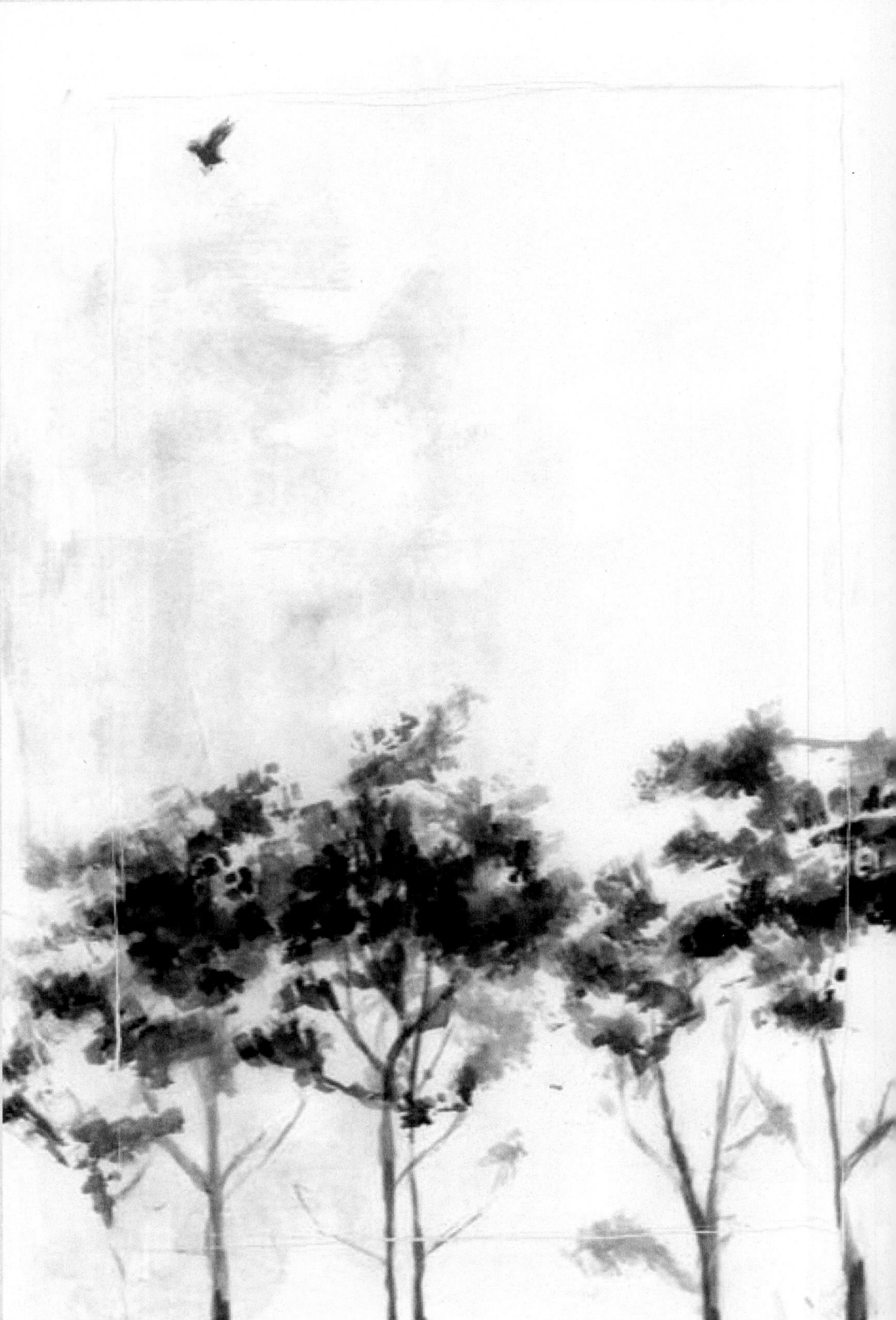

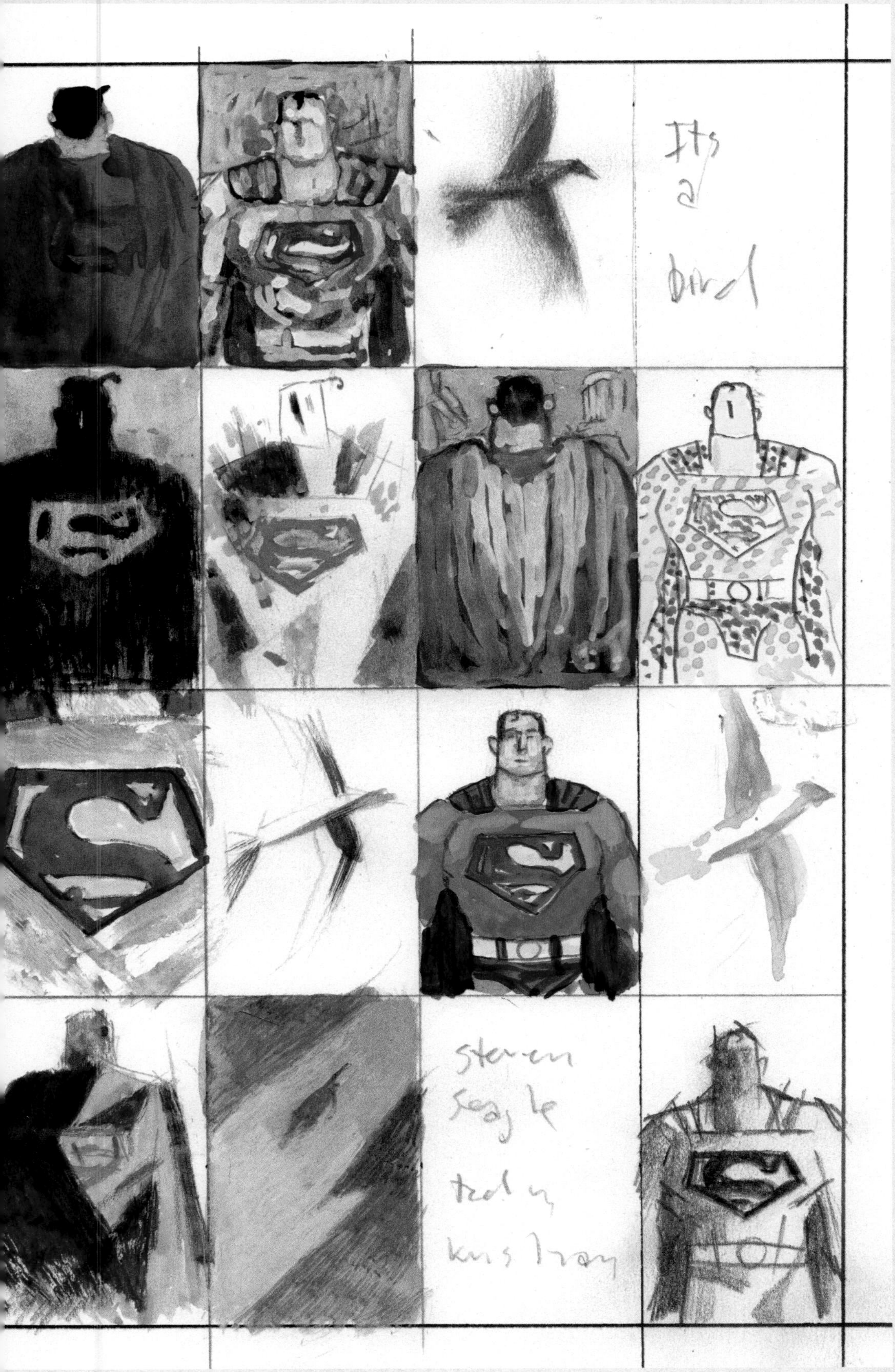
Its a bird
steven seagle

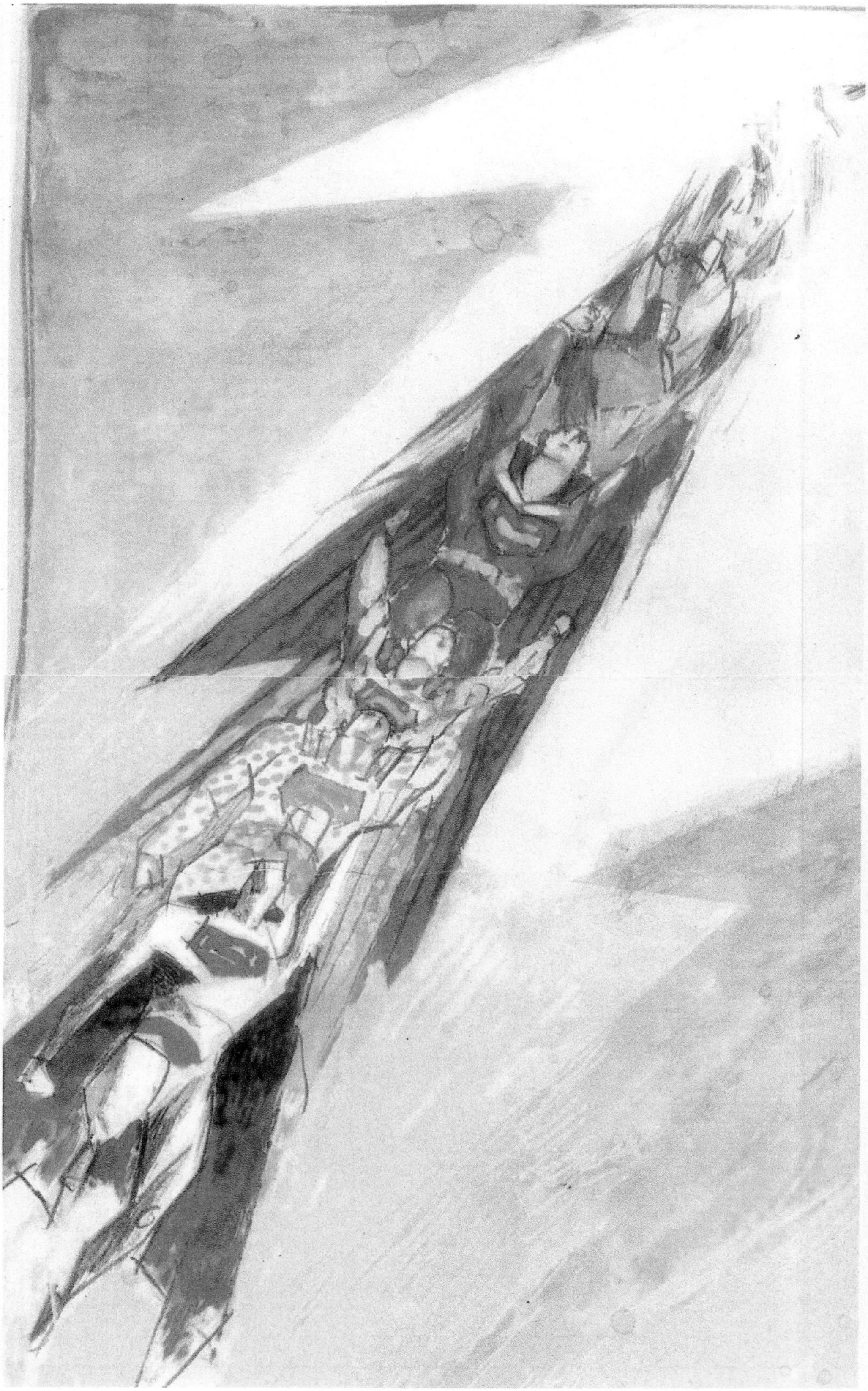

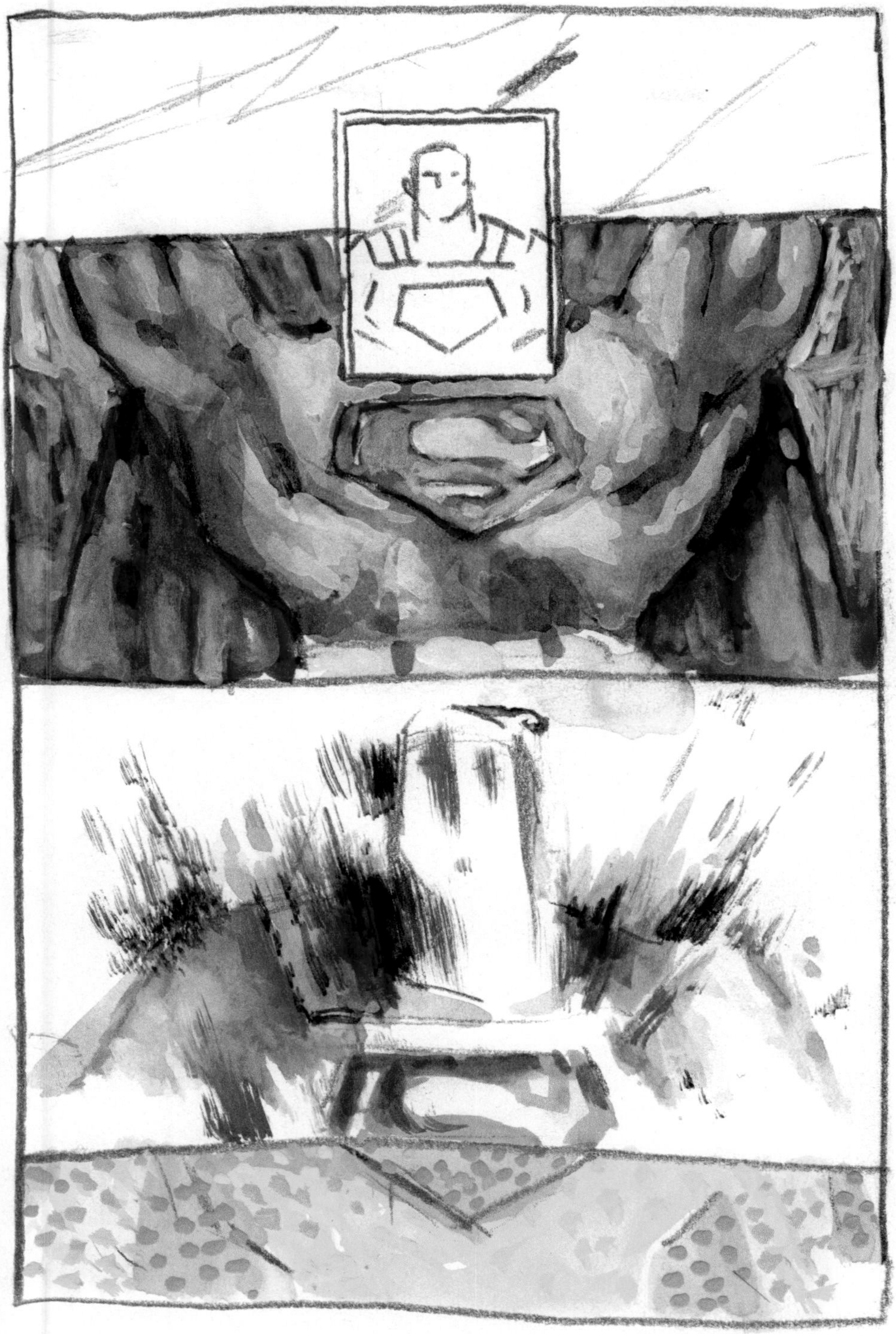

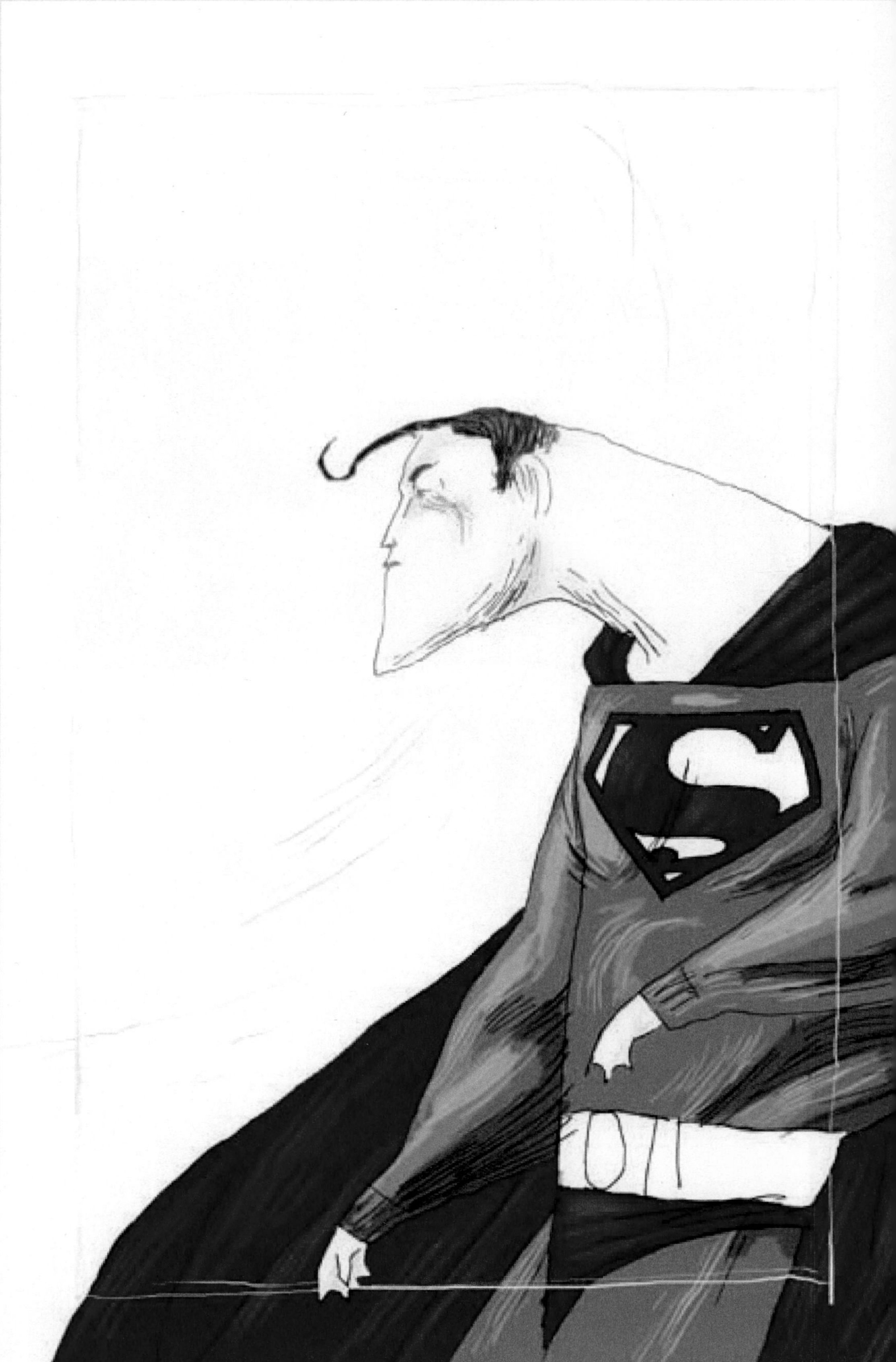

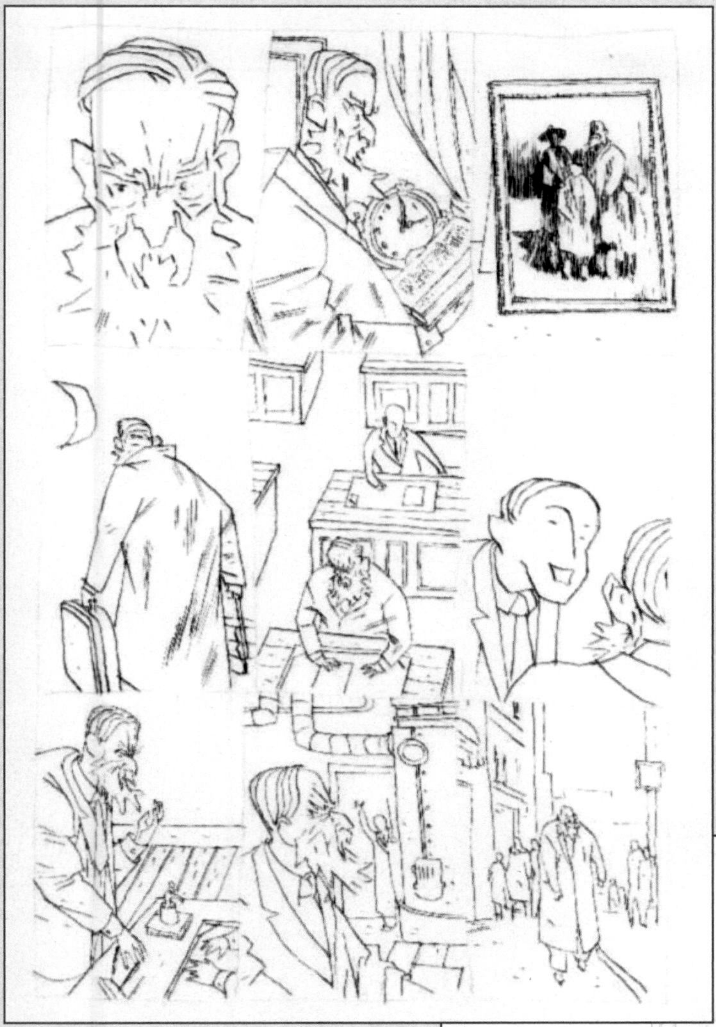

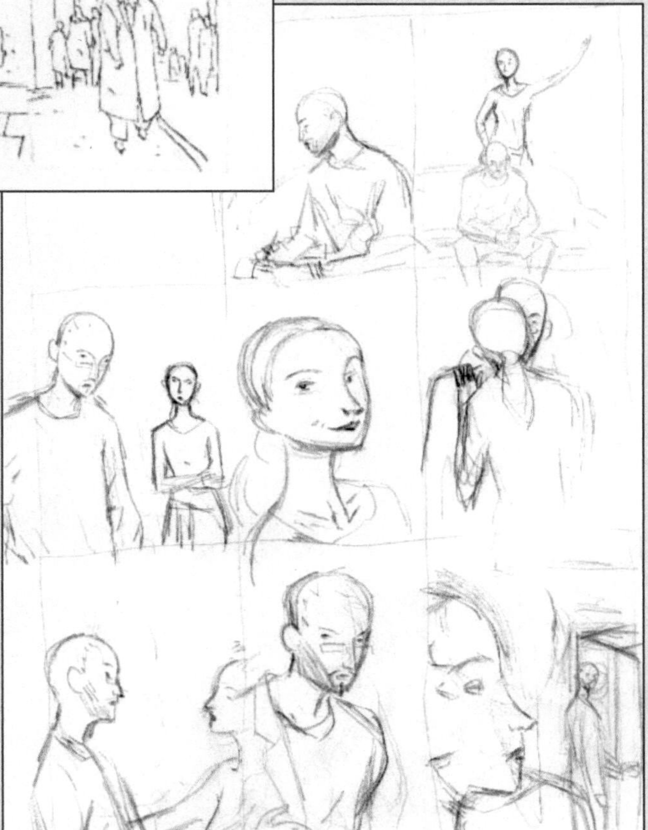
16

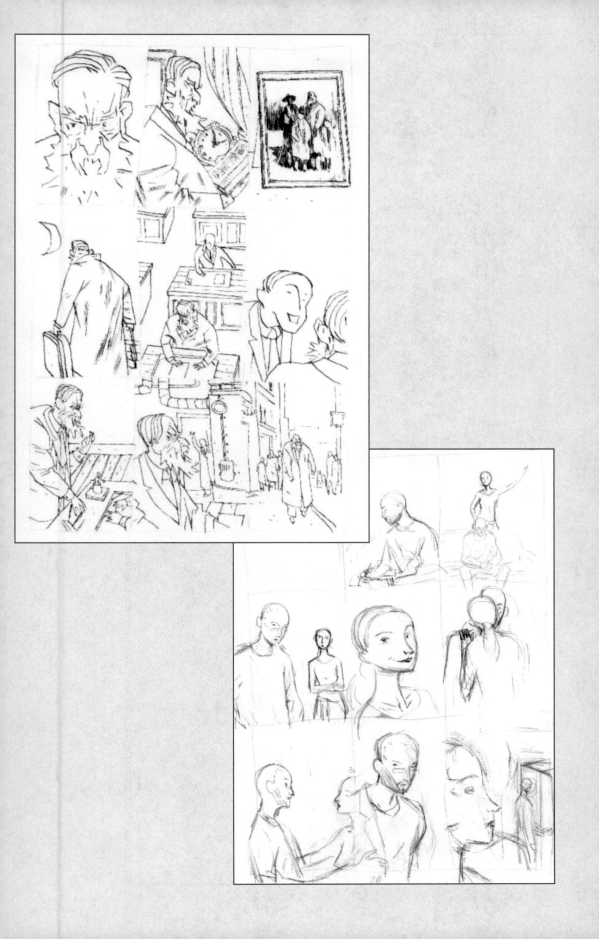

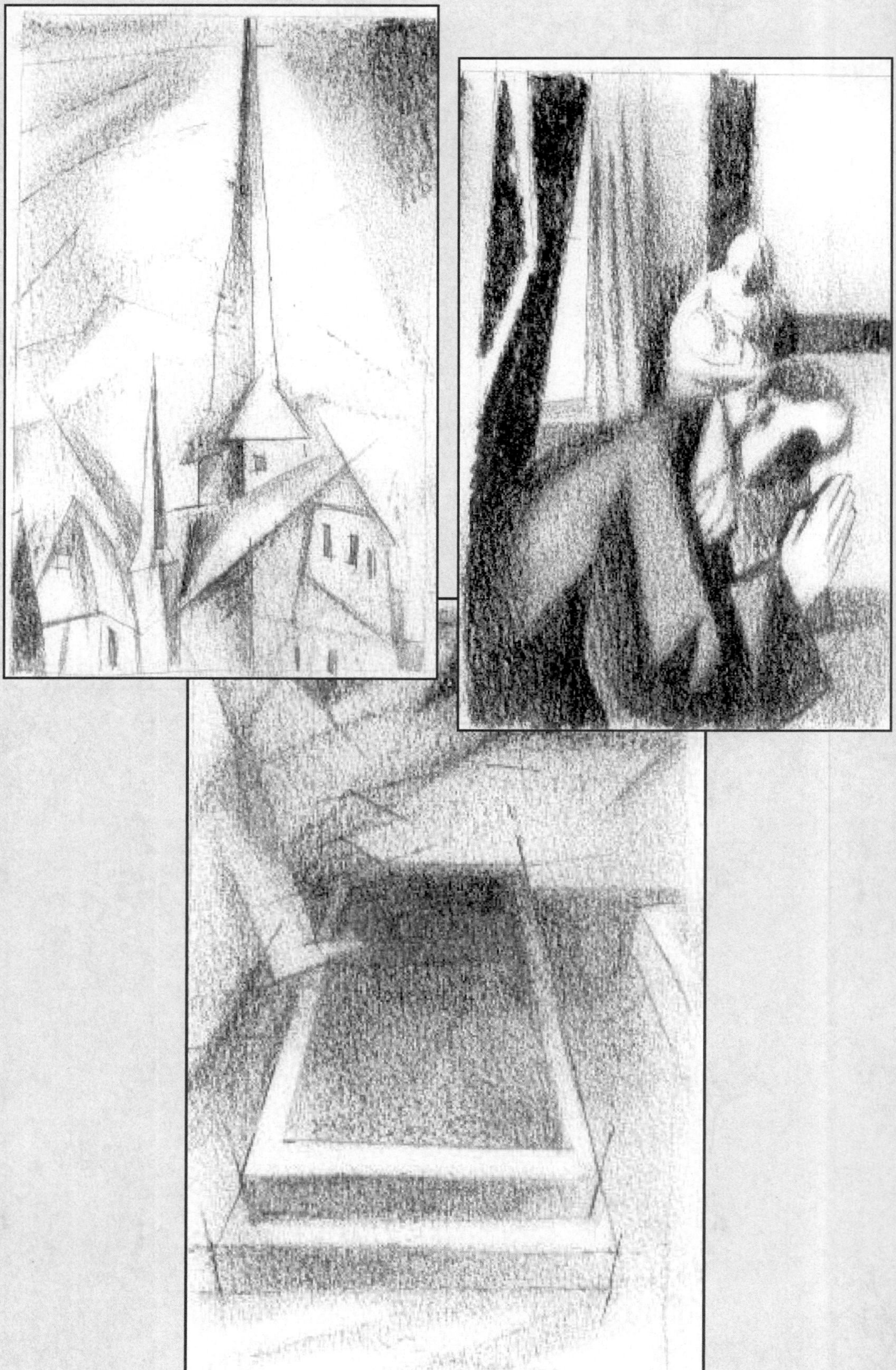

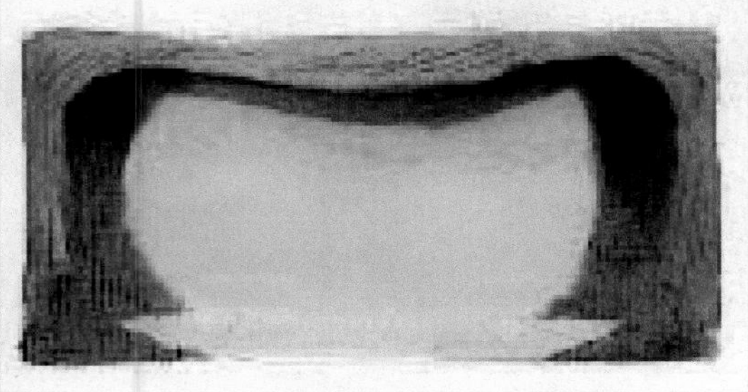

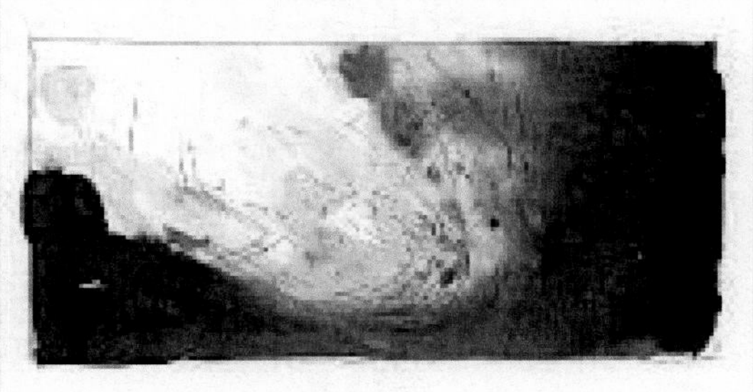

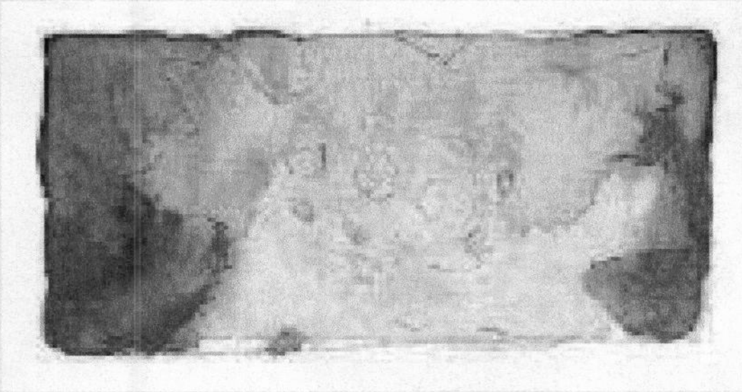

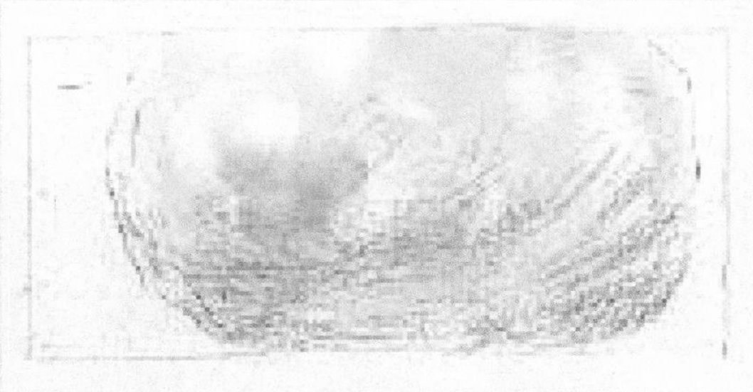

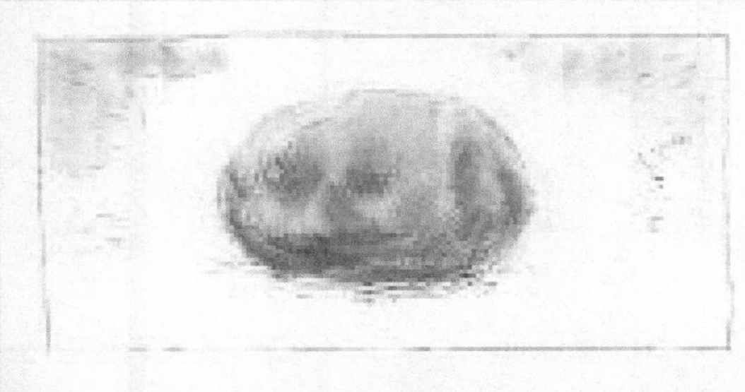

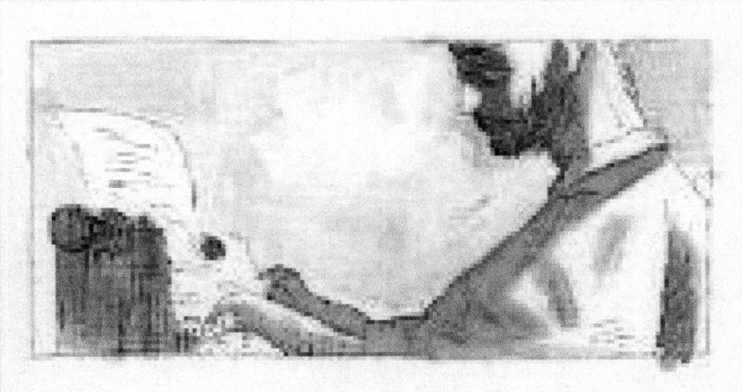

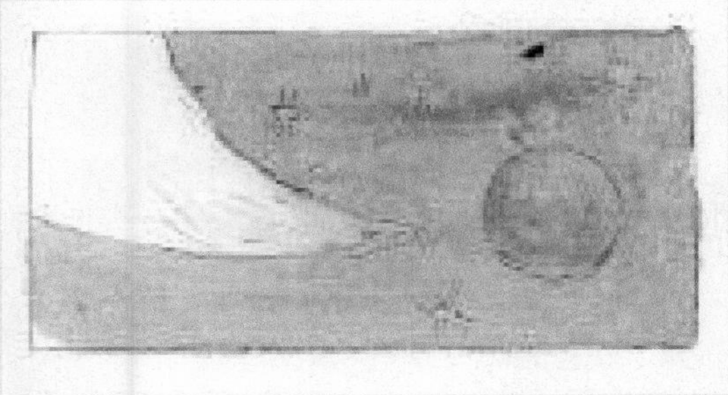

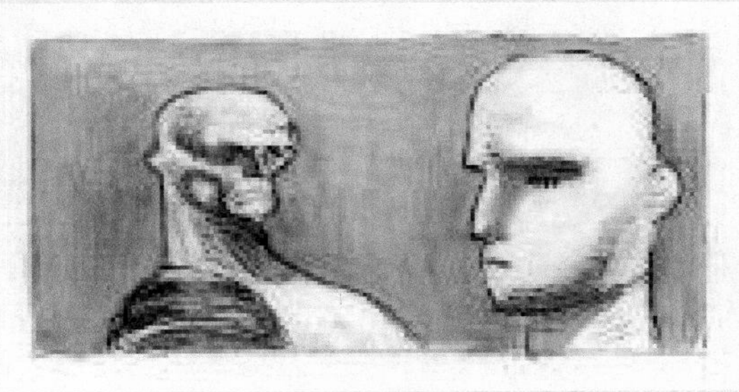

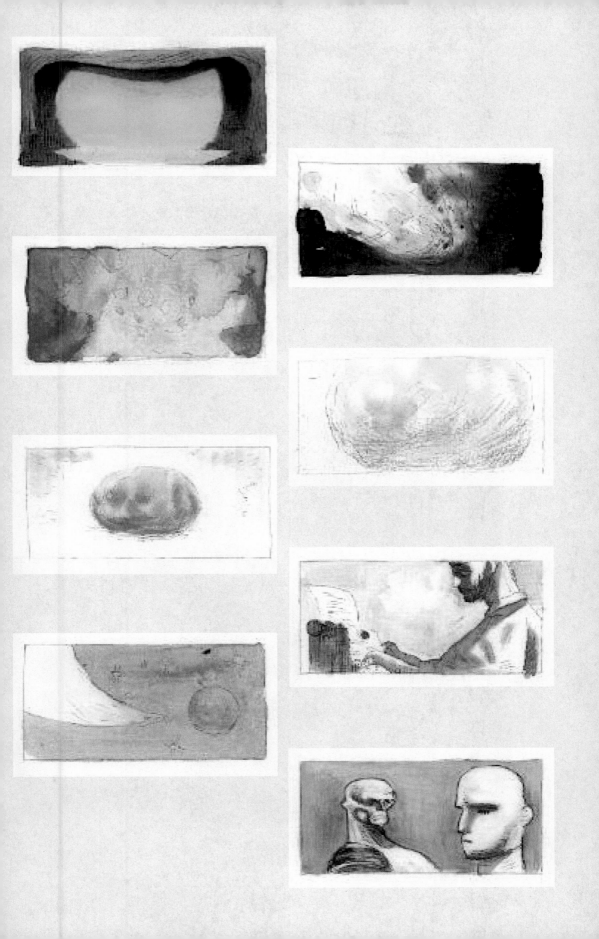

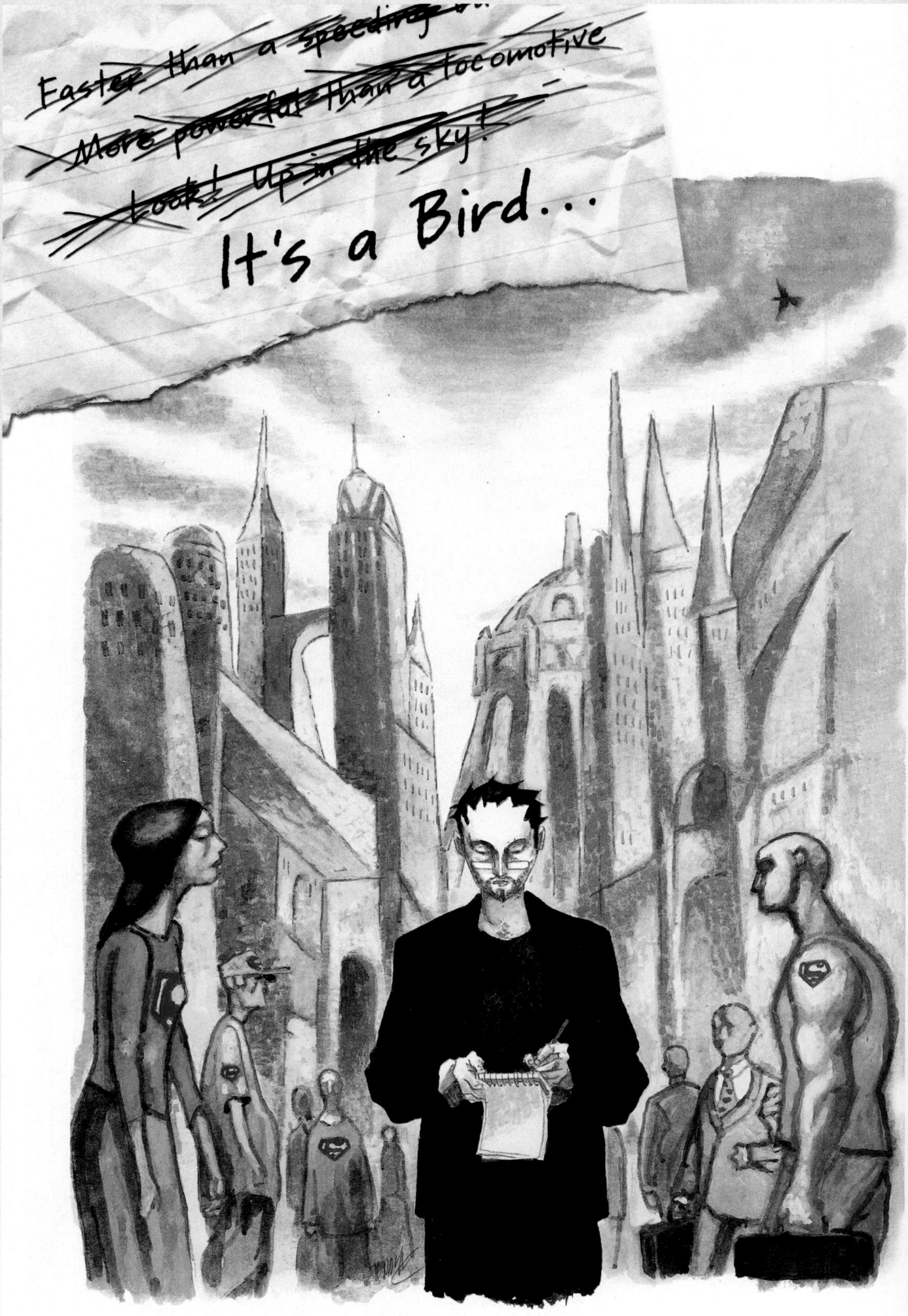
Faster than a speeding
More powerful than a locomotive
Look! Up in the sky!
It's a Bird...

Original cover art for
IT'S A BIRD...

It's a Bat...

IT'S A BAT...

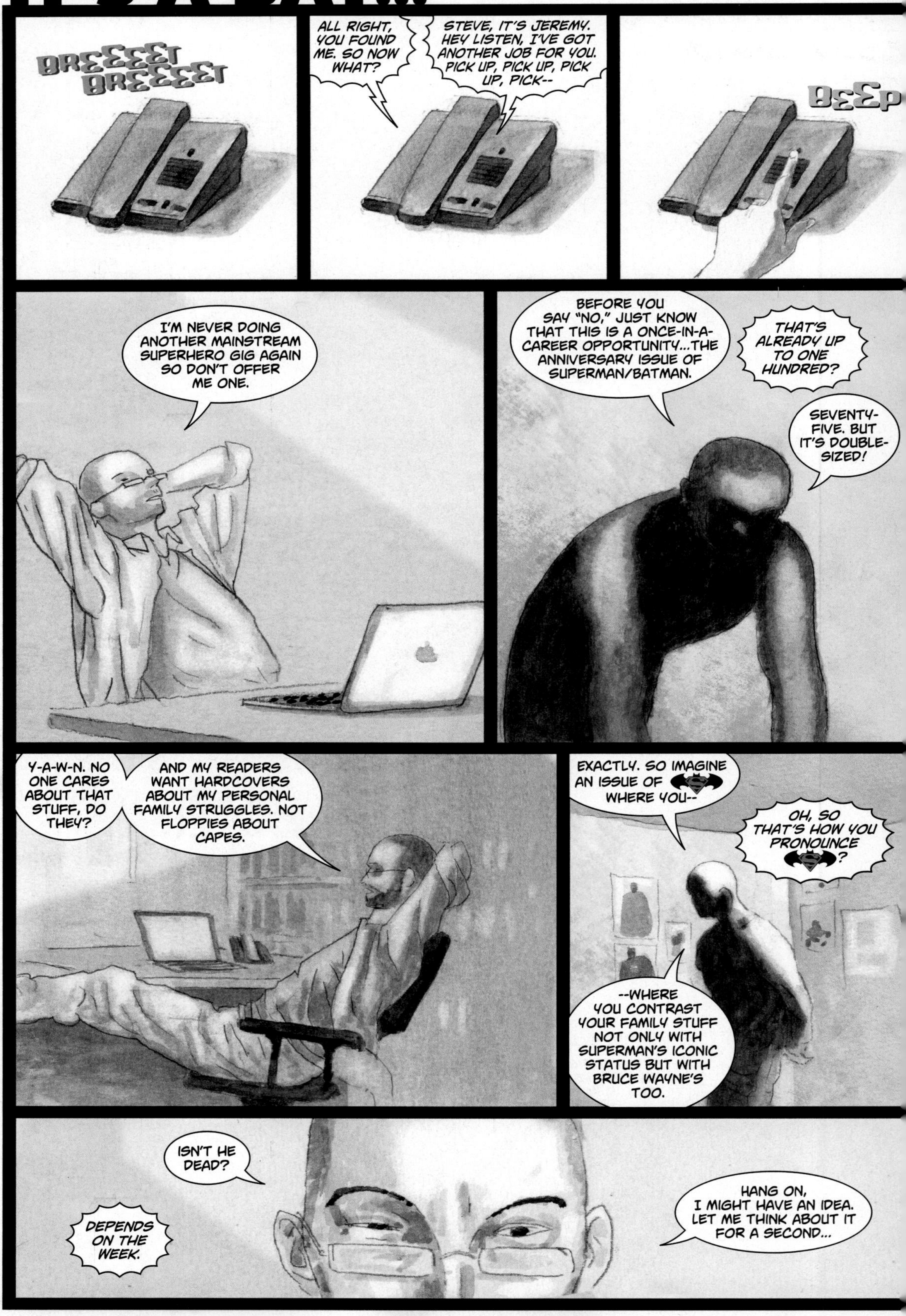

BREEEET BREEEET
ALL RIGHT, YOU FOUND ME. SO NOW WHAT?
STEVE, IT'S JEREMY. HEY LISTEN, I'VE GOT ANOTHER JOB FOR YOU. PICK UP, PICK UP, PICK UP, PICK--
BEEP
I'M NEVER DOING ANOTHER MAINSTREAM SUPERHERO GIG AGAIN SO DON'T OFFER ME ONE.
BEFORE YOU SAY "NO," JUST KNOW THAT THIS IS A ONCE-IN-A-CAREER OPPORTUNITY...THE ANNIVERSARY ISSUE OF SUPERMAN/BATMAN.
THAT'S ALREADY UP TO ONE HUNDRED?
SEVENTY-FIVE. BUT IT'S DOUBLE-SIZED!
Y-A-W-N. NO ONE CARES ABOUT THAT STUFF, DO THEY?
AND MY READERS WANT HARDCOVERS ABOUT MY PERSONAL FAMILY STRUGGLES. NOT FLOPPIES ABOUT CAPES.
EXACTLY. SO IMAGINE AN ISSUE OF WHERE YOU--
OH, SO THAT'S HOW YOU PRONOUNCE ?
--WHERE YOU CONTRAST YOUR FAMILY STUFF NOT ONLY WITH SUPERMAN'S ICONIC STATUS BUT WITH BRUCE WAYNE'S TOO.
ISN'T HE DEAD?
DEPENDS ON THE WEEK.
HANG ON, I MIGHT HAVE AN IDEA. LET ME THINK ABOUT IT FOR A SECOND...

A 2-Page Floppy Parody by Steven T. Seagle & Teddy Kristiansen with Letters by Steve Wands

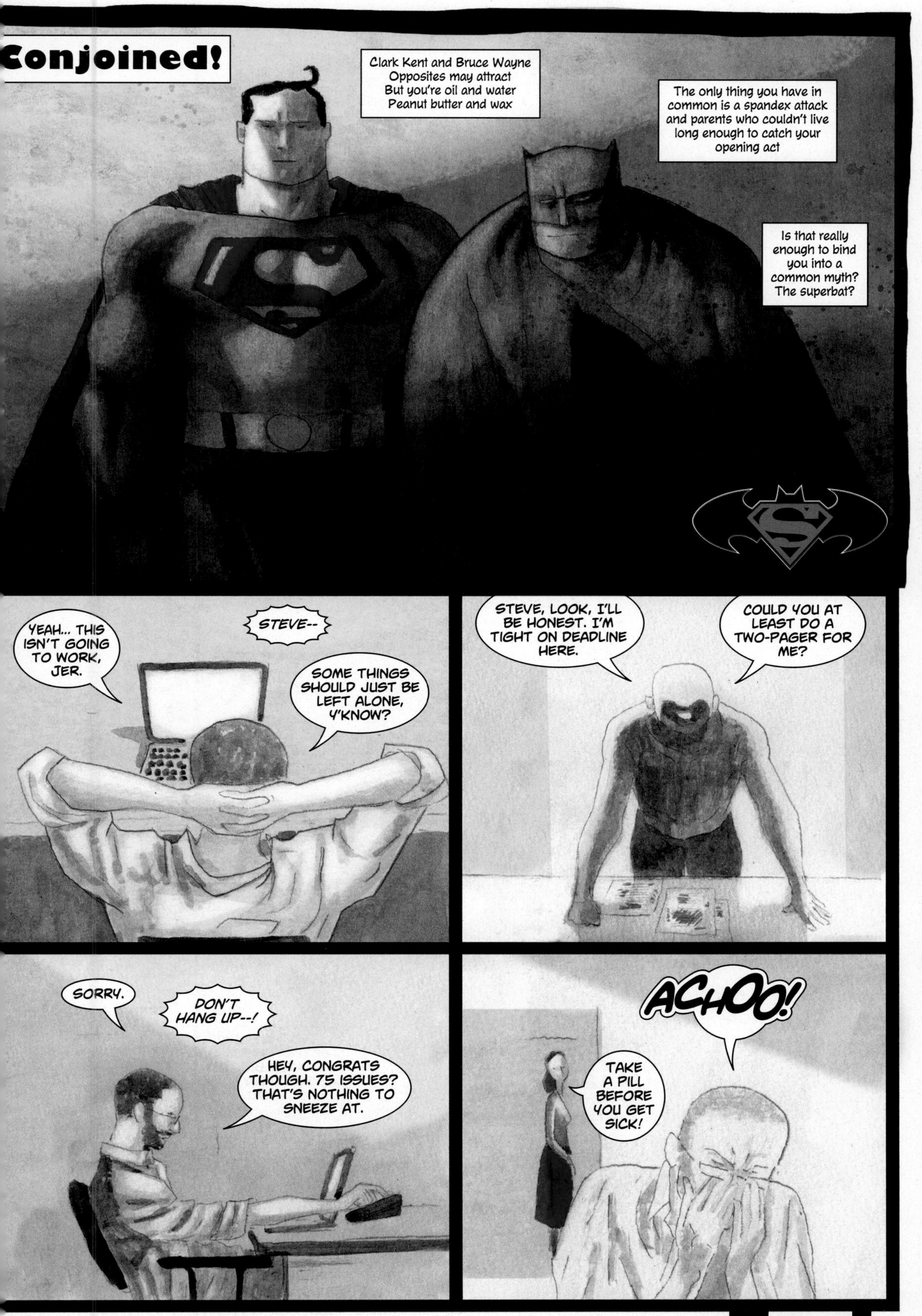
Conjoined!
Clark Kent and Bruce Wayne Opposites may attract But you're oil and water Peanut butter and wax
The only thing you have in common is a spandex attack and parents who couldn't live long enough to catch your opening act
Is that really enough to bind you into a common myth? The superbat?
YEAH... THIS ISN'T GOING TO WORK, JER.
STEVE--
SOME THINGS SHOULD JUST BE LEFT ALONE, Y'KNOW?
STEVE, LOOK, I'LL BE HONEST. I'M TIGHT ON DEADLINE HERE.
COULD YOU AT LEAST DO A TWO-PAGER FOR ME?
SORRY.
DON'T HANG UP--!
HEY, CONGRATS THOUGH. 75 ISSUES? THAT'S NOTHING TO SNEEZE AT.
ACHOO!
TAKE A PILL BEFORE YOU GET SICK!

End.

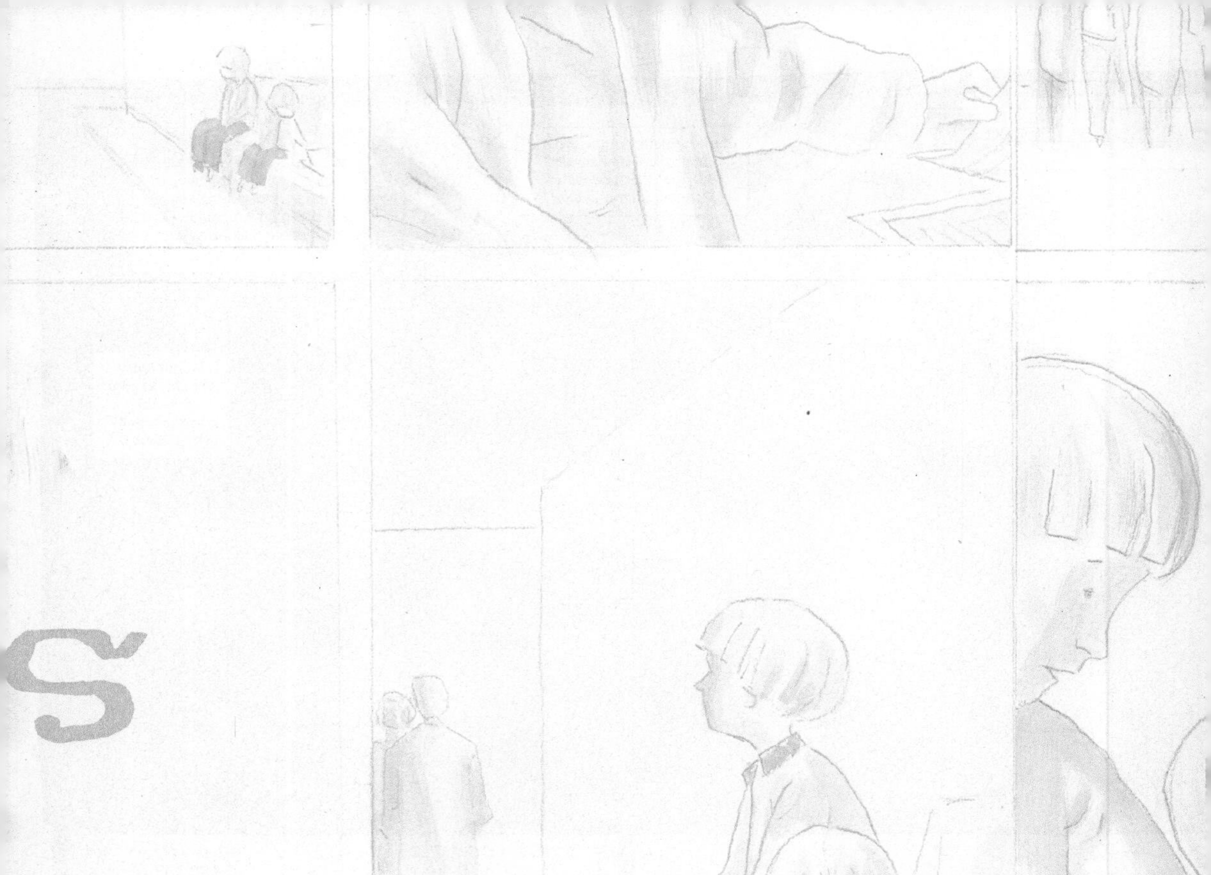

This book is for my Aunt Sarah who, unfortunately, did not get to see it.
—*Steve Seagle*

To Hope, with love and thanks.
—*Teddy Kristiansen*